D0387672

TEAM
TALK

Sporting words
and their origins

SHIRE PUBLICATIONS

TEAM
TALK

Sporting words
and their origins

Julian Walker

SHIRE PUBLICATIONS

Published in Great Britain in 2011 by Shire Publications Ltd,
Midland House, West Way, Botley, Oxford OX2 0PH, United Kingdom.
44-02 23rd Street, Suite 219, Long Island City, NY 11101, USA.

E-mail: shire@shirebooks.co.uk
www.shirebooks.co.uk

© 2011 Julian Walker

Every attempt has been made by the Publishers to secure the appropriate permissions for materials
reproduced in this book. If there has been any oversight we will be happy to rectify the situation
and a written submission should be made to the Publishers.

A CIP catalogue record for this book is available from the British Library.

Shire General no. 2.
ISBN-13: 978 0 74780 834 3

Julian Walker has asserted his right under the Copyright, Designs and Patents Act, 1988,
to be identified as the author of this book.

Text template and page layouts by Bounford.com, Cambridge, UK.
Typeset in Minion Pro.
Printed in China through Worldprint Ltd.

11 12 13 14 15   10 9 8 7 6 5 4 3 2 1

DEDICATION
For Anne, who taught me that I could swim.

Contents

Sport and language

The antiquity of sport and sporting language

Words are essential to competitive sport. The simplest running race between children involves the words 'race', 'win', 'beat' and 'lose'. A competition organised so that it can be repeated under the same conditions involves more words – 'track', 'start', 'finishing line' – for only in this way can all parties agree upon the boundaries of what is and what is not allowed. Further along, a 'starter' is required, and probably a 'referee' and a 'prize'. Even the runner running alone against his or her own expectations has the concept of 'faster' or 'slower' somewhere in his or her head, and, before that, the awareness of 'running' or 'competing'.

On an Egyptian burial chamber at Beni Hassan, built about four thousand years ago, there is a depiction of a series of pairs of men wrestling, using a large variety of holds. Wrestling in this form would have required a declared space, a judge, and recognised stopping and releasing terms; a number of the holds would presumably have had names. Wrestling and racing feature widely in the legends of the ancient Europeans. For example, there is a Greek myth of Atlanta, a fast runner who was prepared to take notice of Melanion only if he beat her in a race. The Roman writer Ovid tells how as she drew ahead of him he threw a golden apple in front of her, three times, which allowed him to beat her. Ovid states that there was a 'starting line', with the signal given by trumpets, a 'victor' and a 'prize'; he does not relate whether she cried 'foul' or accused him of 'cheating'. Horse-racing features in the Old English poem *Beowulf*, and according to Henry Alken's 1821 *National Sports of Great Britain* the French king Hugh Capet sent 'running horses' to Athelstan, the king of England, as part of a tenth-century marriage deal (though in fact Hugh was not born until the year Athelstan died).

Our knowledge of sport in the medieval world comes from sources such as national and local legal documents, which often record prohibitions or limitations on sports; illuminated manuscripts, which show telling details; and court records containing information on payments for goods or services that occasionally give glimpses into how sports were played. Illuminated manuscripts from the twelfth century onwards show scenes from rustic sports and pastimes, and much of our knowledge of medieval sporting activity comes from statutes of prohibition and records of purchases. The cost of a 'running horse' during the reign of Edward III (1327–77) was £13.33, which in modern terms would be not far from the cost of a thoroughbred now. An item in the expenditure of Henry VII in 1498 is for 'threepence, for lost tennis balls', while the early-fourteenth-century Luttrell Psalter has a margin illustration showing archers shooting at a target. From the twelfth century systems of privilege were applied to sport; while the government deemed sport for the poor as a distraction from work and from training for the defence of the realm, it conceded that activities that were the basis of gambling for the wealthy were untouchable. Joseph Strutt in *The Sports and Pastimes of the People of England* (1801) relates how a statute of Richard I banned gambling for those below the rank of knight, and concerns and statutes of the reign of Edward III specify time-wasting as a reason for condemning 'the throwing of stones, wood and iron; hand-ball, football, club-ball; cambucam'. In Edward IV's reign 'coits, closh or claish, kayles or skittles, half-bowl, hand in and hand out' were banned, and in the reign of Henry VIII 'bowling, loggating, tennice, dice, cards, and backgammon' were circumscribed. In the sixteenth century you could build a tennis court on your land freely – if you had an income of over £100 a year.

One way to get round these restrictions was by the use of language. A sport banned by printed statute could be renamed, and Strutt reports how the justices of the peace had the skittle-frames in London destroyed. The game was instantly revised and renamed 'bubble the justice' (to 'bubble' meant to 'cheat').

In English the development of sporting language is clearly documented from the medieval period. In 1801 Strutt wrote that 'there was a peculiar kind of language invented by the sportsmen of the middle ages, which it was necessary for every lover of the chase to be acquainted with'. These terms included the names of groups of animals, the names of animals' hiding or resting places, the actions of hiding, resting or running, the young of animals, and parts of the animals. Many of these terms are established within English and have become separated from the awareness of their origins. We speak of someone having 'gone to earth', of 'giving chase', and of a 'flock of geese' rather than a 'flight of geese'. Books on grammar still contain 'proper terms' (that is 'specific to the creatures') for animals: the 1998 edition of *Fowler's Modern English Usage* has a page of these, including ones in common use such as 'a pack of dogs' and 'a litter of pups', but also less used terms such as 'a siege of herons' and 'a sounder of wild boar'.

Other sports of the period evolved from concepts of conflict and developed their own terminology. Thus tennis, which was imported from France, brought with it many French terms that were to varying degrees anglicised: 'dedans', 'tambour', 'hazard', 'grille', 'racquet'. These developed into phrases such as 'the boasted force into the dedans' and 'laying down chase better than two', which are meaningless, but somehow attractive, to those who know nothing of the sport.

The role of language in sport

Current sports-writing uses specialised language just as much as huntsmen and tennis players did in the sixteenth century. Ken Jones, a leading sports journalist, complained of footballers and football writers who

> never fail to convey the impression that football is an art so involved and technical as to be removed from ordinary knowledge and understanding. In their eagerness to pose as experts they fill the air with fashionable theories and jargon, ignoring an unassailable truth, which is that sport is best served by uncomplicated conclusions... Corners and free kicks have long since become dead-ball situations, and forwards who run intelligently into space are said to be probing the gullies.

This is a fair point, but it deserves more consideration. We have to acknowledge that football is paid a considerable amount of attention, both by the media and by the game's followers. It is a fairly simple game, which can be described in terms of 'A kicked the ball to B, while C tried but failed to stop him from doing so'; or 'A passed to B, avoiding C's tackle'; or 'A's dropped shoulder sold C a perfect dummy and released B'. All of these describe a passage of play, but the third would be intelligible to only a limited group of people. In a sense, it is the simplicity of the game that requires the florid language to ensure that we find new ways of saying the same thing. Equally, we can say that a sport must have its jargon, its specialist terms, to allow aficionados to know exactly what they are talking about – a 'dead-ball situation' is as clear to a football follower as a 'form' was to a medieval hunter. The vast amount of written and broadcast text that sport requires provokes inventiveness in language.

More complex sports require different levels of terminology. Kayaking is a sport that requires distinct kinds of terms that the practitioner acquires as part of the process of learning the sport. These range from simple terms to do with the equipment, parts of the boat, the paddle, and so on, and then terms specific to the sport, the 'spray-skirt' (watertight skirts) and 'throwbag' (bag for floating rescue-rope), and then to terms required to become skilled in manipulating these in the environment of the sport – manoeuvres, such as 'duffek turn', and kinds of water features, such as a 'smoker'.

The more specialist the terms, the less likely they are to be known to the layperson. It is of the nature of jargon that it excludes, and in doing so it creates a group identity. This language-based identity is reinforced by mistakes and differences – the use of 'free shot' instead of 'free kick' marks the outsider, the person who does not know; and the selection of 'goal-tender' rather than 'goalkeeper' by the pioneers of ice-hockey deliberately marked their identity as separate from football. However, the waters can be muddied by the metaphorical deliberate mistake of the professional writer or broadcaster who describes a free kick as a 'free shot'. As people who 'speak the language', we know he knows.

Broadcast sport disrupts this hierarchy of language, showing the highest practitioners in action, mediated by the television commentator. Thus terms such as 'Salchow' or 'Axel jump' are routinely served up every four years to television watchers who have never been near an ice-rink; every summer armchair Wimbledon watchers appreciate 'passing shots', and many who enjoy the cultural contribution of cricket and the chat of BBC Radio's *Test Match Special* rarely stop to wonder what a 'cover drive' really is. Television's ability to show the intricacies of sport via replay and slow-motion creates experts out of those who might otherwise have little interest in sports.

What is sport?

In the examination of the role of language in sport, a contentious starting point is to define what we mean by 'sport'. The problem is as follows: snooker is a game, but we might be uncertain as to whether it is a sport; we 'play' a 'game' of snooker; it would not be out of place in a television programme covering sports, and historically a great amount of sporting money was hazarded on the outcome of particular games; however, it is not a sport included in the Olympic Games. So, we 'play' a 'game' but what do we 'do' as regards a 'sport'? Do 'game' and 'sport' overlap, and how do we distinguish between them?

The status distinction in English between words deriving from Old English and those deriving from Anglo-Norman French is fairly clear in the words 'game' (from the Old English *gamen*, meaning 'play, pleasure, pastime or sport') and 'sport' (from the Anglo-Norman *disport*): 'game' implies something less serious, possibly amateur rather than professional, something done for fun – one 'plays' a game, but not a sport. In late-medieval times 'games' were associated with the words 'glee' or 'solace', so with a sense of fun. 'Sport' at that time might be any kind of diversion (the first documented sport in the *Oxford English Dictionary* is 'redynge' – reading, 1425), or the aristocratic delights afforded by hunting. The *Boke of St Albans* (1496) contains a 'Treatise of Fyshynge', which describes angling as one of a number of 'good dysportes and honest gamys': no distinction

GAME. ſ. [*gaman*, a jeſt, Iſlandick.]
1. Sport of any kind.   *Shakeſpeare*.
2. Jeſt, oppoſed to earneſt.   *Spenſer*.
3. Inſolent merriment ; ſportive inſult. *Mil*.
4. A ſingle match at play.
5. Advantage in play.   *Dryden*.
6. Scheme purſued ; meaſures planned.
7. Field ſports : as, the chaſe.   *Waller*.
8. Animals purſued in the field.   *Prior*.
9. Solemn conteſts exhibited as ſpectacles to
the people.   *Denham*.
To GAME. *v. n.* [ȝaman, Saxon.]
1. To play at any ſport.
2. To play wantonly and extravagantly for
money.   *Locke*.

there. By 1755 the overlap was confusing – Johnson's *Dictionary* gives for the first definition of 'Sport', 'play; diversion; game; frolic and tumultuous merriment'; and for 'Game', 'sport of any kind'. By the mid-nineteenth century, the terms were more or less synonymous.

It may help if we turn the question around from 'What is sport and what is a game?' to 'Is this activity a sport or a game?' Is a certain level of physical activity inherent to a 'sport'? When the Sports Council withdrew its support for darts in 1996 on the grounds that it was not physical enough, critics with some justification complained that a similar case could be made against the Olympic sports of archery and shooting, which had wealthy and officer-class associations. The claim was that the discrimination was essentially one of class, with the British Darts Organisation asserting, 'They're really saying that they don't want to be associated with fat blokes with fags in their mouths, but that is such an outdated image of the sport' (*The Guardian*, 14 February 1996). Pigeon-racing, one of Britain's most popular sports for a long period, involves little exercise at all. Definitions based on ideas of movement or endurance or competition or management of equipment make it difficult to delineate the boundaries of sport or game or pastime. *Competitive Sports in Schools and Colleges* (1951, New York) included picnicking among its 'natural activities'. Are hiking or mountain-climbing sports? Are parkour, bungee-jumping and hang-gliding (all of which can be found in *The Sports Book*, 2007, Dorling Kindersley)? If motorsport is a sport, is it largely about the skills of the car designer as much as the driver, and, if this is a stumbling block, then how do we view the role of the racehorse trainer, or the gymnastics or tennis coach?

Historical developments all tend to confirm a distinction between what we might call the 'deep' meanings of the two terms (not an etymological root but that which helps us decide whether to use the word 'sport' or 'game' in any given situation), though we may still find that it is a distinction that we recognise but cannot define. The Catholic Church in Renaissance Europe came to accept and manage sports, seeing them effectively as games, largely because they were pointless and served no purpose other than entertainment. The Protestants, however, saw their value as pragmatic, a training of the body and the spirit for work, and later the development of a team ethic that could have several applications, from military to industrial. To this the word 'sport' seems more applicable.

Studies in 1984 of how professional footballers and cricketers viewed their status indicated that the respondents thought their professions had a reasonably high status, but specifically they stated that 'the drive for success had also driven the pleasure and the play element out of sport' (quoted in John Hargreaves, *Sport, Power and Culture*, 2005). The idea of 'sport' having any elements of 'play' might seem a little naïve now; but did 'sport' ever involve 'play'? Was it not always essentially to do with 'competing'? But how do we factor in all the variety of connotations deriving from the word 'sport' – a 'good sport', a 'sports car', 'a sporting act', 'sportsmanship'?

In American English a further development comes into play. In the late 1860s sport was dominated by baseball, football, shooting, boxing and racing (foot and horse), but there was also a large following for blood sports – cock-fighting in particular. Henry Bergh, who founded the American Society for the Prevention of Cruelty to Animals, recommended 'healthful and invigorating sports', which would replace the blood sports. In this context there grew a distinction between 'sport', meaning lower-class rowdy fighting-based activities – prizefighting, dog-fights, ratting, cock-fights – and wealthy-class 'sports', those which were based on pushing the human frame to high levels of athleticism. 'Sports' meant training and participation; 'sport' implied betting and spectating. And 'sports', as it is used now in North America, is a singular noun.

So can we say that sport is more 'work' than 'play', and that a 'game' is more 'play' than 'work'? In the seventeenth century Robert Boyle noted that tennis was 'much more toilsome than what many others make work', and the appeal of sports to the nineteenth-century educationalists was the way that work and leisure could be synthesised. Several writers have noted that the history of sport from 1700 is one of growing seriousness, and that it was the introduction of the Protestant work ethic that turned the whole business from 'games' to 'sport'.

For Norbert Elias in *An Essay on Sport and Violence* (1986) one key element is the idea of 'pleasurable excitement'; elsewhere he notes that sport is a process of the gradual control of violence. Controlled danger offering high excitement is expressed in Ellis Cashmore's definition of sport as something that 'offers people the liberating excitement of a struggle involving physical exertion and skill while limiting to a minimum the chance that anyone will get seriously hurt' (*Making Sense of Sports*, 2001). Hargreaves proposes a number of elements that serve to make up 'sport': a ludic impulse, the need to do an activity which serves no purpose other than doing it itself; the development of this into a formalised structure, where everybody knows that there are rules, and people have a fairly good idea of what they are; and the concept of some kind of contest, either between participants or against some abstract competitor – time, distance, weight, number, previous acts or calculated possibilities; and perhaps an existence beyond 'play', some feeling of seriousness. Further contributory elements may be a sense of theatre, the development of ritual practices, and symbolic portrayal of power structures. It will be noticeable that the progression of these ideas gradually tightens the boundaries of 'play', reducing the things that a participant can do; the tennis player has to hit the ball into a particular place, the slalom skier cannot go off amongst the trees, and the footballer cannot pick up the ball and run with it, without forfeiting a foul or a penalty or disqualification. The higher up the scale of amateur or professional achievement the player has reached, the greater the disgrace such an action would entail. It would be 'not being serious', it would be 'playing'; not so long ago it would be 'not playing the game'.

The idea that sport and games are essentially about nothing but themselves is echoed by many sportswriters, keen to assert that sport is not a metaphor for life. Joyce Carol Oates, in her masterly *On Boxing* (1986), states that boxing is 'a unique, closed, self-referential world...', and later, 'Boxing really isn't a metaphor, it is the thing in itself.' While sport may give rise to metaphors about conflict and hunting, and while it may derive from conflict and hunting, and while it may depend on and generate vast amounts of money, it is not anything else but itself. As Simon Barnes says in *The Meaning of Sport* (2006), 'Sport is not supposed to be real life.' It has no terms of reference outside itself; its influence on actions outside are constructed; its structures and mores sit uncomfortably on other fields of activity.

And yet it seems at times impossible not to see sport as a metaphor. Barnes proposes that all non-confrontational sports –

pole-vault, diving, horse-riding, javelin-throwing – are about flying. And all other sports can be seen as metaphors – rugby and football for territorial battles, horse-racing for evolution, tennis for duelling – 'its metaphorical nature is what gives it meaning.' The words of sport – 'win', 'beat', 'smash', 'lose', 'champion' – what do these say about the meaning of sport?

Dr Thomas Arnold, who has been portrayed historically as a pioneer of modern sports, was the headmaster of Rugby School from 1828 to 1841, when the ethos of the public-schools curriculum was beginning to give more weight to sport than academic learning, famously paraphrased later by Kipling as 'the flannelled fools at the wicket, and muddied oafs in goal'. For Baron de Coubertin, founder of the modern Olympics, Arnold gave English schools 'the precise formula for the role of athletics in education'. Yet, in George Orwell's estimation, 'Dr Arnold … looked on games simply as a waste of time', and, though there is evidence of his having occasionally watched, his reputation as a promoter of school sports derived mainly from the fictional *Tom Brown's Schooldays*. Occupying no space but their own space, any relation sports have to the rest of life, for example the self-esteem of a school dependent on its basketball team's successes or failures, is a constructed meaning. As Barnes says, 'perhaps sport matters because it doesn't matter'; if it matters whether someone scores a goal, wins a race or scores a point, it only matters because we make it matter. For Don DeLillo in *Underworld* (1997), 'The game doesn't change the way you sleep or wash your face or chew your food. It changes nothing but your life.' For Nick Hornby in *Fever Pitch* (1992), 'Football was life, and I am not speaking metaphorically.'

What are the processes by which 'sport' becomes detached from 'play'? C. E. Green, elected president of the Marylebone Cricket Club (MCC) in 1905, complained that county cricket had become too serious. R. Holt in *Sport and the British* (1989) quotes him as saying 'There is very little sport in it now', suggesting that the meaning of 'sport' here is 'pleasure'. This was from a period when a gentleman sportsman felt that training produced an unfair advantage. Sport in this environment meant a pitting of natural skills, wits and abilities, and produced contests that were not unlike hunting, natural man against natural man. Clearly connected to the arrogance of those born into wealth, its results reinforced that arrogance, for how could the loser be in any way at fault if it was clearly fate that had decided the outcome of a match? This attitude lasted for several decades among the leisured classes after the fee-paying schools and the universities assumed the mantle of the organisers of sport, in the mid-nineteenth century. As Holt puts it, 'Gym was for Germans. Britons played rather than exercised.'

Rather than reading sport as a metaphor for other activities, we might ask what other activities can be used to explore how we understand sport. The model of ritual activity fits easily on to sport. The way clothes developed over the twentieth century, particularly in sports such as American football, snooker, cricket or figure-skating, shows such processes as accentuating or extending parts of the body, using deliberately antiquated costume (the nostalgic 'baggy green' Australian cap), or the pretend revealing of more flesh; all of these are as much to do with constructing a ritual costume as the performance of the activity. Rituals around championships include the curious curtailing of excitement at the end of Wimbledon after the singles finals while the carpets are laid on court and royalty or their representatives 'come down' to present the prizes, at which point the ecstasy revs up again. Regular sporting events such as the Boat Race, the Grand National and the World Series become ritual events in a national calendar, creating 'Wimbledon fortnight' or 'Cup Final Saturday'.

The introduction in the 1860s of coaches made explicit the application of a work ethic to sports; together with the idea of 'muscular Christianity', promoted by young university graduates going to teach in boys' schools, this led to a dissemination of the idea of athletic prowess as an aspect of religious conformity. This sat comfortably too with the amateur mentality, the idea of doing sports for the sake of something other than money. Several studies of sport highlight the relationship between the rituals of religion and those of sport, and the pervasive view that sport has replaced religious faith in terms of providing what people want, ranging from hope and communal ecstasy to a year's calendar. Other models range from Desmond Morris's view of football matches as 'symbolic events of some complexity' that combine elements of mock-fight, status display and act of faith, to the Marxist view of sport as combining drama, displaced violence and a narcotic effect in a social opiate similar to religion.

Sport as a whole was seen by some quarters in the nineteenth century as class-conciliatory, a rallying point for local patriotism that could unite worker and employer. While some have managed to maintain the paternal view of the nineteenth-century organisers of sport, that sport binds people together in some Olympian family, others have read sport as a great divider. George Orwell saw the visit of the Moscow Dynamo football team to Britain in 1945 (for a series of 'friendlies') as an example of sport as 'an unfailing cause of ill-will'. He felt that it was just possible to play without this emotion so long as no local patriotism was involved, but that 'serious sport is bound up with hatred, jealousy, boasting, disregard of all rules ... People want to see one side on top and the other side humiliated.' In *The Football Man* (1971) Arthur Hopcraft wrote about the 'rancour of the game', and how a referee 'can watch the bitterness develop in a match'.

The idea that sport neutralises or channels conflict is hardly borne out by the intense rivalry between the England and Australia cricket and rugby union teams (at least as it is encouraged in the press), between England and Scotland at football, England and Wales at rugby union, the Canada and United States ice-hockey teams, geographically close football teams, and any number of international pairings in most sports. It is a far cry from the Olympic ideal of the glorification of some kind of disembodied athletic body, whose goal was primarily to extend the achievements of the human frame. But the potential for bonding that sport offers, particularly in the structure of the family or same age/gender group, can be seen as bonding through success or adversity. The most noticeable form of this bonding is in the appropriation of sport in the building of national identity, as a team comes to stand for the nation. By no means a post-1966 notion, this was developing in the period before the First World War, as dominant groups looked to sport as a way of holding together an increasingly disparate Britain – largely successfully as witnessed by the extreme nationalism seen at the outset of the war.

'Science' and 'art' are both used to describe sport. C. B. Fry in *The Book of Cricket* (1899) described George Gunn's method of batting as 'in every way scientific', while 'Captain' Stevens in 1845 described swimming as both an art and a science. Boxing in particular provides this dualistic terminology, in its traditional description as 'the noble art of self-defence' and the term used by Pierce Egan in *Boxing: Sketches of Modern Pugilism* (1818), 'the sweet science of bruising'. For Egan boxing was both 'the art of self-defence' and, in the sense of the application of skill and ability, a 'science' requiring 'level-headedness'. 'Much science was displayed on both sides,' wrote *Baily's Monthly Magazine of Sports and Pastimes* in 1836 of a wrestling match, and *The Preston Chronicle* of 26 August 1837 noted of a cricket match between Preston and Kirkham that 'it was generally expected that the superior science of our townsmen would prevail'. A. J. Liebling's 1956 book on boxing, *The Sweet Science*, is still the best-selling book on sport.

Given the extent of conflict-based violence in sport (attack, defend, hit, beat, shoot), how integral is violence to sport, and how is it sublimated? One interpretation of horse-racing is that it is a deliberate attempt to recreate the excitement of the hunt. The concept of 'pleasurable excitement' mentioned above derives from hunting and its development through the vicarious thrill of watching animals kill each other, to the vicarious pleasures of watching people fight in a controlled way (boxing, wrestling), or in a symbolised and ritualised way (rugby, football), which might involve the attacking or defending of territory, real or symbolised (basketball, netball, cricket, tennis). At times the attempts to control violence in sport give way. American college football in the later nineteenth century incorporated violence, both within and around the game, and regular spinal injuries and occasional deaths were seen as a necessary sacrifice in the game, which encouraged survivors to greater violence. Off the field, the naming of Harvard's football ground as 'Soldiers' Field' forged the link between war and football, as sporting violence became a forum by which young men could assert their interpretation of 'manliness'. In the period 1880 to 1914 football in the North of England was markedly more aggressive than in the South, and when the two regions met the distinctions were clearly visible; the Cup semi-final between Swindon and Barnsley in April 1912 was marked by the deliberate injuring of the Swindon captain. The *Daily Express* commented that 'to stop an opponent by maiming him is not football as understood in the south. It is certainly "not cricket".

One curiosity is fox-hunting, which was permitted while other blood sports were banned in the nineteenth century; the elaboration of rules in fox-hunting (the clothes, delayed starts) served to delay the finish, which was carried out at one remove – the killing being done by dogs. The civilising process of making a sport removes or controls the violence, which is often downplayed when it erupts – rugby broadcasters refer to it as an 'outbreak of handbags'.

But boxing, which is effectively the ultimate concentration of sport, one human contesting against another to see which body is stronger, is, despite the science and the art, violence. 'A lot of white men watching two black men beat each other up' – Muhammad Ali's assessment shows it to be violence on more than one level. Oates's *On Boxing* includes the words of a trainer telling a young boxer: 'You gotta want to hurt him, because he's sure going to hurt you.' *Fistiana, or The Oracle of the Ring* (1845) reported that the prize money was called 'battle-money', and contests were 'battles' not 'bouts'. And yet Sugar Ray Robinson, once welterweight and middleweight world champion, could say with all honesty 'I ain't never liked violence'. Oates viewed it as occasionally bewildering:

> There are times when you risk moments of animal
> panic when watching something that is very ugly,
> and that 'by watching it, one is an accomplice'… At
> such times one thinks: What is happening? Why are
> we here? What does this mean? Can't this be
> stopped?

Sport and conflict

A number of early sports-like activities, which developed not so much for fun as for military training, used the terminology of organised conflict, much of which is retained today in sports. The chivalric codes that grew out of military training were fully expressed at the tournament, a sporting display of 'feats of arms' carried out on horseback or foot. But in the late-medieval period archery, for example, was not seen as a sport that could be applicable to military training: it *was* military training, and became a sport only when rendered obsolete by effective handguns. Towards the end of the nineteenth century it was felt by many that too much sport had distracted young men from the things that really mattered – making money, expanding the Empire and winning battles. It is probable that public health did not benefit from increased sporting opportunities as much as had been hoped by those who proposed that regular sport would drastically improve the nation's health. A far wider perception was that absenteeism was crippling industry at the time of sporting events, that army recruits and industrial employees were unfit and underdeveloped, and that over-indulgence in sport was distracting those who should be leading the nation. It is even likely that the games ethos did adversely affect the attitude to professionalism among the officer class at the beginning of the twentieth century. Of course, at the beginning of the First World War, the same British officers were bound to claim that the honourable British gentleman's love of sports would bring a swift victory, and even at the end of the war there were those who continued to believe that it was the officer class's love of sport that had brought victory through team spirit and dedication to the cause.

The relationship between conflict and sport has been seen in a range of ways. Words in regular use – 'attack', 'defend', 'shoot', 'target', 'battle', 'captain', 'defeat', 'hit', 'rearguard action', 'penalty shoot-out' – create a structure where aggression is normal and necessary. Stronger pressures on the professional urge the player to 'humiliate' the 'opposition', to 'thrash' them, to 'hammer away' at them. Football fanzines talk up rivalries between Manchester United and Arsenal, Everton and Liverpool, talking about teams being 'dead and buried', 'thumping' the opposition, 'killing them off'. In fact, 'kill' alone is seldom heard in sport, as if there is a general awareness that this word goes just too far and takes sport to a place where we know it should not go.

Fouling (originally ramming your boat into another in a race) and hacking (kicking your opponent's shins) were gradually removed from sports in the nineteenth century, to the disgust of some of the administrators. In the case of rowing, it was the professional watermen who protested most against the removal of 'fouling', but amateur clubs supported its retention too. 'Hacking' was the matter most discussed in the football meetings in the 1860s and 1870s that resulted in the separation of codes. There is a suggestion that as part of the long process of civilisation through sport the tools of war have been sublimated into rackets, bats and clubs; some argue that the larger ball (football, volleyball, netball, etc.) is a symbolic head, and that the smaller one (hockey, cricket, baseball) is a symbolic fist. There is documentation of a head used as a football: that of Jeremy Bentham, founder of University College London, was reportedly used as a football by students in the 1920s – it had been preserved and kept on display, in accordance with his wishes.

But the 'civilising impulse' can have effects the opposite of those desired. The controls on boxing – the gloves and the headguards – actually allow greater violence. The 16-ounce glove massively increases the force of the fist, allowing the boxer to go on hitting without damaging his fist, while the headguard makes his head a larger target. The head is hit more, and with greater force, than is the case in prizefighting (bare-fist fighting), and probably more boxers die now than did nineteenth-century prizefighters. The unprotected fist can stand only so much punishment, and is likely to come off worse against the bones of the head, while the gloved fist can pummel the head for hours, with little distinction as to the damage it does to the brain whether the head is unprotected or protected. Boxers do die in the ring or because of it, the structure of the fight and the importance attached to will ('bottle', 'spirit', 'guts') being such that there is little incentive for the boxer either to surrender or to know that he is being irreparably damaged.

In the United States a supposed linguistic difference between football and baseball emphasised the military nature of the former ('bombs', 'hits', 'helmets', 'territory') against the more comfortable terms of baseball ('parks', 'pastures', 'home', 'base'). From the outset, college football was run on a semi-military basis, to the extent that in 1905 the President of Harvard stated that football was 'a fight, and its strategy and ethics are those of war'. Harvard's football team at the beginning of the twentieth century used to dip their shirts in animal blood before a match. During the 1970s violence became associated with both football and baseball, with incidents on and off the pitch; but these only echoed regular incidents reported from a hundred years earlier.

When organised sport and organised conflict do meet the results are perplexing. There are several reported incidents of footballs being kicked to signal an attack during the First World War, the best-known being when Captain W. P. Nevill of the East Surrey Regiment ordered four balls to be kicked forward on the first attack of the Battle of the Somme. This, rather than the Christmas truce matches between opposing soldiers in 1914, was more typical of the way the establishment viewed sport at this time; though there was much recruiting at football grounds, it was felt appropriate to shut down the Football League from 1915, along with county cricket and amateur athletics meetings and the Boat Race. Robert Graves reported playing a game of cricket with improvised equipment (including a bird cage) during the Battle of Vermelles in 1915, and, a century earlier, officers of the Brigade of Guards played cricket before the Battle of Waterloo. There is even a report of a British officer arranging a cricket match to divert a conflict between opposing forces in Afghanistan in the 1930s.

Sport and hunting

The Salish, a people of the north-west coast of North America, were reported in 1909 as playing a game that consisted of shooting an arrow through a rolling hoop. It would be difficult not to see this as training for hunting, but sport and hunting have a much more complex relationship.

For centuries the word 'sport' was synonymous with hunting. The persistence of this idea can be seen in the large number of books published before 1940 with titles like *Sport* or *The Language of Sport*, which deal exclusively with fox-hunting, fishing, shooting, and so forth, more recently described as 'field sports'. For example, the introduction to *The Language of Sport* by C. E. Hare, published in 1939, contains the following:

> The term 'sport' is here used in the modern sense of
> 'field-sports', connected with the (killing or) hunting
> of animals. It is not concerned with organised games,
> horse-racing or the prize-ring.

But animals shot as 'sport' were 'game', shooting large animals was 'big-game hunting', and fishing for large seafish is 'game-fishing'; in 1674 *The Compleat Gamester* described cock-fighting as 'a sport or pastime so full of delight and pleasure, that I know not any game in that respect is to be preferred before it ...' *The Compleat Sportsman* (1718) is a book entirely about hunting, in which all animals are 'game', whether edible or not. In the nineteenth century Russian adopted the English words 'sport' and 'sportsman' to apply to the contexts of hunting and fishing.

Any survey of the culture of sport must address blood sports, since for hundreds of years these were for many people the primary experience of what historically was called 'sport'. By the end of the nineteenth century three-quarters of each monthly issue of the *Badminton Magazine of Sports and Pastimes* was devoted to various forms of removing animals from their natural environment dead or alive. For hundreds of years up to then cock-fights, bull- and bear-baiting, ratting and dog-fights attracted vast numbers of spectators, and betting at ruinous levels. Though banned in the early nineteenth century in Britain and the United States, many of these activities continued – cock-fights and ratting were especially popular, and dog-fighting continues; the use of the term 'dog-fight' for 'aerial combat' in the two World Wars no longer depends on the metaphorical association with dogs fighting, indicating how the term has become part of mainstream English.

Many of the terms used in blood sports cross over into 'legitimate' sports, particularly when those sports share aspects with or developed from the blood sports. Greyhounds racing round a track now chase an 'electric hare'; for centuries greyhounds were set to race after a live hare in such coursing competitions as the Waterloo Cup, whose results were regularly reported in the national press. The 'ring' by 1400 was the term for a circular space for display or sport, applicable later to both bull-baiting and boxing. The Luttrell Psalter (1330) shows a bear being baited by four dogs; the dogs were expendable, while the bear was not, so this would have been a highly managed spectacle. The bear-handler is equipped with two sticks, one of which is being brandished at a dog, while his other hand is laid gently on the bear's back. The *Boke of St Albans* (1496) shows fishing to have been highly developed at that stage; reels were not in use, but the description of how to tie distinct and carefully described flies indicates a set of skills that would have been desirable and honed through practice. 'Bait' itself as 'food used to entice prey', used in fishing from the early fourteenth century, derives partly from the Old Norse word *beita*, meaning 'to cause something to bite', which developed into bear and bull 'baiting'. 'Sport' itself can still be used to mean 'teasing' or 'tormenting', or watching this activity.

The Cruelty to Animals Acts (1835 and 1849) put an official end to blood sports (though not fox-hunting); and certainly cruelty had been the driving impulse behind much of the baiting and setting animals against each other. At the time, dog-fights and cockmains were advertised in *Baily's Monthly Magazine of Sports and Pastimes* (1829). Wild shooting and hawking, which had been supplements to the food supply, had disappeared, and, as the urban middle class exercised its power, those who lost out in these matters were the rural working class and aristocracy. It must be remembered that in the eighteenth century it was felt that animals that died in pain provided more tender meat; bull-baiting was required by law in some areas, to improve the meat. A red mist seems to have descended over people's eyes when it came to relations with animals. The phrase 'cock-shy' comes from the habit of tying to a post cocks that would not fight, and stoning them to death. Horse-racing retains the name 'National Hunt' racing for races with fences or hurdles, in memory of its origin in fox-hunting.

Boxing's detractors regard it as a controlled blood sport (the term dates from 1895), on the grounds outlined above. Newer combat activities such as martial arts, cage-fighting and kick-boxing hover near the limits of acceptable violence. Greco-Roman wrestling is an Olympic sport, while professional wrestling, particularly in the United States, is more to do with entertainment, performance and partisan support.

Cashmore gives a model for understanding sport as a way of reconciling the speed of humankind's mental and social evolution with that of our slower physical evolution, the pleasurable excitement of 'artificial hunting' satisfying the need to hunt for food. The answer proposed by this model is that sport is a development of the interim idea of hunting for its own sake, 'having no purpose apart from its own existence'. Sport, Barnes suggests, is not an urge to recreate the hunt, but to tell the tales of the hunt.

Winning

The control of competitiveness was a long-held tenet of amateur British sport. Within the context of colonialism, competitiveness was seen as less important than perseverance, team spirit, resoluteness and discipline. The concept of 'fair play' and 'playing by the spirit of the game' (now enforced negatively by charges of 'bringing the game into disrepute') was intrinsic to the gentlemanly nature of the way amateurs approached all sports at the end of the nineteenth century. The process of writing rules that kept competitiveness in check was seen by many as an affront to the amateur sensibility, an explicit acceptance that there were people who did not know how to behave or to limit aggression and the will to win. C. B. Fry, a major sporting figure of the early twentieth century, complained in 1911 about the assumption, implicit in rules against those who would 'trip, hack and push their opponents and behave like cads of the most unscrupulous kidney', that sportsmen would need to be told how to behave. Despite the supposed 'gentlemanliness' of rugby union, the rules are enforced ruthlessly, as maybe is the 'gentlemanliness' itself: obedience to the referee is maintained by moving penalty kicks forwards by 10 metres if they are disputed. There is an inference here that this level of 'sportsmanship' has to be maintained through a kind of punishment that would be interestingly inflammatory in football.

By the time of the 1932 'Bodyline' cricket series, when English bowlers were directed to bowl at the Australian batsmen rather than the wicket, the concept of competitiveness was at the heart of this most mannered of sports. The Australian popular press left its readers in no doubt that the tactic was 'not cricket', and that the 'win at all costs' mentality was not appropriate to the nature of cricket.

Extreme competitiveness is often thought of as a modern aspect of sport, absent in an earlier age when sport was more concerned with skill, finesse and spectacle based on 'playing the game well'. Derek Birley, writing in 1979 about the myths of cricket as portrayed in cricket writing, contrasts the 'display element that was once greatly admired in cricket and team games but nowadays tends to be subordinated to competition and excitement'. This would seem to imply that something has been lost, that a golden age of sport depended on love of the game rather than love of winning. In this context, trying to win competitions came to be described as mere 'pot-hunting'. In American sports history, argue Gorn and Goldstein (*A Brief History of American Sports*, 2004), the need to win has always been inherent in organised sport, far stronger than ideas of sportsmanship, recreation, or even patriotism. Money has often underlain this, but the idea of 'making a good game' rather than going out to win has never been a major impetus in American sports.

And yet public perception of 'the win' in the past sometimes shows a difference from the present; England's World Cup win in 1966 was not the major headline in the following day's *Sunday Telegraph* and occupied no more than a quarter of the front page of *The Guardian*; Chattie Cooper is said to have cycled home after gaining one of her five Wimbledon championships, to be ignored by her brother, who went on cutting the hedge.

Historical post-match activities and pre-match agreements indicate the degree and nature of competitiveness and its relation to building a culture of sport above the details of winning and losing. International club matches are still often preceded by the exchanging of club pennants, there is a strict protocol for creating a channel of applause for opponents to pass through at the end of a rugby match (winners applaud first), and hands are shaken all round and shirts exchanged. In the seventeenth century it was acknowledged that the winners of a tennis match would pay for the use of the court, firewood, assistants and the post-match drinks. To a certain extent these customs ritualise checks on the all-out desire to win.

But of the first sixty-two cricket matches between Oxford and Cambridge, in the nineteenth century, only three were drawn, and these because of rain. Despite there being different rules for declaration and following-on, this would seem to indicate that players generally went for the win. In cricket there are definitely complications – 'going for a draw' may mean avoiding defeat, which in 'saving the match' can be a turn-around in the direction of a match, which feels as good as a victory.

The growth between 1920 and 1935 of non-competitive sports – hiking, cycling and rambling – echoes the early organisation of hockey in the late nineteenth century. In 1892 the Hockey Association decided that there was no room in the sport for leagues, competitions or prizes. The magazine *Hockey* approved of this move as one which would 'save hockey from disaster and being sacrificed upon the altar of popular, but ruinous, competition'. International matches continued in a spirit of 'gentlemanly friendliness' and seem to have been modelled on the idea of making a good spectacle based on intelligent placing of the ball, rather than tactics that would stop the opposition from scoring.

An alternative, more cynical – or realistic – approach embraces the rules and the role of the referee in the tactics of playing the game. In football there are ways of moving or putting special pressure on a team, particularly near the goal, that can draw an opponent into fouling; when done successfully, it is often described as 'winning a penalty'. Inducing your opponent to foul is not seen as cheating unless there is a clear pretence of having been fouled. For the person who is induced into fouling, the opponent is suddenly not the other team but the fooled referee. Compare this with the way referees 'manage' rugby matches, talking to the players, warning them that they are in danger of being caught off-side, and telling them to stay on their feet.

For the individual competitor, at crunch time competitiveness may have to be left aside, its frenzy left to the spectators. Egan's point about the 'science' of boxing was that the boxer depended not on his emotion so much as what he knew about how to defend himself and overcome his opponent's defences. If a player 'cares' too much, emotion can be a cause of mistakes, ill-judged moves and bad timing. Competitiveness in this case becomes more about calculation and judgement than an all-out will to win. Though some competitors, especially teams, may be deliberately fired up before a match, for the individual the desire immediately before the event is often to be alone and empty of emotions to do with competitiveness. The racing driver Jackie Stewart said: 'By race time I should have no emotions inside me at all – no excitement or fear or nervousness … I'm drained of feeling, utterly calm.' Boxers since Muhammad Ali have proved the exception to this, to the extent that the competition starts long before the fight proper. Whipping up feeling seems to be more directed at the spectator, who has no outlet for it other than making noise; for the partisan supporter, the 'result' governs the experience of the match. From the beginning of the twentieth century football results newspapers began to be published in the early evenings, encouraging the viewing of sport as a matter of results, to be pored over and compared; many of the papers contained advertisements for pubs, obviously keen to attract a clientele whose Saturday evening conversation would be based on the day's sports results, despair and elation being equally strong incentives to the consumption of alcohol.

Early on in the documented history of sport in England, William Fitzstephen wrote in Latin of a game, *lusum pilae*, being played regularly. At the heart of organised sport lies the fact that winning a contest is not the end of the matter. A club may walk off the field of play holding a cup, but at the beginning of the next season it has to start again. The triumphalist 'We are the champions', sung at football cup finals, is balanced by the tradition since 1927 of singing the funereal 'Abide with me'. The Olympic champion starts on the same line as everyone else for the next race, the champion skier must race against the same stopwatch, and the winning horse emerge from a box like every other horse. Sporting triumph is a plateau, at the top of the hill, but with another hill beyond. And there is an element of self-destruction in the process. Professional footballers look old before their time, sports injuries cripple athletes for life, while concussion and brain injuries are common in boxing and American football. For the fan, every success is tinged with the promise of future failure, while being a football supporter can be having a companionable forum within which to contain disappointment. Add to this the desire for the press to create and destroy heroes, and the fact that for every person who succeeds in professional sport many fall away early on, and it is possible to read sport as a quest for success with the inevitability of failure at its core: failure in victory, victory in failure, a fate deeply seated within the nature of sport. Captain Matthew Webb's victory was the source of his ultimate failure. He was the first person known to have swum the Channel, which he said left him with a feeling similar to that which he might feel after the first day of the cricket season; but he was condemned by his success to a career of exhibition swims till he died trying to swim across the pool of Niagara Falls in a bid to make enough money to be able to give up swimming professionally.

The fugitive present and uncertain future compare poorly against the myth of the golden age in the past, the so-called 'glory days' of all football clubs, and most other sporting groups, from school netball teams to national Olympic teams. The term 'glory days' in a sporting context appeared just a few months after England's World Cup win in 1966. Al Silverman in *The Twentieth Century Treasury of Sports* (1992) saw two 'golden ages' in twentieth-century American sport, the 1920s and the 1960s. Single achievements stand out from months of mediocrity and in doing so raise the status of the past; sport is a fertile field for nostalgia and, but for today's winners and their supporters, resentment of the reality of the present.

Money, money, money

From the seventeenth century money began to play a major part in organised sports. Robert Burton in the *Anatomy of Melancholy* (1621) noted that horse-racing and its variations were 'good in themselves, though many gentlemen by that means gallop quite out of their fortunes'. Betting put greater pressure on the need to win and increased cheating, which in turn caused the decline and reinvention of a number of sports. Though prizefighting was declared illegal in 1750, there were too many of the great and the good who were financially involved, and it continued until 1820, when a number of thrown fights brought about a collapse in confidence among backers and punters. A collapse in the world of betting threatened to bring down horse-racing at the beginning of the nineteenth century, and cricket around 1825, until the MCC banned betting from Lord's Cricket Ground (the *Laws* published in 1774 included rules for betting, and in 1835 a rule was introduced forbidding betting by umpires). In the late eighteenth century the cricket matches played at the Hambledon club were being played for £500 a side, a vast sum for the time; side-betting would have raised more money. For the betters and bookmakers there were fortunes to be made by paying players to throw matches, and the decline in cricket during the first part of the nineteenth century was largely due to this. From this time and this culture come many slang terms – 'pony', 'punter', 'bookie' and 'leg' – some of which are still in use.

Money underlay both amateur and professional sport, as prizes were usually low compared to the quantities of cash that changed hands between punters and bookmakers. But the idea of open payment for performance was anathema to the amateurs, who felt that as soon as money was involved there was a possibility of the 'purity' of amateur sports being tainted. Payment for performance drove a wedge between professional and amateur that lasted till the end of the twentieth century. Professionalism became increasingly linked to betting, to 'thrown' matches and underhand tactics. In March 1906 the *New York Times* reported that J. E. Sullivan 'has induced several of the best men to go [to an international tournament] who could ill afford to spare so much time for such a trip, and, what is more important, he has prevented the attendance of some who, while they might have been athletically capable, bore reputations none too savory for pure amateurism'.

To add to the mix, the long-lasting link between sport and betting was reflected in the use of the word 'sport' to mean 'bet'; for example, Pierce Egan in *Boxiana* (1821) writes of one early-nineteenth-century prize-fight that 'it is reputed that not less than twenty thousand pounds were sported on this occasion'. And current terminology applies 'gaming laws' to the world of legalised betting.

The introduction of charges for football spectators in the 1880s coincided with the decline of the hopes that sport would create a more healthy and relaxed working class. 'Spectatorism' (used from 1889) exasperated the gentlemen amateurs at the same time that increased consumerism in other fields of entertainment was disappointing social reformers and socialists who hoped for the working class to be more involved in activities that affected them.

The need to make sport attractive as a commercial commodity has led to changes in rules – notably the 1925 change to the off-side rule in association football, but also the number of tackles rule in rugby league, the various forms of limited-overs cricket, and the penalty shoot-out and the 'sudden death' ends to cup-ties in association football (though 'sudden death' in games has been in use since the 1830s). The commodification of sport can be seen not just in the way the state buys into its potential for making money (witness the ruinous scramble to hold regular international events), but also in the ways that sports clothing is widely accepted outside the sporting arena, and the emergence of such concepts as 'guerrilla advertising' at sports events, and the consequent ring-fencing of phrases (e.g. 'London Olympics') for the benefit of official (i.e. fee-paying) sponsors, with threats of fines for unauthorised usage.

A number of thrown prize-fights and some corrupt financial deals led to a loss of faith in the sport by punters after 1820 and again in 1840, and, as it declined, so did the language attached to it. When the sport was revived, with gloves and rules, it was no longer 'prizefighting', the word 'milling', meaning 'fighting', had largely disappeared, and 'the Fancy', the social group made up of the followers and financiers of the sport, had dispersed.

Writing the rules

The stages of the development of sport in Britain up to 1914 can be divided roughly into the following general stages:

Up to 1600: rural games, military training, courtly sports including tennis, tournaments and hunting.

1600 to 1750: competitive games, and the beginning of organised cricket, horse-racing and foot-racing.

1750 to 1830: the development of prizefighting, cricket and the emergence of public-school sports and governing bodies.

1830 to 1870: public-school and university sports, writing the rules, the emergence of amateurism.

1870 to 1914: divergence of codes, decrease of popular professional sports.

Between 1850 and the First World War the culture of sport in Britain was extensively transformed. During the preceding hundred years watching and playing sport had been common to all classes, but the numbers were erratic and attendance was localised. From the middle of the nineteenth century the number of people involved in sport increased dramatically. As the *Madagascar Times* put it in 1885, 'the nineteenth century amongst its numerous developments has produced nothing more extraordinary than the extension and generality of our out-door sports.' There was less interest in some sports – rowing, shinty, pedestrianism (professional running) – but their places were taken by sports that had greater potential for participants and spectators, particularly fee-paying spectators.

In this environment codification and writing the rules assumed considerable importance. The writing of laws for sports had begun before 1800: in bowls from 1670, cricket from 1727, golf and prizefighting from the 1740s, curling from 1795. Governing bodies existed too – the Jockey Club from 1751–2, the St Andrews Society of Golfers (later the Royal and Ancient) from 1754, the Marylebone Cricket Club (MCC) from 1787. Modifications were made: the rules of cricket were formalised to ensure parity in determining the outcome of matches, but they were revised in 1744, and again in 1755.

Sport had been practised in schools before the nineteenth century: school football dates from the seventeenth century, and cricket from the eighteenth century, with inter-school matches from the 1780s. Between 1830 and 1860 the attitude towards sport in public schools changed, from indifference and antagonism to support and incorporation into the school curriculum and ethos. The codification of football emerged from the public schools, with several schools playing their own codes in the early nineteenth century. By 1846 it was clear that the Eton and Rugby codes were incompatible, and that this reflected a conflict between the aristocracy and the wealthy bourgeois class. As a result of a series of meetings at Cambridge University the followers of the Rugby code became isolated in 1848. But it was 1857 before a football club was established, at Sheffield, outside the public school/university environment, using primarily dribbling rather than handling.

The second half of the century was characterised by codification, institutionalisation, the growth of sponsorship, professionalism and spectating. Where middle-class involvement was regular, in sports such as angling, bowling, curling in Scotland, golf and cycling, club structures were well funded and secure. In rowing, cricket, association football and sports where working-class support was uppermost, institutions tended to be temporary or enjoyed only irregular support.

Advances in transport, the availability of rubber, improved gun technology and new filaments, changes in working hours and levels of money available – all of these had major effects on the number of people who devoted time to watching or participating, and the potential achievement levels. New sports became available – badminton, lawn tennis, polo, hockey, cycling, table tennis. There was a massive growth in bowls, golf and curling, and in angling, cricket and fox-hunting. In 1910 there were possibly 650,000 regular soccer players in England and Scotland, 250,000 anglers, 178 fox-hunting packs, and 600,000 crown-green bowlers in northern England. Attendance at a county championship cricket match in the 1900s could be as high as 25,000. By 1909 a million people watched soccer on Saturday afternoons, and in 1913 the attendance at the Cup Final in London was 121,919, and the semi-final of the Scottish Cup was watched by sixty thousand in Glasgow.

The main strand for rule-writing was the increasingly important role that sport came to play in the nineteenth century, first at the public schools and then at the universities. From these two strata of institution, the rules flowed from the middle classes to the working classes, either by emulation or by the direct process of education, through clubs and churches. This process does not explain the increase and spread of sports, but the success of sports practised in this context showed the value of the institutionalisation of rule-making. In this context in the United Kingdom, sports rules as passed down in rugby, football and amateur athletics can be seen as enforcing the moral authority of the middle classes, and the later takeover of rugby league and football by the working classes as a class reaction to this.

While rules and codes were being worked out, compromises sometimes involved half a match being played under one code and the other half being played under another, or consecutive matches being played under different codes. This happened particularly in American universities in the early 1870s, when the codes for football were developing. The new rules led to the adoption of new terms – 'touchdown' and 'try' in 1876, 'guarding the runner' in 1879, 'scrimmage' and 'safeties' in 1880, 'running interference' in 1888, 'boxing the tackle' and 'splitting the line' in 1888, 'shoving wedge' in 1889, 'pushing wedge' in 1890, and 'the plough' in 1892. This development of language both facilitated the game and created an identity among followers and players.

The wide growth of newspapers in the last two decades of the nineteenth century spread this language throughout the United States and made entrepreneurs aware of the economic potential of sports. The National League was founded in 1876 and quickly took control of baseball from the players' association, as baseball became big business; but there were gains for customers as spectators – the 'raincheck', part of a ticket retained in case the game is washed out, to be used against a later ticket purchase, dates from the 1880s. Albert Spalding's sports equipment business and sports publishing firm became the main supplier of equipment by 1900. Aside from college football, athletics and rowing, private business played the controlling role in the United States that was being performed in Britain by the universities and schools and their offshoots.

The processes of codification gradually brought about the creation of terms that have become synonymous with sport: the Northern Rugby Football Union (1895, becoming the Rugby Football League in 1922), the Ivy League (1935), Formula One (1946). The first football club to use the name 'Wanderers' was Wanderers FC, who won the first FA Cup in 1872; the first 'United' was Hanover United, formed in 1873.

The separation into different codes can mask the influence one sport may have had on others. There has always been a temptation to create lineages for individual sports: to say, for example, that modern football derives from the Roman *harpastum*; or the opposite, for example, to say that baseball was invented in the early-nineteenth-century United States. Both impulses are based on a 'legitimising' principle, on the basis of either history or invention. Guy Campbell in *A History of Golf in Britain* (1952) urges the idea that the forerunner of golf was *paganica*, a Roman game, the strongest evidence offered being that the ball was stuffed with feathers (as were early golf balls). The early use of a word can be 'claimed' as proof of the antiquity or ancestry of a sport – this happens a lot with the search for the beginnings of 'cricket', whose antiquity is claimed in the words 'creag', 'crycce' and so on.

What seems more likely is that new sports develop out of a number of strands, but unravelling them across time and space can be difficult. Tutball, a forerunner of baseball, was a Shropshire folk game like rounders, also called 'stob-ball' and 'stoolball'. But 'stoolball', first mentioned in the sixteenth century in Wiltshire and Gloucestershire, was a game which Strutt described around 1800 as 'golf or bandyball, the *paganica* of the Romans'. Another writer described it as 'similar to cricket played by women in East Sussex'. It was also, according to Edith Mendham, 'played by milkmaids on their return from milking', using a high board as a wicket (as in stoolball as played currently in Sussex). But in Lancashire children used a stool as a wicket, and their hand as a bat, while in Colditz prison-camp during the Second World War stoolball was a mixture of basketball, American football and wrestling, with a goalkeeper sitting on a stool.

The *Oxford Companion to Sports and Games* proposes that 'hockey is thus the forerunner of all modern sports played with an implement'. It is more likely that the actions of hockey, tennis, golf, shinty and cricket are all interconnected, and it is codes and rules formulated by words that created sports out of them. So it is not surprising that terms like 'hat-trick', 'shoot', 'triple crown', 'strike', 'sprint' and 'grand slam' transfer between sports. A smash hit by a jumping tennis player is called a 'slam-dunk smash', adopting 'slam-dunk' from basketball.

Class

The sports and pastimes of middle and late medieval society were specific to certain groups: the nobles had tournaments, hawking and tennis, but would be unlikely to participate in wrestling or football; the yeomen would be required to practise archery; and monks appear to have been involved in some of the early versions of fives.

There were restrictions as to who could play what. The Beggars Act of 1495 prohibited apprentices, farm labourers and others from playing backgammon, tennis, a kind of croquet called 'closh', dice, cards and bowls, except under supervision at Christmas.

By the eighteenth century sport was on the whole not deliberately socially exclusive. Only the wealthy could afford to race horses of course, or to play tennis in the specially constructed courts, but there were versions of these sports for the less well-off. Golf was played in Scotland across the population, boxing and cock-fighting brought together rich and poor, and cricket in the south of England would find dukes and shepherds on the same team. The Tory squirearchy in the countryside generally retained an involvement and a patronising role in rural pursuits, mostly based on hunting. Prizefighting was largely a sport carried out by the poor for the amusement and betting of the rich, but it brought them together in mutual dependence.

British social class structure primarily governed the division of sports between professionals and amateurs. By about 1850 pedestrianism was, according to Neil Tranter in *Sport, Economy and Society in Britain 1750–1914* (1998), 'the most extensive working-class sporting interest'; when in 1866–7 the Amateur Athletic Club drew up its first rules for athletics, it 'specifically excluded mechanics, artisans and labourers from participation in an attempt to divorce amateur athletics from professional pedestrianism and preserve the former exclusively for the upper and middle classes'. The 'mechanics clause' caused significant antagonism between amateurs and professionals, which lasted well into the twentieth century. In 1907, when the International Olympics Committee met to organise the 1908 London Games, the 'artisans clause' was cited in drawing up the rules for the rowing events, having been adopted by the Amateur Rowing Association in 1882. In 1895 twenty-two clubs met to discuss the Rugby Union's refusal to let them pay players who had to take time off work to play ('broken time payments'); this led to the formation of the Northern Union, which eventually became the Rugby Football League in 1922.

The reorganisation and reconstruction of British sports which occurred in the second half of the nineteenth century and the first quarter of the twentieth involved the dissemination of an ethos, which was partially accepted and partially rejected by different groups. The public-school and Oxbridge influence on football, rugby, rowing and athletics provided models for the organisation and playing ideology that led to structures of organisation and also to ideas of how and why sport should be played. From this derive such concepts as 'sportsmanship', 'fair play', 'team spirit' and 'the spirit of the game', which are still in use, and 'manliness' and 'muscular Christianity', which, though now abandoned, had great influence on sports. Inevitably, given the proselytising process by which Oxbridge graduates took sports to churches and clubs, this sat firmly within the class structure of society as a whole, particularly the philanthropic desire to bring the benefits of society to the poor. It was felt that sport was an effective way to bring awareness of the benefits of working together for the common good, a key tenet of the 'team spirit'. The figure of the athletic clergyman was central to attempts to bring sport into urban areas, with many football clubs attached to churches. In the urban United States, in the first half of the twentieth century, this came to be known as the 'Angels with Dirty Faces effect', from the 1938 Michael Curtis film of that name, in which poor boys were drawn into church-based sports clubs.

In Britain local businessmen followed the churches' example, as a way of maintaining a happy and healthy workforce. The hope that sport would promote some sort of fusion in society was explicit, as seen in the satisfaction of the president of the Football Association in seeing that the Sheffield team at the Cup Final in 1877 'was a mixed one of gentlemen of the middle classes and working men'.

But despite attempts to use sport as a way of fusing society together, the working classes were unlikely to accept gratefully suggestions as to how to behave politely and in a gentlemanly fashion. The nineteenth century had seen the municipal curtailing of street sports in towns, and the removal of what had been felt were the poor's privileges of rowdy behaviour on certain days. Foot-racing on roads was banned in areas in the 1850s, and in 1866 a man foot-racing in Bolton was prosecuted using indecency laws because his legs were showing. In the twentieth century there were instances of the police treating street football as a breach of the peace.

The working class's refusal to accept a model of amateur sportsmanship was one part of the divergence between the two strands of sport, while Tony Mangan suggests that the middle-class adoption of sports in the later nineteenth century was part of a process of social improvement, of moving more towards the sport practices of the public schools, with the adoption of their language, and away from the sports of the working-class areas. It was through sport that one could most easily learn the rules of becoming a 'gentleman', and the public-school elevation of sport with its etiquette, ritual and instilling of notions of proper behaviour was the prime conduit for teaching this. 'Manliness' in middle-class amateur thinking came to mean restraint, good behaviour, acceptance of the rules and participation; for the working-class person it came to mean aggression in the cause of winning, and as a spectator being associated with a winning team.

In the United States the growing fascination with sports among the wealthy led to the foundation of several expensive amateur athletics clubs from the late 1860s. Exclusive by their nature, they purported to be defending athletics against the dangers of corruption, but in effect they became socially exclusive and class-divisive, part of a system in which cricket, yachting, racquets and rowing clubs were exclusive men's organisations. On a smaller scale the same thing happened in Britain, with tennis and golf clubs operating on an invitation basis with high membership fees. American college football was in the nineteenth century the exclusive preserve of the wealthy elite, but its violence caused problems. The *National Police Gazette* in 1889 mocked the pretensions of college football followers' attacks on prizefighting, noting the level of aggression and the kinds of injuries that occurred regularly in football matches. Somehow the class that could afford to send its sons to college managed to create an enclave of upper-class violence that was different from the violence of prizefighting and cock-fighting. The same dichotomy survives still in the description of rugby as 'a game for hooligans played by gentlemen'.

Words continue to reflect this class distinction in sport in ways that stand out, and in ways that are less noticeable. How likely is it for a professional footballer to use the word 'deem'? Yet almost every broadcast of *Match of the Day* includes a discussion between ex-footballers about the off-side rule, with them quoting from the rules stating that a player 'has to be deemed by the referee not to be interfering with play'. Slang variations on football and rugby also act as class indicators – 'footie', 'soccer', 'footer' and 'rugger' have all been used by and can be identified with specific groups.

The association of particular sports with particular social classes changed during the nineteenth century. Partly this was for simple financial reasons; until the 1860s white-collar and skilled manual workers did not have the income level to allow them to participate in sports at any but a basic level, and it was not until the 1880s that unskilled workers could afford to watch boxing, cricket and football matches. Yet there was some social mobility of the sports themselves, being taken up by and associated with the wealthy, or the labouring poor, or the middle classes, only to be taken up by a different class under a different set of rules. The hostility to professional rowing by amateur clubs led to the sport being restricted to the middle classes; hunting attracted more than just the wealthy; amateur boxing became very much a working-class sport in the 1890s, as did rugby in South Wales from the 1870s, cricket in the North, and football throughout England and Scotland. At the same time sports clubs set up by and for the wealthy or the middle classes were careful to exclude those less well-off, so that the very words 'golf club' and 'tennis club' came to have exclusive class associations during the first half of the twentieth century.

The association between class and sport encompasses ways of watching sport (quiet contemplation of cricket versus the 'Barmy Army', or the 'appropriateness' of the Mexican wave at Wimbledon), who does what sport, and the notion of who owns sport. Horse-racing may enjoy support across all classes, but could the same be said of tennis, darts or polo? The question of how the amount of money earned by footballers and boxers affects their social status depends on various interpretations of class in the contemporary world, but one of the longest-lasting themes in boxing has been the way it has been seen as 'a way out of the gutter'; Chris Eubank's challenging of what this level of wealth confers, with the extra factor of race to consider, shows that we are still questioning whether financial success as a result of sporting prowess allows class mobility. Certain sports, such as polo or real tennis, whippet-racing or boxing, may operate as class-based 'closed shops'. Sport as an expression of class in the United Kingdom is still with us.

Amateur and professional

In Britain the frantic attempts by the amateur controllers of sport to maintain amateurism (done with the best of intentions, that of keeping financial corruption out of sport) led to absurdities of control. In both Britain and the United States amateur institutions worked strenuously to exclude professionals and to penalise anyone who it was found had taken any money for performing.

In rowing there was fierce discrimination against professionals and working men (there was a fear that this would be a contest between brute strength and doing the sport for the love of it). In 1846 the Lancaster Regatta organisers consulted with *Bell's Life* as to the

protocol of whether to admit a boat crewed by tradesmen; the response was that 'tradesmen' were acceptable so long as they were not 'journeymen or mechanics', in which case they were to be called 'landsmen', 'to distinguish them from gentlemen amateurs and professional watermen. If the oarsmen in question are master tradesmen the decision should stand; if journeymen or mechanics, they should be defaulted.' 'Landsmen' was a term that had been in use for some years by that stage, to indicate someone whose normal employment was on land. The Isleworth Regatta in the same year had races for apprentices, landsmen, amateurs and watermen. The discrimination increased from the 1870s when American and Canadian crews started to participate in British regattas, their amateur status being regularly challenged. In 1874 the Bolton and Bingley Rowing Club was disqualified from the Agecroft Regatta when it was found that there were artisans in their crew. The rules for the Henley Regatta in 1879 stated that 'no person shall be considered an amateur oarsman or sculler who is or has been by trade or employment for wages, a mechanic, artisan or labourer'. At various times the Amateur Athletics Club and the Amateur Rowing Association adopted similar clauses, though the Amateur Athletics Club dropped theirs after fourteen years, under pressure from members; in 1890 the National Amateur Rowing Association was formed by clubs who found that several of their members would not pass the amateur qualification regulations of the ARA – the two did not amalgamate until 1956. In 1900 the National Cyclists' Union banned from their race meetings prominent English cyclists who had recently been racing on the Continent. The 'Artisan Golfers' Association' was formed in 1920. The 'mechanics clause' survived the longest – it still applied for rowing in the 1908 London Olympics. Henley Regatta as late as 1920 banned an American rower who had once been a bricklayer, and banned the Australian Olympic eight in 1936 because they were policemen and therefore could not be amateurs. Whatever the intention, the 'mechanics clause' came to be seen as an act of class exclusion and resentment.

In this context amateurism offered a route for social aspiration, being as much about social values and class-based institutions as it was about payment for participation. But the association between amateurism and wealth was not absolute; working-class amateurism has always existed and has occupied a place in society, even if only in aspirational terms, such that between 1941 and 1991 several boys' comics ran the tales of 'Alf Tupper', the working-class amateur athlete, who regularly beat the trained professionals.

The professional background

Sport has formally employed servants since the sixteenth century at least. In France in the seventeenth century there were people who looked after tennis courts and started the games – enough of them for them to form an association; at the time there were professional jockeys and trainers in England. Most swimming in the first half of the nineteenth century followed the example of pedestrianism, with races and demonstrations and endurance tests for wagers, and money to be made from spectators. Professional swimmers were called 'professors', a usage that had nothing to do with teaching, but announced their profession. Cricket in the nineteenth century employed club servants, who would be at the members' beck and call to bowl for those wanting to practise their batting; however, their basic earnings in 1900 were about twice that of a skilled manual worker. The 'golf pro' had a very circumscribed role, part teacher, part servant, part shopkeeper. Professional footballers comprised for the most part young men who were 'on the books' of a club but seldom got more than a year's employment and a few games in the reserves. Professional quoiters and bowlers in the late nineteenth century might make a fairly good living, but the profession could support only very few at the top level.

County cricket until 1945 maintained a resolutely non-commercial stance in which the spectators were little considered. The county clubs were in effect a string of gentlemen's athletic clubs, their debts covered by the members and wealthy backers, with Australian team tours bringing in a boost every four years. With falling attendance figures and rising costs, eventually the ethos of amateurism had to change, but the absence of an alternative summer spectator sport, other than the brief and London-based Wimbledon championship, meant that its pre-industrial idyll continued longer than other sports. The last quarter of the nineteenth century saw the development of the bitterness surrounding the two-tier system of 'players and gentlemen' in county cricket. Though 'players' were theoretically there to 'help out' the 'gentlemen' and the club, in practice this meant different entrances to both the ground and the field of play, meals for the 'gentlemen' and their own sandwiches for the 'players', and the players having to provide for themselves over winter. Nor was the pay for professionals always adequate – they were often unpaid over winter, and watched their amateur counterparts make more money in 'expenses' and gratuities than the professionals' salaries (W. G. Grace was a brazen demander of money for playing, though an amateur, and made around £120,000 over forty years up to 1910). Bobby Abel, the Victorian Surrey 'player' batsman, asked to turn amateur so that he could make more money. The system lasted until 1963, when they were eventually all classed as 'cricketers', the last symptom being that players were indicated in match programmes by having their initials after their surnames; it was a long-standing tradition that status could be distinguished linguistically – in 1864, in a match between Cambridge University and Surrey, the 'gentlemen' had 'esq' after their names. Not long before its demise, the system was producing absurdities that, were it not for their offensiveness, would be looked on as quaintly eccentric. At a match at Lord's in 1961 an announcement was given on the public address system: 'Your score cards show at No. 8 for Middlesex, F. J. Titmus; that should read, of course, Titmus, F. J.'

As amateur sports maintained a hold over their activities that prevented big business from becoming involved, business opportunities were instead sought in the world of professional sports: pedestrianism for publicans, and football directorships for the commercial and industrial managerial class, with some involvement of the skilled working class. It was very much the semi-skilled and 'respectable' working class that provided the mass following for sport

ESSEX		1st Innings	
1	DODDS T C	st Catt b Pettiford	121
2	AVERY A V	b Dovey	50
3	T E BAILEY	b Ridgway	41
4	HORSFALL R	st Catt b Pettiford	66
*5	D J INSOLE	b Pettiford	16
6	VIGAR F	b Pettiford	60
7	GREENSMITH W T	not out	14
8	SMITH R	st Catt b Pettiford	16
†9	TAYLOR B	ct Wilson b Pettiford	10
10	J BAILEY		
11	PRESTON K C		
	Extras	b-5 lb-9 nb- w-	14

in the first half of the twentieth century. Professional football between 1890 and 1914, as it was taken over by the working classes, became an area where the rich, politicians and royalty 'visited' to provide manifestations of support without becoming involved.

The introduction in 1885 of a wage for professional footballers was originally meant to allow waged men to be paid for the time taken off work in order to play football. The intention here was to allow all players the possibility of playing at the highest level. Certain controls meant that players could not be poached from smaller clubs by richer ones, but the introduction of a maximum wage was clearly influenced by the mentality of those players who could afford to be amateurs. Despite how we may feel about the rates of pay given to top-level footballers, there is still widespread disapproval of highly paid sportsmen (the same disapproval of modern footballers' cars was aimed at nineteenth-century prizefighters wrecking their carriages). Regardless of the physical injuries sustained, the short career, and the size of audience, there is still a sense that the profession is overpaid.

There were areas in which the distinction between professional and amateur was less than clear. The Oxford and Cambridge rowers in 1839 established three principles between them – that a 'gentleman' should steer (but at that time they would have all been gentlemen), that fouling should be abolished, and that 'victory should be its own reward'. Fouling was the emphasis of the sport for professionalism – you won a race not just by speed, but also by any means that you could put your opponent off. But money changed hands after the races between amateur clubs on the Thames, who also employed fouling.

The Welsh Rugby Union was extremely generous in its interpretation of 'reasonable expenses', with the result that attempts to introduce rugby league to South Wales failed, and fewer skilled players moved to paid jobs in rugby league in the north of England. After a crisis of inspection of the management of the amateur code in 1907 led to the cancellation of international matches, the Welsh Rugby Union let it be known that it would be ruled by itself alone, and the comfortable 'amateur' status of Welsh rugby, with full squad training sessions comparable to professional training, gave the game a status and a success level that continued to the 1980s.

'Shamateurism' in the 1990s was the term applied to amateur rugby union players whose income from endorsing products and similar secondary sources made it obvious that they were not amateurs, but neither were they professionals. The acceptance that the game would eventually become professional at least stopped the drift of talented union players over to rugby league, where they could play and be paid openly for their skills. The Amateur Athletic Association has retained its name, though condoning the payment of athletes through various forms.

Soon after the Marylebone Cricket Club (MCC) had resolved the distinction between players and gentlemen, Wimbledon admitted professional tennis players to the championship, and footballers managed to get the maximum wage abolished. The association of the term 'professional' with club servants, kowtowing to the members who paid their wages, disappeared as professionals began to be seen as consummate entertainers essential to their clubs' financial success. The incentives for top-level athletes to gain a reward appropriate to the level of both their skills and their audience attraction can clearly be seen in the prizes previously available: for winning the Ladies' Singles at Wimbledon in 1966 Billie Jean King was given a Harrods gift voucher for £45. Two years later, as champion she received £750, though this was still only three-eighths of the amount won by the men's champion.

But the word 'professional' still retains a meaning 'done with a calculation to improve the chances of winning'; a 'professional foul' is done after calculation that its consequences are less than that of losing a point/goal/wicket. H. A. Harris in *Sport in Britain* (1975) was so outraged by the gap between sport done for enjoyment and sport done to attract paying spectators that he coined the word 'spenter' for the latter; any scheme of reform would have to accept the fundamental difference between the two – '"Spenter" must be left to look after itself, and sport must make a clean break from it.'

Codes of conduct

English has many expressions using the word 'sport' that are to do with honourable or generous behaviour: 'that's very sporting of you', meaning 'you are honourable to be prepared to surrender that'; 'you're a sport'; 'sportsmanship'; 'sportsmanlike'. Certain assumptions that derived from the team ethos as promoted by team sports in the public schools combined with 'good manners' to create a certain kind of 'sportsmanship' in team sports such as cricket and football. In cricket this survived perhaps until the 'Bodyline' Ashes series of 1932. In football it created amateur and professional approaches that sat uncomfortably beside each other into the early twentieth century. Corinthian Casuals football club was founded in 1882 to preserve the cream of England's public-school players and, it seems, the best manifestations of sportsmanship: when the penalty kick was introduced in 1891, they introduced the practice of withdrawing the goalkeeper, on the grounds that if a foul had been committed that warranted this punishment its full consequences should be taken unquestioningly.

However, this notion of the sovereignty of fair play needs to be seen in context, and C. L. R. James was in a good position to highlight the potential paradoxes. As a Marxist historian, Trinidad nationalist, cricket fanatic and former public-school boy, he writes in *Beyond a Boundary* (1963) of how absolute the rituals of fair play were on the cricket field, but within a school environment where boys cheated and were aggressive and intolerant. The public-school system itself was renowned for its institutional bullying and produced the system that in Trinidad organised cricket along racial lines:

> The British tradition soaked deep into me was that
> when you entered the sporting arena you left behind
> you the sordid compromises of everyday existence.
> Yet for us to do that we would have had to divest
> ourselves of our skins.

However, it may also be argued that cricket allowed exploration of the discipline of fair play where it might not be explored elsewhere, and without it the discipline might not have been touched on at all.

The colonial environment echoed the 'civilising' effect of the nineteenth-century public school, teaching obedience, team spirit and fair play. In June 1922 the *Gold Coast Independent* published an article, signed by 'Fairplay', affirming these sentiments:

> If we really wish to shift our country to any higher
> level of civilisation we must get in hand young men
> who are smart, bright and social; who have a love for
> comradeship and who have the real understanding of
> duty. There is no institution capable of achieving
> these better than Cricket and Football.

Of course, much of the 'gentlemanly conduct' was empty ritual. *Lillywhite's Guide to Cricketers* (1853) includes advice to captains in a section on 'management', which is clearly about how to organise the activities of a team, for example when to eat, in order to maximise the chances of winning.

Control

Questions of governmental control have for a long time influenced sport, for, while late-twentieth-century sport became increasingly drawn into politics, sports have always been a tool and an expression of governmental policy. Roman emperors negotiated their relationship with the mob by means of violent spectator sports; Henry VIII and François I jousted, wrestled and shot their way through the diplomatic summit of the Field of the Cloth of Gold in France in 1520; and in the twentieth century a variety of governments used the Olympics as blatant political showcases. Much of what we know of early sports comes from documentation of their being banned – football in the thirteenth century, half-bowl in the fifteenth, tennis in the sixteenth, bowling alleys in the seventeenth, and billiards in the eighteenth. Court documents recording fines for unlawful playing of sports tell us what games were played when, where, and who was allowed to play them. The governmental suppression of sports, the question of 'who plays what', and the drawing up of rules have in Britain all had an effect on the language of sports and on language applied to sports.

Terraced standing viewing was lost after legislation to change the design of football stadiums, following lethal disasters in the 1980s; the change to all-seater stadiums has meant the gradual loss of terms such as 'on the terraces' or 'the word from the terraces', replaced by 'in the stands'. The term 'chinaman', for a deceptive spin ball in cricket, currently recognised as unacceptable, will probably

TEAM TALK

disappear, and the technique will be renamed or merged with another. Following legislation to ban hunting with dogs in the 1990s, few now would describe hunting as 'sport'.

From the mid-sixteenth century sport was a target of puritans, who saw it as pointless at best, and an inducement to evil-living at worst. For one minister in the seventeenth century, sports were 'these dunghills and filth on commonweals'; the suppression of sports on Sundays was one of the clearest influences of puritanism from the sixteenth century to the twentieth. The temperance movement in the nineteenth century, however, provided sports in the form of mass walks, cricket matches and outings to horse-races, as an alternative to drinking and the sports activities connected to pubs.

In 1573 Philip Stubbes complained in the *Anatomie of Abuses* of the 'prophane exercises on the Sabbath day', including 'bowling, tennisse-playing, football playing and such other devilish pastimes'. One of our earliest surviving records of cricket is found in the documentation of a court case (often the best sources of early information). In 1622 the Consistory Court of Chichester Cathedral fined five men for playing cricket in Boxgrove churchyard on a Sunday ('contrary to the seventh article', that is the seventh commandment, to keep the sabbath holy), for breaking the church windows with the ball, and 'for that a little childe had like to have her braynes beaten out with a cricket batt' – clearly fielding too close. In seventeenth-century Scotland golfers were regularly prosecuted for 'profaning the Sabbath'.

James I encouraged some activities – dancing, leaping, archery, and some seasonal festivities – but he banned the Sunday enjoyment of 'all unlawful games ..., as bear and bull-baiting, interludes, and at all times in the meaner sort of people by law prohibited, bowling'. The problem with bowling, and many other sports, was that they encouraged gambling, which threatened the status-quo of honest, if back-breaking and soul-destroying, labour for wages, necessary to a lawful and ordered society. But there was a sort of gloating in such publications as the broadsheet *Divine examples of God's Severe Judgments upon Sabbath-breakers in their Unlawful Sports, collected out of Several Divine Subjects* (1660):

> On January 25 1634 being the Lord's Day in the time
> of the great Frost, fourteen young men presuming to
> play at Football upon the Ice on the River Trent near
> to Gainsborough were all drowned.

Nineteenth-century social reformers managed to have a number of blood sports banned – bull-baiting, ratting, cock-fighting. Most of their success came in urban areas, where these had been associated with the working classes; in rural areas fox-hunting and badger-digging continued. The feeling among some municipal authorities was that sport had to be controlled to preclude the dangers of crowds getting overexcited and out of control. Municipal control kept sport to clearly defined areas, which meant no sport in public spaces and parks. The churches managed to exert their influence over many urban sports clubs: in 1870 a quarter of the football clubs and half of the cricket clubs were based on churches, so the structure for control was clearly understood by all concerned. While in southern European countries the Church sanctioned sports on Sundays, thereby maintaining some control over public behaviour, in the Protestant areas no such dispensations were allowed. Church attendance was required by some employers in the nineteenth century, and as late as 1842 boys were being fined for playing cricket on Sundays. In the United States the National League prohibited professional baseball and gambling on Sundays from the 1870s until the 1930s, while in the United Kingdom Sunday racing was banned until 1992, and at first no on-course betting was allowed.

Sport and the language of morality

Thomas Arnold's aim at Rugby School between 1828 and 1841 was to create a class of men who would be disassociated from the aristocracy, the greed of the industrialists and the claims of the disenfranchised who threatened to disrupt society. Disciplined, self-reliant, socially responsible Christian gentlemen, who would govern society well, fairly and enthusiastically, were the ideal product, and through a succession of headmasters Rugby School intended to produce them; sport came to be perceived as the ideal means. In 1864 the Earl of Clarendon spoke in the House of Lords about the report of the Public Schools Commission, stating that 'games' tended 'to make the English gentleman what he was, and what he would, it was to be hoped, long remain'. Games were, according to the report, 'creators of health' and developed 'some of the most valuable social qualities and manly virtues'. 'Manliness' was a word that originally meant 'kindness', but came to acquire connotations of male adulthood as well. By the 1820s it was being used to describe sports. 'Manliness' and 'athleticism' were

seen as a flair for games and an instinct for fair but firm colonial government. Manliness was playing the game fairly, but trying to beat your opponent. Manliness was stopping immediately anyone was hurt. Manliness was being prepared to wager money on your own skill, but not to be paid for your actions.

Manly sports were the subject of much discussion through the Victorian period; according to *Cassell's Book of Sports and Pastimes* (1907), cricket, swimming, boxing and pingpong were manly; shinty, ice-hockey, javelin and lawn tennis not. Cricket was consistently described as a manly game. Athletics was manly, rugby football was manly, and amateur rowing was manly. But, as the century progressed, 'manliness' came to have different meanings for different social groups; for the middle classes it meant amateurism, participation rather than spectating, playing by the 'spirit of the game'; for the working classes it meant watching your team do anything to get a win, aggressiveness, professionalism.

In the mid-nineteenth century the United States saw the ideological inclusion of active sports in the building of the nation, the Protestant and bourgeois ethic embracing athletics and gymnastics in particular as a way of reinforcing self-control and self-improvement. Later in the century, new conceptions of masculinity embraced manly sports as supplying the ideal view of themselves desired by white middle-class males in a rapidly changing country. As cricket did in Britain, so baseball defined manliness for the United States. Rounders was, for Henry Chadwick, champion of baseball, 'devoid of manly features'; a baseball player had to 'possess the characteristics of true manhood' (*Dime Book of Baseball*, 1867).

Spalding's catalogue in 1911 listed the manly sports as fencing, boxing, wrestling, tumbling, jiu-jitsu, Indian clubs, dumb-bells, pulley-weights and 'how to punch the bag'. The widening appeal of American football beyond the colleges drew it into the manly sports, especially on account of its physicality. 'Manliness' now is perhaps more to do with the acceptance of the vicissitudes of sport, from defeat to injury. Frank DeFord, one of the United States' premier sports journalists, questioned the 'health and safety' approach to sport in terms of manliness: 'Is the game no longer worth the price of admission to manhood?' (National Public Radio, 17 October 2010).

A related expression that emerged from the public schools at the same time as 'manliness' was 'muscular Christianity' – an ideal personified by the Oxford crew that won the first Boat Race in 1829, all of whom became clergymen. 'Muscular Christianity' proposed the cultivation of the body as a metaphor of moral fitness, allied to social Darwinism, in which the 'terrible laws of natural selection' (Charles Kingsley) could be used for the good: physical prowess was the outward sign of moral decency, which itself would be a proselytising influence on society. This implied a moral duty to exercise, and through sport any aggression could be managed, directed and controlled. A key part of the thinking behind this was that training in moral behaviour on the sports field could be transferred to the world beyond; this was the pattern that young men graduating from the universities took to the sports clubs and boys' clubs in urban areas, particularly those attached to parish churches. The sentiment gave rise to a literature of tracts and moralising novels such as Kingsley's *Alton Locke* (1850) and Hughes's *Tom Brown's School Days* (1857). Rudyard Kipling saw through much of this in *Stalky and Co* (1899), his attack on muscular Christianity, which indicated that sport might teach duty, but not make people brilliant or insightful.

In the United States the same sentiments were expressed through the open-air culture proposed by Thoreau and Emerson. The American version of muscular Christianity deplored the utilitarian view of pioneer America, that gardening should be preferred to sport. The moral character needed nutrition, which could be provided by team sports and communion with nature.

An echo of this exists in the deal that requires highly paid sportsmen to be role models. Barnes contrasted this with the freedom available to musicians; 'sports stars must be better, not worse than the rest of us. It all goes back to the Victorian notion of sport: that sport teaches you to be a better person.' Most practitioners appear to accept the role-model deal, though the moral authority of the sports' governing bodies does exert an unspoken pressure, dependent on the need to keep their own houses in order for sound commercial reasons. In some cases part of being a role model involves just doing what you are told, often doing public relations for the club and the sport. One of the worst offences in this regard is refusing to talk to the press, this being part of 'playing the game'; a professional sportsman or -woman has to comply and participate in all the aspects of the profession. Some sportsmen and -women have objected to this – Charles Barklay said, 'Just because I dunk a basketball doesn't mean I should raise your kids', and footballer Joey Barton protested that 'You might be good at that (sport), but you might be crap at life'.

Identity

The language of sport serves to create group identities. The histories of cricket and golf go back beyond the sports themselves, as people have looked for named antecedents that may provide the honour of antiquity. The folk ancestors of football, more to do with ritual territorial capture and defence and male bonding, have a barely discernible connection with football as played today, but these may be seen as preferable to a view of the game being created from chaos at a handful of privileged Victorian schools.

In some cases this involves myth-making. The 'invention' of baseball was sought with the fervour of the quest for the Holy Grail in the late nineteenth century and, though the story of its invention by Abner Doubleday was thoroughly debunked, the myth took a long

FLANNELETTE FOOTBALL SHIRTS.

time to die, and the National Baseball Hall of Fame contrived to name its online catalogue the 'American Baseball Network for Electronic Research', ABNER for short. And though the myth of William Webb Ellis's picking up the football and running with it is equally debunked, Rugby School still has a plaque in his memory, and the trophy of the Rugby Union World Cup is the Webb Ellis Cup.

The building of the group through language happens most noticeably in the knowledge of jargon, the specialist words. This itself takes a number of forms: the preciseness of cricket field-placings and the names of different kinds of bowling; the supposed impenetrability of certain rules – off-side in football, leg-before-wicket in cricket; and the development of metaphors from the terminology of sports. 'Inside terms' arise, such as the 'inside baseball' term 'sprinkle the infield' for buying a round of drinks, from the process of watering down the dust between innings.

Spectatorism builds group identity, from school to national levels. The coincidence of geographical location allows this to operate across other divisions – class, age, gender, race. Governments have long known that the success of national sporting teams is of great value in an economic crisis; it makes people feel better, and that means less criticism of the government. Harold Wilson felt that one of the major factors in his defeat in the 1970 general election was England's defeat by Germany in the World Cup four days earlier. In Britain this sense of nationalism in supporting the English cricket or football or rugby team grew stronger till the 1930s, and was perhaps abandoned when it came into contact with the nationalist fervour of Germany in the 1936 Olympics. The sound of 'England' being chanted has created the word 'Engerland', so far not in the OED. Within the United Kingdom the support for national teams representing England, Wales, Scotland and Northern Ireland allows several concepts to be explored: surrogate nationalism, real national identity and difference, and chosen nationality – the sport identity of 'British' is always there if the other fails. Colonial cricket tours by English teams were thought to have eased transition to independence for countries whose success added to their self-esteem.

The use of terms of national stereotyping in sports commentating – 'Gallic flair', 'dour Scottish defence', 'clinical German build-up' – creates easy patterns which become expected clichés. In defeat the British are 'lion-hearted', in victory the Germans are 'clinical and effective'. Individuals take on national or regional characteristics: Bjorn Borg is 'ice-cool', Harry Redknapp 'a diamond geezer'. Coverage in the media of major sporting events adds to the sense of a national way of life, with the creation of phrases such as 'England batting collapse' or 'They think it's all over', all-embracing in their misery or joy, and comforting in their ritual use (for a curious coincidence, see Egan's description of a prize-fight in 1821: 'The spectators left their places and ran towards the ropes, thinking it was all over...'). Martin Polley in *Moving the Goalposts* (1999) describes the metonymic use of the name of the country as something we accept unquestioningly – 'Great Britain gets a medal in the Olympics' does not need the qualifying 'an athlete representing...'

The creation of 'the national game' tends to happen retrospectively; we do not know that a sport has emerged with these laurels till long after it has happened. One reason why baseball is perceived as the national game of the United States is the vast amount of literature it has produced, the way it is used as a forum for the exploration of feelings and relationships. The same is said of cricket in England, though others would claim football as England's 'national game' (partly perhaps a way of claiming it back from those who

57

regularly beat England). Despite consistent success at rugby union and cricket, Australians consider rugby league as their national game. In Ireland in the 1880s the delineation of national sports by the Gaelic Athletic Association led to 'the Ban', a direct challenge to the hegemony of British sports, whereby anyone who had played British sports was banned from any GAA-organised event. Gaelic games became a symbol of Irish nationalism, both at home and abroad.

Women or ladies?

Those following Wimbledon in the early 1970s would have been accustomed to hearing 'Game Mrs King, Mrs King leads by three games to two'; a few years later it would have been 'Game Borg, Borg leads by three games to two'. Was this a case of civility extended to ladies, or an assumption that one sex was a more natural player of the game? This designation of Miss or Mrs before women's names in sports reporting has a long history – hockey players in 1936 were referred to as 'Miss ...' or 'Mrs ...' in *The Guardian*, and the only women to feature in the sports pages of the Scottish *People's Journal* in the 1930s seem to have been the daughters of football club coaching staff, writing long appreciative articles under the name 'Miss Hindle' or 'Miss Nicholl'.

Women were excluded from attendance at the ancient Greek games (see 'Clothing'), and many historians of sport have pointed out the fundamental 'maleness' of team sports. Typical of this was Cornish hurling, seen by Richard Carew in the seventeenth century as a training for conflict, or as excused outright conflict itself. The danger and damage to the individual here was subsumed in male bonding through violence. Manliness set the tone for the predominance of maleness in nineteenth-century sport, with all the rule-writing being a male preserve. For much of the twentieth century women's roles involved watching, washing men's kit, and making sandwiches for cricket tea intervals (though it was noted in 1907 that there were as many women as men in the stands at Aston Villa's matches).

Until the nineteenth century women's participation in sport had raised few eyebrows; it was less than men's participation, but proportionately more than women's participation in other activities, such as business or politics. Women are known to have played tennis in medieval France, and are shown playing cricket, practising archery and shooting in prints from the late eighteenth century. In Scotland golf was played by women from the sixteenth century on, but this was an exception to the rule. The mania for games in the English public schools in the nineteenth century was part of a process that successfully separated 'ruling class' males from females, who were generally educated at home, with few opportunities for sport beyond archery, croquet, riding, skating and, eventually, badminton and tennis. The first women's hockey club, Molesey Ladies, was founded in 1887, with women's basketball and netball appearing in the 1890s.

Roedean, a girls' public school founded in 1885, followed the boys' school model, with two to three hours of exercise daily. The following generation saw a big increase in female sport, with cycling, rowing and walking all involving women participating in public spaces. Much of this was the result of sociological thinking at the time that an increase in female fitness would lead to

healthier babies, and would counter the mental strain believed to affect women now more included in education.

But the period also saw the seeds of the failure to get women participating on an equal basis to men. Female football and cricket failed spectacularly, with two professional female cricket teams collapsing after one season in 1890. Rounders and netball did not have enough participants to establish governing bodies until the 1920s, and the Football Association distanced itself from women's football in 1921. Promotion of women's sport at the end of the Victorian era also fell into the trap of linking sport with fashion, with scandalous sporting gear such as bloomers catching the public's attention more than their wearer's tennis or cycling skills. The Women's Amateur Athletic Association, founded in 1922, and the Women's League of Health and Beauty, founded in the 1930s, show people addressing the need to regularise and provide sports for women, but also the mainstream absence of women's participation up to this point.

For most women in the first half of the twentieth century sports were abandoned after education, and football, snooker, rugby, quoits, sea-fishing and cricket excluded female participation almost absolutely. More individual sports such as golf or tennis were acceptable, and non-contact team games such as hockey, netball and lacrosse. However, women did manage to play rugby and football in spite of the FA's saying that 'football is quite unsuitable for females and ought not to be encouraged.' Even hockey had to fight against the (male) Hockey Association, who opposed the setting up of an All-England Women's Hockey Association. When women did get to play cricket, from 1926 under the Women's Cricket Association, they were expected to revert to the old underarm bowling style, despite the inconvenience to players wearing skirts.

Until 1984 there was no marathon for women in the Olympics, and women first ran openly in a public marathon in 1967. Kathy Switzer entered the Boston Marathon as K. V. Switzer, later claiming that she did not know that women were barred and had just given her usual signature, though it is clear that she was deliberately challenging the male hegemony, as she ran wearing lipstick. 4 miles into the race the organisers caught up with her, and she was attacked by the race director but managed to escape and finish. Roberta Gibbs, who ran in the same race, was prevented from finishing by a match official. *The New York Times* described her as 'a willowy 23-year old blonde whose father is a chemistry professor at Tufts College'. Incredibly, people still believed that women did not have the powers of endurance to run a marathon. Women had been admitted to the Olympics first in 1928, but until the 1948 Olympics there were only three track events for women, all of them up to 100 metres. J. J. Coakley in *Sport in Society* (1978) suggested that if women had been responsible for writing the Olympic motto it would have been not so much 'Faster, higher, stronger', but rather more to do with balance, flexibility and endurance.

For Silverman it was ultimately tennis player Billie Jean King who broke the mould with her demand that women athletes should be treated as athletes, 'not as symbols of women's lib'. From 1972, following a legal challenge, the Jockey Club staged flat races for women, though at first applying the name 'jockettes' to female jockeys. Popular culture in the 1980s and 1990s began to examine women's roles in sport, with films such as *Gregory's Girl* (1981) and the television series *The Manageress* (1989–90). But the overriding assumption is still that team sport, as labelled, is a male activity. We have football and women's football, rugby and women's rugby, cricket and women's cricket, boxing and women's boxing.

On the other hand there is a long history of sports from which men were excluded. At Inverness there was a Shrovetide folk-football match for women only. Netball developed from basketball as a 'women's version'. Some gymnastics disciplines seem to be dominated almost exclusively by young teenage girls; and figure-skating was for a while so associated with women that in many people's minds the sexuality of participating men was compromised. Some female sports participation, both historically and currently, is so little-known that it seems to be deliberately ignored. Women's boxing, currently acceptable, had a long history as an exhibition sport from the eighteenth century; 'lady boxers' appeared at prestigious municipal venues until the 1920s, and women's boxing was an exhibition event at the 1904 Olympics before being banned in most countries. Mixed boxing has never been officially sanctioned, but until 1962, when the male competitors of the Tourist Trophy unanimously voted to ban them, women competed with men on equal terms in motorcycle racing.

The general problem of assumptions in English words that women are included within terminology that is demonstrably male (e.g. 'mankind') is very noticeable in sport. In 1994 Tonya Harding was stripped of her national figure-skating title for 'unsportsmanlike behaviour'. It is noticeable that while the signatories to the *Rules of Stoolball* (1909) were all women, and the game is clearly described in *Recreation and Physical Fitness for Girls and Women* (1937), the people who face the bowling are all 'batsmen'. By 2010 the word 'batters' was being widely used in cricket, a year after 'Miss' and 'Mrs' were dropped from Wimbledon scores.

There are still curiosities in the gender separation and mixing of sports: United Kingdom competitive angling has male and female categories. Though mixed games were common from the start of lawn tennis in the 1870s, more recent high-profile exhibition contests between men and women on not quite equal terms were labelled as 'Battles of the Sexes'. While female boxing has had a long and little-known history, the thought of mixed boxing instantly crosses several boundaries of unacceptability, though we may be hard put to define them. That the whole question of gender in sport is still in a state of flux is shown by the fact that gender-testing still goes on and has taken forms that appear to treat women as second-class citizens.

At the European Track and Field Championships in 1966 every woman competitor had to be seen naked by a panel of female doctors, while Princess Anne was the only female competitor who did not have to undergo a sex test at the 1976 Olympic Games.

Spreading the word

The commentary on a horse-race is one of the most distinctive methods of communicating sports information, but we might be forgiven for wondering what exactly is being communicated. Is it the excitement of the race, or clear and concise information about which horse is winning? Is it possible to visualise where the ball is while listening to a tennis commentary? Oates in *On Boxing* states that the 'ringside announcers give to the wordless spectacle a narrative unity', and, if applied to other fast-moving sports, the commentary is about the overall story and the atmosphere. Details of place and person are essential primarily so that we know that the commentator is *there*; perhaps it is the 'there-ness' that is being conveyed primarily. Sports broadcasting ('sportscasting' from about 1930) tells us more than the score, as does the communicating of sports in literature, journalism and drama.

Sports broadcasting creates a special relationship between broadcaster and audience mediated by language; it embraces character (John Arlott in cricket, Eddie Waring in rugby league), continuity (John Snagge and the Boat Race, 1931–73; the football results read on Saturday afternoon BBC television), tomfoolery (Brian Johnston for *Test Match Special*), and clichés, gaffes and senseless comments (David Coleman, who was commemorated in *Private Eye*'s 'Colemanballs'). Ultimately phrases like 'They think it's all over' provided an irrevocable link between sport and broadcasting, and a communally recognised linguistic understanding of the event. Sports broadcasting until the 1950s might make assumptions about the identity of its prime listeners; Adrian Beard points out the case of cricket updates, which would be preceded by: 'For those of you who have just come in from the office', an assumption of work status and income levels. But at the same time live broadcasting made sports accessible and immediate to a vast number of people whose previous access had been through newspaper reports.

Before broadcasting, journalism had over a hundred years created a removed spectatorism and provided a forum for news, challenges and analysis, ranging from simple results to the writings of William Hazlitt and Pierce Egan. The 'pink 'uns' (newspapers carrying sports reports), which began in the late Victorian period, gave poetical reporting along with the news, a style of writing that sports reporting has retained. Hargreaves points to the current 'lexical poverty' of sports journalism, how it reverts to clichés and expected epithets in which tackles are 'bone-crunching', opponents are 'crushed', goals 'slammed', and so on. This restricted code he calls 'sportuguese', the attempt to use sensationalist language in order to retain the audience's attention and loyalty. Journalism shows us language changing; in 1921 *The Times* reported on a team written as "Spurs", but by 1922 the inverted commas

had gone, as the name had ceased to be a specialist term among fans and become one which readers of *The Times* would recognise. Some writing was almost breathless; this is from the *Daily Express*, 11 June 1936:

> Spinners of Mitchell had Gloucestershire reeling. He
> didn't start too well. Began with a wide; soon
> conceded another; and had 11 runs hit off him
> before he 'got' Barnett at 64. What he did after that
> was a shame. Look:–O 10 M 3 R 26 W 7.

In the United States in the 1920s sportswriting was exciting, brash even, with a number of journalists known as 'gee-whizzers' for their direct enthusiasm particularly boosting the persona of the sporting hero. Throughout the twentieth century sportswriters on both sides of the Atlantic were obsessed with the hero (Babe Ruth, Jack Hobbs, Dixie Dean, Muhammad Ali, Martina Navratilova, Olga Korbut), particularly the hero to be made and unmade (Ian Botham, Paul Gascoigne, David Beckham). It was the 'writing down' of the hero that expressed the real power of the written word, with headlines such as 'Rock-Botham – Reckless Ian to blame as England crash' (*Daily Mirror*, 19 February 1981).

Club magazines and match programmes for football clubs appeared at the end of the nineteenth century, the first known programme being at Watford in 1891. Football fanzines, which appeared in the 1980s as a development from punk writing, could afford to be more allusive, more 'inside'. The earliest of these was *Foul*, produced by Cambridge University students in 1972, followed by *Terrace Talk* (York City) and *Wanderers Worldwide* (Bolton Wanderers). The best of them show in their titles an inspired gallows humour – *The Hanging Sheep* at Leeds (the coat of arms of the city of Leeds shows a golden fleece), and *What a Load of Cobblers* at Northampton, whose editorial for December 1993 began: 'Can it get any worse?'

During the nineteenth century sport increasingly became the subject of literary writing and reportage, with Dickens writing about horse-racing and cricket, Pierce Egan and William Hazlitt raising the status of prizefighting by their enthusiastic and informed work, and Byron celebrating his own swim across the Hellespont (though fairly casually):

> My dripping limbs I faintly stretch,
> And think I've done a feat today.

This period also saw the beginning of an industry of sports books for children and teenagers, both fiction and non-fiction, creating a heroic sporting world, epitomised by C. B. Fry, both a great sportsman and a great sportswriter. The twentieth century brought the full acceptance of sport as a worthy subject of literature, particularly in the United States, where sports fiction became a major medium whereby the country explored its own identity.

For some writers, the interpretation of sport as an art form came naturally; Neville Cardus wrote about cricket in the summer and music in the winter (he was the *Guardian* critic for both) and often used musical metaphors for cricket. In a famous essay in 1920, *The Cricketer as Artist*, he implied that in the cricket of the time technique was rightly accorded more importance than winning. For others, the fact that there are resemblances between art and sport is merely coincidence. 'Style', in batting, passing, running, can easily be read into sporting technique, though it is more likely to be projected on to the actions of a winner than those of a loser.

For others, the idea of any compatibility between thinking and sport is still confusing. After a violent incident in 1995, the footballer Eric Cantona baffled a press conference with the words: 'When the seagulls follow the trawler, it is because they think sardines will be thrown into the sea.' In a sport that was notorious for the low intellectual ability of its practitioners, this immediately classed him as a devotee of obscure French philosophy. What was expected of footballers was a string of clichés such as 'I'm gutted' or 'We was robbed'; appreciation of the French footballer's skills was usually expressed with the chant 'Oo-ah-Cantona'.

Though there are more books on golf than any other sport, it has not engendered great literature so much as humorous story-telling. Contemplative writing about cricket has attracted many writers in England and the Commonwealth, and yet there are not many memorable fictional accounts, and no top-rate novels to compare with those about baseball in the United States. Fiction based on American football has addressed the increasing commodification of the sportsman, while in Britain *The Loneliness of the Long-Distance Runner* by Alan Sillitoe (1959) and *This Sporting Life* by David Storey (1960) used sport as the theatre for exploring the struggle for identity.

Swimming has been seen as the human body committed to managing two competing environments. It is acting both with and against air and water, for the body can move horizontally through water yet hardly at all through air; yet it needs air to survive, while water supports it. In this environment like no other, the body competes with and is fully aware of itself, as strain becomes relaxation, and the lack of impact heightens the consciousness of time and rhythm.

Little wonder then that it inspired Shelley and Byron, the first so desperate to swim that he threw himself into water and lay at the bottom waiting for his body to rise, and the second so at ease in the water that his homage to ancient texts took the form of swimming the Hellespont, recreating the mythological swim of Leander. In the contrast between these two there is an awareness of a contest against death; for the swimmer there is always the shadow of the threat of not being able to keep afloat, of meeting the fate of Shelley, cast up on the shore drowned. And yet it is precisely the water, and its difference from the body, that keeps the body afloat. For John Cheever in *The Swimmer* (1964) swimming is the ultimate metaphor for the quest and failure to know the self.

Cricket seems more than most games to extend a potential for almost any kind of interpretation. Its continuity is a comfort, the fact that such a complex game has changed so little acts as a kind of deep justification; every boy walking out to bat feeds the culture of cricket, and carries on that justification. Cardus mythologised it (too floridly for some), Priestley understood the work of it, and C. L. R. James understood the politics of it; John Arlott saw the poetry in it, describing a Gary Sobers six as 'the stroke of a man knocking a thistle top off with a walking stick'. C. B. Fry read it as a dance narrative, while Derek Birley warned of the dangers of reading cricket as art. Perhaps some of this came from the complexity of the game, particularly the changing pace of time within a test match, the way the balance changes inexorably or freakishly, the much remarked-on 'Englishness' of it.

Baseball is 'our game – the American game', said Walt Whitman, and it could be said that no game belongs more fully and exclusively to a country than baseball does to the United States. Perhaps the best example of the description of sport as 'a story about ourselves that we tell ourselves', baseball 'dominates most American sport literature' (*Oxford Encyclopedia of World Sport*, 1998). Novels of the calibre of *You Know Me Al* (1914–16) by Ring Lardner, *The Natural* (1952) by Bernard Malamud, *Bang the Drum Slowly* (1956) by Mark Harris, which was the source of a genre of 'literate' sports films, *The Celebrant* (1982) by Eric R. Greenberg, and *Underworld* (1997) by Don DeLillo, show the tradition of baseball fiction to be producing major works throughout the century.

Though Hemingway's *Death in the Afternoon* (1932) is a *tour de force* of aficionado writing about bullfighting, few sports have been explored so revealingly through writing as has boxing. Leonard

Gardner's *Fat City* (1969) examines the nestorian despair inherent in losing skill and power with age, while Norman Mailer's *The Fight* (1975), about the Muhammad Ali versus George Foreman fight, and Joyce Carol Oates's *On Boxing* (1987) provoke the reader to consider boxing in terms of hatred, bewilderment, fanaticism and tenderness. Here is Mailer on Foreman's second, Dick Sadler:

> Sadler works on him, rubs his breasts and belly, Sadler sends his fingers into all the places where rage has congested, into the meat of the pectorals and the muscle plating beneath Foreman's chest, Sadler's touch has all the wisdom of thirty-five years of Black fingers elucidating comfort for Black flesh, sensual are his fingers as he plucks and shapes and shakes and balms, his silver bracelet shining on his Black wrist.

And Oates writing about a sportswriter's 'intermittent disgust for the sport he has been watching most of his life':

> Yet we don't give up on boxing, it isn't that easy. Perhaps it's like tasting blood. Or, more discreetly put, love commingled with hate is more powerful than love. Or hate.

In writing time can be slowed down, and this is very much the case with boxing – Mailer, and Pierce Egan 150 years earlier, were very aware of this, as was W. C. Heinz in *The Fighter's Wife* (1955). And it can accept the violence for what it is – from Ring Lardner's *The Champion* (1916) right back to the brutal fight between Epeios and Euryalos in the *Iliad*, one of the first recorded sports reports. A. J. Liebling's *The Sweet Science* (1956) has been recognised as the 'number one sports book of all time' (*Sports Illustrated*, 2002).

Sport and words

As well as developing from earlier words, sporting terms derive from people's names, from places, from clubs and practitioners. Imported terms come with imported sports, such as tennis and fencing. But English also is a great exporter of sporting terms. French has *le turf, le steeplechase, le jockey* and *l'outsider*, no doubt much to the dismay of the Académie Française; while Russian has *boksor* and *nokaut* as direct terms, and *atakujushciy* (attacker) and *tennisistka* (tennis player) as terms 'made into Russian'. As British trading and colonising activities took sport around the world, they also took English as the language of sport.

But sporting language has also been very inventive. 'WAGs' (footballers' wives and girlfriends, from 2006) are accompanied by 'punters' in horse-racing and 'alicadoos' (former players) in rugby union. Local terms for football include 'togger' (Manchester), 'nogger' (North Staffordshire, archaic), 'fitbaa' (Aberdeen), while Bobby Moore and Glenn Hoddle both became rhyming slang terms (for 'score' and 'doddle'). The expression 'to lose your bottle' came from prizefighting, as 'bottom' (spirit) became removed to 'arse', rhyming with 'glass', and extended to 'glass bottle'. Twentieth-century boxers acquired fighting names, as Walker Smith became Sugar Ray Robinson and Jake La Motta became Raging Bull, much the same as nineteenth-century pedestrians had used names such as the Suffolk Stag and the Crow.

On the other hand, sport is renowned for its use of tired language, meaningless phrases and clichés. The demands of broadcasting have produced spectacular phrases such as 'a game of two halves'. *Private Eye*'s 'Colemanballs' has collected these for decades, scapegoating David Coleman, who was indeed responsible for 'A truly international field, no Britons involved', but whose contributions pale beside 'He's in front of everyone in this race except the two in front of him' (Murray Walker) and 'She finally tastes the sweet smell of success' (Ian Edwards). Broadcasting has produced extreme wit and subtlety though, from John Arlott's descriptions of the field-placings occupied by pigeons in the cricket field to Brian Johnston's discreet assessment of unsuccessful batsmen who leave 'without troubling the scorers', a model that extended to Olympic commentators talking about competitors who leave 'without doing damage to the medals'. A lot of the more unfortunate terminology was a continuance of the florid melodramatic style that had been popularised by the 'gee-whizz' style of American sports-writing in the 1920s; in Britain this produced football writing that used such awful phrases as 'leather spheroid' and 'hapless custodian'. Later self-referential terms like 'Roy of the Rovers football' were more comfortable, possibly thanks to nostalgia, with the wholesale red-top adoptions of 'Gazza' (Paul Gascoigne) and 'Sheri' (Teddy Sheringham) working their way quickly into spoken English. Sports-writing's invention of words may be externally referential, for example 'Bloodgate', the story of an injury scam, referencing Watergate; or internal, as in 'WAGs', from the celebrity-creating stories about footballers' wives and girlfriends.

Lost sports, lost words

Is it fair to judge the extent to which a sport enters the psyche of a nation by the number of terms it gives to speech outside the context of sport? We would possibly be able to create a statistical table, but what it would show might be clouded by the fact that some sports involve more specific terms than others, and that an older activity now out of favour, for example hawking, may have given words that have embedded themselves deeply into the language.

Sport has given hosts of phrases to English: 'below the belt', 'own goal', 'level playing-field', 'keeping a straight bat', 'stepping up to the plate', and so on. Many of these retain their connections to sport, while others have become disconnected. 'Cadge' and 'haggard' come from falconry, the first having been a wooden structure for carrying birds for sale, and the second originally describing a young adult bird. 'Hoodwink' is often thought to come from the same field, but this is disputed. A 'stalking horse' was a horse that acted as a moving hide for a wildfowler, while 'heckling' came from cock-fighting (it meant 'pecking out the neck feathers').

Several terms have changed: 'high leaping', from 1870, is now 'the high jump', matches no longer 'come off', and the 'Siamese twin race', reported at the Temperance Gala in the *Blackburn Standard* for 31 August 1878 would now be a 'three-legged race'. And some of the sports are more or less gone – 'purring' (shin-kicking), potshare bowling, long-bowling, goal-running, 'the stride' – a gymnastic

apparatus like a maypole that allowed fantastic circular leaps. Shovelboard, popular in rich Tudor homes, became a game for the poor and has now migrated to the decks of expensive cruise ships. Several games did not quite make it: vigora, cricket played with tennis bats and a hollow rubber ball; hazena, popular in the Czech Republic, and recommended for girls' PE in Britain in the 1930s; closh, a kind of croquet, banned in 1495 and abandoned; pushball, played between two teams each trying to push an enormous ball into the other's territory; tip cat, like knurr and spell, but played with a piece of wood rather than a ball; and balloon, a kind of volleyball played with wooden braces on the arms and a strong ball, adopted at Princeton after duelling was banned. Local games survived into the twentieth century, often in schools or colleges, such as 'codeball' and 'blitzball' in American colleges, or the Eton wall game. But the success of 'keepie-uppie', recorded from 1983, shows that some games can make it, with their own words, from the playground to the training ground.

The future of sporting language

When at the 2010 Winter Olympics Shaun White performed his 'double McTwist 1260', some thought that the name of the manoeuvre must be linked to the name of a product by a well-known fast-food chain using the 'Mc' prefix as a marketing sign. The fact that it was not (it was named after Mike McGill, who devised it) was a relief, but raised the spectre of commercial sponsorship of manoeuvres in new sports, by which the sponsor's name would be part of the manoeuvre. Such a move would not be odd; Lord's Cricket Ground was named after its owner, effectively a sponsor of cricket, and most major privately owned sports grounds and professional championships carry sponsors' names. Why should not a company sponsor a competitor to perfect a technique, give it the company's name, and

73

follow the established practice of sponsorship deals? An actual extension of sponsoring into language is seen in the protection of sponsors' exclusive rights to combinations of words to do with the Olympics, designed to combat 'ambush marketing', but with unclear guidelines that cause concerns about the potentially ruinous illegal use of 'protected' phrases.

Equally there is a strong movement of American sporting words into office-speak, with 'throwing a curve-ball', 'team players', 'ball-park figure' and 'left-field thinking' commonly heard in management meetings. As new sports gain more coverage, the words from those will probably be brought into English-speaking offices.

As existing sports develop and new sports emerge from existing ones, new terms will be required. Skateboarding has a number of terms for manoeuvres most people will not know about – 'stalefish', 'mute air' and 'gay twist' (coming from the usage of 'gay' as 'fake'). Martial arts, from Thai boxing and kick-boxing to taekwondo (Korean for 'breaking with the foot'), will bring to English words from Chinese, Korean and other oriental languages, as well as 'fight club' and 'white-collar boxing'; 'cage-fighting', or 'mixed martial arts', for women as well as men, uses 'sprawl' and 'takedown' as technical terms. The rise of private gyms over the past decade has produced familiarity with 'treadmills', 'personal trainers' and 'power cages', an area where commercial incentives will produce more specialised equipment and training styles.

And within American English the film industry will occasionally produce phenomena like dodgeball, massively popularised by the 2004 film of the same name, and now played in United Kingdom schools. If rollerball, as in the 1975 film, turns out to be a film-fiction game that becomes reality, it will confirm the worst fears of those who are concerned that television coverage of 'cage-fighting' presages the return of gladiatorial combats. But the linguistic developments will be interesting.

Sports

Aerobics

An expression that originated in the United States, 'aerobics' is low-intensity, long-duration exercise, designed to use heightened intake of oxygen to improve cardiovascular activity. Derived from Greek words meaning 'air' and 'life', the word is recorded from the mid 1960s.

American football

American football, or 'gridiron football' (just 'football' in the United States), spread from Harvard and other colleges as a response to the apparent chaos of localised codes of rugby during the 1870s, involving running with the ball rather than kicking (the Harvard version was then known as the 'Boston game'). The key colleges at first were Yale, Harvard, Princeton and Columbia, which in 1876 adopted rugby rules for a championship; Walter Camp at Yale, the 'Father of American Football', was responsible for various subsequent modifications to the rules, including the award of continuous possession to the team holding the ball after a tackle, with a back-pass through the legs (a 'snap-back') as part of a 'scrimmage', a line of players combating each other across the field. The next change was the 'down', in which the team in possession had three attempts to move forward 5 yards or yield possession. The 5-yard lines crossing the pitch, which show the progression of the movement of the ball needed to make legitimate 'downs', led to the name 'gridiron football', in use from the 1890s.

The involvement of 'running interference' at the scrimmage led to high-impact tackles and a massive increase in injuries, which led to charges of brutality aimed at the privileged classes playing football. Deliberate and open physical assault typified the scrimmage line, and fatalities and spinal injuries became frequent. A 'win at all costs' mentality both fed off and increased the violence – in the early 1880s a player was legally allowed to punch another three times. A series of conferences, the first called by President Theodore Roosevelt in 1905, forced the colleges to reform or abandon football, and in some places it was banned. The death of a player in 1905 led to a further crisis, and rule changes to make brutal play less rewarding. The addition in 1906 of the forward pass and the lengthening of the yardage needed to retain possession led to the game becoming more about running and less about impact.

The development of the game away from the colleges followed the colleges' lead; amateur teams began to pay their players, and then industries began to sponsor teams in the period after 1918. Most of the star players of professional teams were former college boys, and eventually college teams became 'feeder' teams for the professional clubs. Football organisation was modelled on industrial and military organisation, with Camp himself claiming in 1910 that the game taught 'obedience to authority'; time management and discipline became an essential part of the game, as it became an echo of American industrial efficiency. At Yale this was carried out so thoroughly that the college lost fewer games than one a year over a period of thirty-three years. Following the Second World War, professional football edged college football out of the limelight, with increased investment, rival franchises, and television coverage from 1939 making football more of a nationwide spectator sport. Many tactical terms date from the 1930s, such as 'zone defense', 'T formation' and 'three-end offense'.

Of all the forms of football, American football does the most to indicate that the origin of football lies with its being done on foot rather than with the foot. Kicking does occur, but drop-kicks were eliminated in the 1930s, and, apart from kicking for goal, it is secondary to running with the ball.

Angling

Leaving aside the question of whether angling should be considered a blood sport, it has long been thought of as a sport. The *Treatise of Fyshynge* (1496) describes it as a 'good dysporte and honest game' and introduces it as 'anglyng with a rod or a yarde, a lyne and a hooke'. The 'rodde' was to be 'a fadom and a halfe longe', with the injunction to 'frette him faste with a cockshotecorde' – a line used for making the nets for bird-catching. This, with the line of white horse-tail, split and retwined, and the 'baytes', 'hoke', 'flot' and 'plumbe' (weight), made up the 'harnays' or tackle. The tying of flies was fairly advanced at this time, with instructions for tying specific flies to match insects landing on water at specified times of the year. For August the writer instructs:

> The drake flye: the body of blacke wall; and lappyd
> abowte wyth blacke sylke; wings of the mayll [outer
> feather] of the blacke drake, wyth a blacke heed.

'Angle' originally meant a 'fishing hook' and developed from the Old English *angul*, which was connected to similar words in Germanic languages, pointing towards an Indo-European root word meaning to 'bend' – this was also the root of the Latin *angulus*, meaning a 'corner', adopted into English in the fourteenth century. There is a story that this word is the origin of the word 'English'. This proposes that the area of Schleswig that the Angles came from was called *Angul* because it was hook-shaped. Unfortunately, the boundaries of this area in the period before the fifth century are unclear, and the mapping technology required to observe such a resemblance was not known at that time.

Aquatics

Aquatics was the name given to sports on water, but primarily rowing, in the nineteenth century – some rowing clubs gave themselves the name of 'aquatic club'; *Bell's Life*, the nineteenth-century sporting paper, ran a section called the 'Aquatic Register'. Modern 'aquatic clubs' are all to do with swimming.

The Tynesider Harry Clasper, who died in 1870, and whose funeral was attended by 130,000 people, was known as the 'father of modern aquatics'.

Archery

Archery has been called this since the beginning of the fifteenth century; one previously used term was 'shooting' – *scotungum* in Old English. Given the importance of archery in medieval warfare, especially during England's wars in France, there is some obscurity about the term for 'archery' at this time. The word 'archer' or 'archar' was in use in the thirteenth century, and is documented as being used for arrows as well as archers (and was an alternative name for the bishop in chess). The Latin word *arcus* meant 'bow, arch or curve'.

As soon as guns began to have more certain effects in warfare, archery became more of a sport than a means of national defence, though statutory regulations to maintain skills and equipment remained in force in the seventeenth century. Archery as a pastime was maintained by those with wealth and land, and by the mid-nineteenth century the sport began to be adopted by middle-class women, having long been practised by aristocratic women.

Archery terms include those in Roger Ascham's five points, as presented in *Toxophilus* ('Lover of the Bow', 1545): standing, nocking, drawing, holding and loosing. 'Nocking', setting the notched end of the arrow on the string, refers to the 'nocking point' on the string where the arrow is set, though the 'nocks' are the points at either end of the bow where the string is attached. 'Loose' was reputedly the command given to military archers, and is now the term for letting the arrow go, and the instruction given to competition archers when it is safe to shoot at the target; the word 'fire' is very much frowned upon in this situation.

Roger Ascham's contribution to archery is commemorated in the word 'ascham', denoting a cabinet for bows and arrows. Other specific terms include 'fistmele', the distance from the string to the grip of the bow, from the Old English *fotmal*, literally the 'distance of a foot', in which 'foot' was probably changed to 'fist' to make sense of the word.

Athletics

In 1850 the annual horse-race run at Exeter College, Oxford, proved unsatisfying to the competitors, who were of the opinion that it would be equally demanding to run the course on foot. The suggestion was taken up, a steeplechase course was delineated, and entries were taken. Equally important to the proceedings at this stage was the betting, for betting was integral to amateur as well as professional sport in the nineteenth century. The runners curiously ran under the names of horses (but see Pedestrianism: Birmingham medical students in 1838 ran under the kinds of names used by horse trainers and foot-racers). The steeplechase was preceded by some shorter 'flat' races, and the whole process was called a 'set of athletics'.

This is usually given as the beginning of 'athletics' in the United Kingdom as an amateur sport, though the word was in use occasionally beforehand, an 'athlete' mostly being thought of as a wrestler up to this point; and contests of running and jumping have been part of human physical activity since early antiquity. Athletics took off at the universities in the 1850s, and then the public schools, maintaining both an amateur ethos and a proselytising 'muscular Christianity', with a few eccentricities that are recognisably English. For example, Marshall Jones Brooks took the English Championship at high jump in 1876 with a jump of 6 feet, 'without removing his hat'. Early divisions between the Amateur Athletic Club and the Athletic Society of Great Britain (the Liverpool Athletics Club) were reinforced by rival meetings in London in 1866, various attempts to enforce extreme views of what constituted an amateur, and attempts to form rival organisations, which were eventually resolved with the foundation of the Amateur Athletics Association in 1880.

'Athletics' in North America is 'track and field', the term in use since 1905 (*OED*).

Badminton

Evidence for this game has been found in ancient Greece. Badminton was supposedly developed into a rival to other racket games by the

British Army in India, where it was known as 'Poona', after the town where the rules were first codified in 1870. The game is thought to have been brought to Badminton in 1873, though there is no documentary evidence for this (which has not stopped the elaboration of the story with details such as that the original hourglass shape of the court derived from the idea that there were doors halfway along the sides of the room where it was first played). The rules were finalised in 1893.

Balloon

According to the first edition of the *Encyclopaedia Britannica* (1768–71), in the game of 'balloon' an inflated leather ball was 'driven to and fro with the strength of a man's arm fortified with a brace of wood'. The same description appears in Strutt's *The Sports and Pastimes of the People of England* (1801), possibly taken from the *Encyclopaedia*. This seems to be a reinforced version of volleyball, given that the ball, to be inflated, would have to be above a certain size. The word and the game came from France in the sixteenth century, though a version called *Pallone* is recorded as having been played by Italians living in London in 1776; it was known to the locals as the 'Olympic game'.

Bandy

Bandy was an ancestor of hockey, played between two teams, and popular from the sixteenth century to the nineteenth; among its regional names were 'bando', 'bandy hoshoe' in Norfolk, and 'hawkey' in Suffolk. Bandy was similar to football in its organisation, and the two games were often played by the same players; Nottingham Forest Football Club was at one stage the Nottingham Forest Football and Bandy Club. In the nineteenth century it developed into a game

played on ice using a rubber ball, with a National Association formed in 1891 to regulate the game. Sets of rules were published in 1882, 1889 and 1896, similar to those of soccer, and in *The Field* for 16 February 1895 it was reported that 'bandy has quite taken the place of football at Oxford'. It was exported to Holland, the United States, Canada, Scandinavia, Germany, Poland and the Czech Republic, and in cold winters it is still played on frozen fens in East Anglia.

The game took its name from the curved stick called a 'bandy', as opposed to the straight stick, called *cric* in Old English. Golf clubs were occasionally called 'bandies'. The origin of the word is obscure, but it may be connected to the word 'band' in the sense of a 'team', but its first use in English, in the sixteenth century, is in the context of tennis, where the ball is 'bandied' to and fro; the phrase to 'bandy words with someone' retains this sense.

Barleybreak

Barleybreak (sometimes 'barley break' or 'barley brake') was a common English sport in the eighteenth century and is referred to in earlier works, such as Sidney's *Arcadia* (1590) and Burton's *Anatomy of Melancholy* (1621). It involved three mixed couples standing in three areas in a line, the outer two having to cross the central space while holding hands, or 'breaking', while the central pair tried to stop them. The central area was known as 'hell', giving rise to the phrase 'the last couple in hell'. In the Scottish version only one person stood in the middle, and those who were caught had to assist the catcher in the next crossing; effectively this is 'British bulldog', which is known as such since the mid-twentieth century, while barleybreak is known from five hundred years earlier.

Baseball

'Base-ball' is first documented in *The Little Pretty Pocket Book* (1744), as another name for 'rounders'. One of the first books published directly for children, *The Little Pretty Pocket Book* is an alphabetical sequence of rhymes and morals, which was published in North America in 1762. One of the rhymes goes:

> The ball once struck off,
> Away flies the Boy
> To the next destin'd Post,
> And then Home with Joy.
>
> Moral
> Thus Britons for Lucre
> Fly over the Main;
> But, with Pleasure transported,
> Return back again.

In this rhyme we see two terms which baseball has retained – 'strike' and 'home'. The word 'post' has been replaced by 'base', though the illustration shows that the 'bases' are fairly substantial waist-high lumps of wood or stone. Jane Austen's *Northanger Abbey*, written in around 1815, contains the next well-known reference to the game:

> It was not very wonderful that Catherine, who had
> nothing heroic about her, should prefer cricket, base
> ball, riding on horseback, and running about the
> country at the age of 14, to books.

The relationship between baseball and rounders has excited some passion in the past. Henry Chadwick's 1867 *Dime Book of Baseball* states that the game is 'of English origin', a development from rounders, 'a school game', 'entirely devoid of manly features'; baseball players must 'possess the characteristics of true manhood', because 'rounders is a game that boys, and even girls can play without difficulty'. In Britain *The Observer* on 9 August 1874 noted that baseball 'is a thoroughly well-balanced game, though obviously developed from rounders, ... but exciting'. But the first rules for baseball are found in a German text by Johann Gutsmuths from 1796, as *Ball mit Freystaten, oder das Englische Base-ball* ('ball with free-station, or English base-ball').

In 1908 a commission set up to investigate the origins of baseball conveniently ascribed the invention of the game to an American Civil War hero, Abner Doubleday, in 1839; Doubleday, it was claimed, had taken the game of 'townball', not unlike English campball, and turned it into baseball. Chadwick's tales of the development from rounders were put down to his having migrated from England as a child. The American creation myth of baseball was too good a story to be abandoned outright, though other more viable claims were put forward, and the Doubleday story was entirely discredited. It now seems likely that rounders and baseball (and 'townball', 'one old cat', 'tutball', 'munshets', 'stoolball', and, dare one say, cricket) were different names for very similar games with slight variations. However, as early as 1858 it was very clear that baseball was perceived as *the* American game.

Supported by Irish and German immigrants, baseball was notably more prevalent than cricket in prisoner-of-war camps during the

American Civil War – it appears that more Northern baseball club members than cricket club members joined the armies. The *New York Times* in November 1864 reported a cricket match, 'notwithstanding the absence of hundreds of our fellow citizens who are absent on the field of battle'. In a prison-camp game, more players were involved simultaneously in the action, the roughness of the ground was not a problem, games were long, spectators were closer to the action, and less space was needed. This has been put forward as the key to why baseball grew so quickly in the period after 1865, while cricket became associated with first-generation immigrants; also, the scoring in baseball is supposedly simpler. Gorn and Goldstein suggest that another reason for baseball's appeal was the number of ways in which the word 'home' occurs in the game, appealing to an immigrant population building a new home, and it has been said often that immersing oneself in baseball was a clearly visible way for immigrants to gain acceptance. The amateur period, until the 1870s, was characterised by manliness and team spirit, with a respectable working-class following bringing to the game terms from work and craft – 'strike', 'hand', 'count' and 'pitch'. After the introduction of full professionalism in 1869, the Cincinnati Red Stockings being the first openly professional team, baseball quickly became a major business operation, gradually developing its own language. Many terms have entered common English speech, without the speakers having any idea of the original frames of reference: 'left-field thinking', 'raincheck' and 'curveball' particularly have become common in management-speak.

Basketball

James Naismith, a Canadian physical education instructor at the International YMCA Training School (later Springfield College), invented basketball in late 1891, as a ball-game that could be played in a gymnasium. The original intention was to use square wooden boxes for a game, but, in the absence of boxes, peach baskets were used, nailed to the walls. For some time the base of the hoop remained closed, until the open-ended net design was adopted. The game was instantly popular, the peach baskets being quickly replaced by wire baskets, and then hoops with hanging baskets underneath. Generally accepted as a purely North American invention, basketball gave rise to netball in Britain.

Naismith started from a specific set of aims for the game, including absence of physical contact, and the removal of any possibility of defending the goal; these may have stemmed from awareness of how these two kinds of action in college football provoked violence and lack of movement. Naismith was working very much within the context of muscular Christianity, the use of sport for the improvement of health, and the potential social benefits of sport. Though there was some initial disapproval, basketball for women developed quickly. Certain facets of the game in its early days, requiring a set supervised space and raised baskets, led to the growth of supervised and organised play in urban environments, and in particular provided the YMCA with opportunities to provide non-school activities for the growing immigrant population of the United States.

Battledore

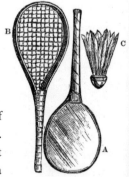

'Battledore', or sometimes 'shuttlecock', is documented from the sixteenth century, generally as a children's game, which consisted primarily in knocking a shuttlecock back and forth with the aim of keeping it in the air as long as possible. 'Battledore' was also the name used for the bat used for playing the game – previously a 'battledore' was a wooden bat used in washing clothes and then for smoothing them out, and from this the tool developed into one used for pushing loaves into an oven; the tool was also known as a 'beetle'. Though the word may be related to 'bat' and 'beat', the 'dore' part has not been satisfactorily explained.

'Battledores' used in the game of pingpong, according to the laws published by the manufacturers J. Jacques & Son in 1902, were long-handled with faces made of stretched parchment or gut. 'Battledore' and 'Shuttlecock' are passages of the bobsleigh Cresta Run.

Billiards

On early billiards tables there were six pockets, called 'hazards', an ivory 'port' (a hoop), and an ivory 'king' (a stake); cues were held over the shoulder with the ball being hit with the club end (players 'stroked' or 'stroaked' the ball). *The Compleat Gamester* (1674) gives useful and direct advice and information:

> The Gentle, cleanly and most ingenious Game at
> Billiards had its first origin from Italy … As this is a
> cleanly pastime, so there are Laws or Orders against
> lolling slovenly Players, that by their forfeitures they
> may be reduced to Regularity and Decency … If you
> smoak and let the ashes of your Pipe fall on the table,
> whereby oftentimes the Cloth is burned, it is a
> forfeiture. Have a care of raking … Beware when you
> jobb your Ball through the Port with the great end of
> your Stick that you throw it not down … There is
> great art in lying abscond, that is to lie at bo-peep
> with your adversary, either subtlely to gain a pass or
> a hazard… [This seems to indicate a precursor of a
> 'snooker'.]

Billiards was known as the 'French game', indicating its supposed origin; the word came from the French *billard*, meaning a 'stick', as in the English word 'billhook'. 'Trucks', which originated in Italy (from *trucco*), was the usual name for the game with the hoop and king (it was shaped like a cone). This game lasted into the eighteenth century and involved going round and through the hoop without knocking it down.

Professional billiards emerged in the nineteenth century, following the usual professional practice of challenge matches, spectators, exhibition matches and cash prizes, taking place in billiards 'academies'. On 28 January 1888 *The Penny Illustrated Paper and Illustrated Times* reported that:

> D. Richards and H. McNeil at the Marble Arch
> Rooms, 524 Oxford Street, on Monday commenced a
> match of 10,000 up, … on even terms, for £100 a
> side. Richards led off in capital form. The scores at
> the close on Monday were – Richards 1688; McNeil
> 1569.

With breaks of up to 300 and matches lasting days, eventually the crowds tired of the repetitive success and from 1930 professional billiards gave way to snooker.

Bowls, bowling

Indoor bowls in medieval times was repeatedly banned by royal decree, probably because it so easily lent itself to gambling. Restrictions were eased for people with large incomes, and the laws seem not to have been strictly enforced. The oldest bowls club in England is believed to be in Southampton, where the green was reputedly laid in 1187. 'Bowls' appears twelve times in the works of

Shakespeare, where we find the first recorded use of the word 'jack' in a bowls context. He also makes it clear that women played bowls in late-sixteenth-century England. 'Ninepins' is first found in 1580 (*OED*). Bowls could be a matter for strong feelings – in 1660:

> At Baunton in Dorsetshire, some being at bowles on
> the Lord's day, one flinging his bowl at his fellow-
> bowler, hit him on the eare, so as the blood issued
> forth at the othere eare, whereof he shortly died. The
> murtherer fled.

The word 'bowl' comes from the French *boule*, and before that the Latin *bulla*, meaning 'bubble', and thus 'sphere'. There is no connection to the other 'bowl', meaning 'large round vessel', which comes from a Germanic rootword. The 'bias' in a bowl (the weight on one side) probably relates to the curved line of movement of a bowl, which is weight-loaded on one side – 'bias' was from a French word meaning 'oblique'. Around 1715, a song, 'The Oxford bowlers', indicated the antiquity of some bowling techniques:

> There's ne'er a set of Bowlers so far & near renown'd,
> We twist, we screw, & with Grimace we coax the
> bowl around,
> And a bowling we will go.

Kegling is another name for 'bowling', more common in the United States than Britain. It derives from the German *kegler*, meaning 'skittle player', and is related to the word 'kayles' or 'cayles', a word for 'skittles', mostly found in southern English dialects, but now rare. 'Club kayles' used a stick instead of a ball, and other name variations included 'cloish', 'loggats' (which appears in *Hamlet*), 'kittle-pins' (which probably became 'skittles'), 'Dutch pins' and 'Dutch rubbers'.

A further variation, called 'half-bowl', involved playing with a hemisphere, which had to roll behind the pins before hitting them. 'Nine-holes' used holes instead of pins.

'Crown-green' bowls, popular in the Midlands and North of England, is played on a green originally with a raised centre, known as the 'knob'. In this game, bowls are 'run', and the 'jack' is called the 'block'.

Boxing

There is a similarity between the English word and Middle Dutch *boke*, Middle High German *buc* and Danish *bask*, all meaning 'to hit', but no clear sense of how 'to box' developed from these. The word appeared at the beginning of the fourteenth century. For Wilson (*Ultimate Sporting Lingo*, 2004) the idea of the 'box' made by the closed fist dates from 1719. Certainly during the nineteenth century the term 'boxing' replaced 'prizefighting', as the practice of using wrestling throws in fights disappeared. Philips's *New World of Words* (1671) gave the world the word 'pugillation', which lasted for about a hundred years, but Pierce Egan, writing in the early nineteenth century, popularised the terms 'pugilism', which had been used from about 1790, and 'boxiana' to describe the whole culture of boxing, its supporters and its financiers. Joseph Strutt in the early nineteenth century looked at the term 'shadow boxing', defining it as 'fighting with a man's own shadow', and giving it a Greek-derived name, 'skiomachia'. 'Shadow boxing' came to mean 'sparring against an imaginary opponent' as a form of training. Actually training against a shadow must have been interesting.

The first rules of boxing were drawn up by Jack Broughton, 'by whose superior skill and ability pugilism obtained the rank of a science' (Egan). Broughton's rules, approved by a group of 'gentlemen', were set out in 1743, soon after a bout between Broughton and George Stevenson, who died a month after the fight. Broughton had been backed by the Duke of Cumberland, and Stevenson by the Prince of Wales and Captain John Godfrey, who later wrote *A Treatise upon the Useful Science of Defence*.

In the eighteenth century prizefighting allowed a number of wrestling holds, such as the 'Tipperary Fling', by which Patrick Henley threw John Francis, alias the Jumping Soldier (nicknames for pugilists are not new). Continued aristocratic support for prizefighting was largely based on its potential for gambling (when Egan was writing about fights his round-by-round commentary included changes in betting odds), and the Fancy grew up as a pool of enthusiasts – 'amateurs' – who followed the sport devotedly. Such was the regard in which boxing was held, despite being banned in 1750, that in *The Principles of Taste* in 1808 Richard Payne Knight wrote: 'Not only is boxing the best guardian of the morals of the common people, but, perhaps, the only security now left, either for our civil liberty or political independence.'

Pierce Egan, at the beginning of the nineteenth century, wrote about boxing imaginatively and with excitement, using phrases such as 'with a celerity unequalled' alongside the common terminology of pugilism, raising the status of the jargon of the sport. For example, 'Belcher's display with Tom Jones convinced the amateurs of his peculiar science, spirit and bottom'; 'spirit' here means 'assertiveness', while 'bottom' means 'staying power, endurance' (it was replaced by 'heart' in the United States). Jim Belcher used to wear a spotted handkerchief, which came to be called a 'belcher', with boxers adopting their own colours, by which they were known.

Corruption and scandals led to a slump in the support for prizefighting in the 1840s, after revised rules in 1838 had outlawed head-butting, biting and hitting below the belt, but the Marquess of Queensberry's rules of 1867 set out boxing much as it is currently. Prizefighting, away from the Queensberry Rules, declined markedly in the 1890s. The new rules meant that boxing could be taken up as a manly pursuit by the promoters of muscular Christianity (it had been maintained as a sport in several public schools), and it became a regular activity in church clubs, boys' clubs sponsored by universities, and the YMCA, in the last quarter of the nineteenth century; it was also proposed as an amateur sport to be included in the activities of the new Amateur Athletics Club in 1867 until the Amateur Boxing Association was set up in 1880. The first uses of names for the main hits in boxing are recorded from a short period of time, 'uppercut' from 1897, 'hook' from 1898, 'jab' from around 1900, and 'cross' from 1906. These precise and short descriptive terms contrast with Egan's 'severe blow', 'wading off' and 'sharp hit'.

Officially illegal in England, in the early nineteenth century boxing had to be staged in temporary rural locations, where it could be quickly disbanded and restaged. In the United States it was the sport of the urban poor, based more on street-fighting than fair play, and fights often descended into anarchy or were the basis of corrupt betting. Boxing was remade by Richard

Kyle Fox, a newspaper proprietor, who realised that boxing made good copy, but that it needed to be regulated for it to build up a real following. The adoption of the Queensberry Rules ensured this, and boxing's new respectability was confirmed by the presence, and even amateur participation, of powerful and distinguished supporters such as Theodore Roosevelt, William K. Vanderbilt and Jack London. Popular ideas, particularly social Darwinism, saw boxing as a genuinely American answer to perceived decadence, and its commercial potential was fully exploited; much of the public's awareness was centred on John L. Sullivan, who from 1879 became American boxing's first celebrity; though previously a prizefighter, he came to acknowledge and advertise the value of the Queensberry Rules.

In a sense boxing is the quintessential sport, in that it pits one person against another in the most basic form, to see who should prevail. In this, as a developed sport, it has the potential to show us exactly what sport does, as a pathway to reach back to something aggressive and dangerous inside ourselves, and simultaneously to see the civilising process in action. It is both horribly violent, compelling, ritualised and referential to basic communal existence.

Holt sums up the paradox:

> As a display of complete athleticism a great boxing
> match is a supreme sporting event, the purest
> expression of skill, strength and courage. But it is
> undoubtedly dangerous and often cruel, stirring not
> so much the boxers but the crowds who watch them
> to a pitch of savagery quite incompatible with the
> notion that boxing is 'the noble art of self-defence'.

At a 'dinner show' in 1982, two boxers fought in a ring surrounded by wealthy diners at the Grosvenor House Hotel in London's Park Lane.

Six months later one of the boxers died, never having come out of a coma. The conventions of the event show sport at its most ritualised, grotesquely so: no sound was allowed from the spectators during the rounds, and only polite clapping at the end of the round; the diners sat close enough to the ring to be hit by spilt blood. After this bout the winning boxer, deeply distressed by the outcome, was challenged that it was his priority to render his opponent unconscious. 'No,' he replied, ' it remains primarily a game of self-defence. For me and many others, boxing is the greatest of any one-to-one sport' (*The Guardian*, 25 October 1995).

Callisthenics

A nineteenth-century creation, callisthenics was a system of gymnastics designed specifically for girls. Distinct from 'gymnastics', it typically involved light exercises designed to promote graceful movement, usually without any equipment, though sometimes with hand rings and wands, and E. B. Houghton's *Physical Culture* (Ontario, 1886) recommends the use of Indian clubs. The 1972 *Chambers Twentieth Century Dictionary* defines 'callisthenics' as 'exercises for cultivating gracefulness and strength', repeating the order of the constituent parts of the word, *kallos*, meaning 'beauty' and *sthenos*, meaning 'strength'. It could be performed in a 'callisthenium', a word constructed along the pattern of 'gymnasium'.

Campball

In the eastern counties of England football was known as 'camp-ball' or 'camping', from the Old English *campian*, meaning 'to fight'. An 1823 description of campball shows the game had developed variations, using large or small balls, with closer goals, teams limited to fifteen, and points called 'notches', or 'snotches' in Suffolk. Strutt in 1833 described the game as one in which 'the ball is driven about with the feet instead of the hands', and it is often thought to have been a version of folk football, though 'camp' in Suffolk was a hands-only game. In some areas, if a large ball was used it was called 'kicking camp', and if played wearing shoes it was ominously called 'savage camp'. As Shearman points out after giving illustrations of medieval local forms of the game, 'the football itself was hardly essential'. In East Anglia, local place-names such as Camping Close record the existence of the game.

Clay-pigeon shooting

Clay pigeons were substituted for live pigeons in the target-shooting sport in the late nineteenth century, though live-pigeon shooting in this context was not made illegal in the United Kingdom till 1921. The sport retains much of the terminology of live-pigeon shooting: a clay pigeon is still referred to as a 'bird' as well as a 'target', a hit is called a 'hit' or a 'kill', and a miss is called a 'bird away'. Many of the different kinds of ways a target can be sent out of the trap are named after animals or birds – 'turkey', 'rabbit', 'nested pair'. The first substitutes for live birds were glass balls, sometimes filled with feathers, then balls made from silt and tar; currently 'clay' pigeons are usually made from pitch and pulverised limestone. 'Skeet shooting' uses the same targets but the shooter has to move to different positions and the targets are not released until two or three seconds after the signal is given. 'Skeet' was chosen as the winner in a competition run by an American sporting paper to find the name for the 'new' sport in 1926, and was supposed to be an old form of 'shoot'; but it may have been more to do with an older Dutch word for a long-handled scoop for throwing water over sails.

Club-ball

A picture in the Bodleian Library, Oxford, dated 1344, shows a woman about to bowl a ball about the size of a dinner plate to a man holding a roughly made club. This is believed to be the earliest known image of people playing what Strutt in 1801 called 'club-ball'. Another picture shows the person with the club about to hit the ball. These do not give us enough information to know the actions involved in the game: Strutt's use of the word here is the first recorded, and the idea that this was a precursor of cricket is based on very little evidence.

Cricket

The wardrobe accounts for the reign of Edward I (1272–1307) show a payment being made to Johanni de Leck 'ad creag et alios ludos' ('for creag and other games'). This is thought to be one of the first references to an early form of cricket; 'creag', 'cryce' or 'cricce' derived from an Old English word for a 'club' (a French word *criquet*, dating from the fifteenth century, was used for the stick bowled at in *jeu de boules*). Documents refer to 'creag' being played in Kent in the early fourteenth century, though 'creag' in other contexts appears to have been a name for 'ninepins'. The first reliable documentation for the game dates from 1598, when a dispute over a plot of land near Guildford included John Derrick or Denwick describing how he had played 'at Creckett and other plaies' there as a child. In 1611 two men were prosecuted for preferring cricket to going to church.

Early versions of the game involved a hole rather than a wicket, the wicket developing as two stumps and a crossbar, though an engraving from 1648 shows a three-legged stool called a 'cricket'. There have been other names and derivations for cricket: a nineteenth-century Yorkshire version of cricket played against a wall was called 'bad', while Joseph Strutt in 1801 claimed that medieval 'club-ball' or 'cambuca' was the 'parent to cricket', and John Nyren in 1833 proposed that the word 'cricket' was derived from the Welsh *clwppa*. Samuel Johnson's 1755 *Dictionary* defined cricket as 'a sport, at which the contenders drive a ball with sticks in opposition to each other' – strange that so typical an Englishman should get so English a sport so wrong.

Cricket is first recorded in America in 1710, and by the middle of the nineteenth century it was fairly widespread, meriting an entry in

Webster's 1828 *American Dictionary of the English Language* – 'a play or exercise with bats and ball', slightly better than Johnson's definition. There was still a clear English influence: the first New York club was called the St George's Cricket Club. The game blossomed in Canada in the mid-nineteenth century, and in 1867 the Prime Minister stated that it was Canada's national sport. The first international match was in 1844, between Canada and the United States, fifteen years before the first international tour, of an England team against United States and Canadian teams. At the match played at Hoboken 25,000 spectators arrived, not apparently a partisan crowd, but rather driven by curiosity. In 1860 there were about five hundred cricket clubs in the United States, and many players played under both cricket and baseball codes. Despite the assumption that from the rise of baseball in the 1870s cricket in the United States went into decline, in 1911 there were well over a hundred cricket clubs all over the country, including in Los Angeles, Arkansas, Akron and Salt Lake City; the game was still played under the rules of the MCC (Marylebone Cricket Club). Cricket is still played in New York, now embracing players of several nationalities.

Cricketing documents from around the year 1800 show a number of differences between then and now, both in the way the game was played and the terminology. A broadsheet printed in Nottingham in 1800, *A Correct Statement of the Grand Cricket Match played at Worksop 3rd–5th November, 1800*, shows 'the Nottingham Club' and 'the Sheffield Club' competing for a prize of 200 guineas, but Nottingham fielded eleven players against Sheffield's twenty-two. Players were 'bowled out' and 'catched out'. In the first match at Lord's, on 31 May 1787, players wore no pads or gloves, but did wear a tricorn hat.

Rules and Instructions for Playing the Game of Cricket (1800) contains a reference to 'the game at four corners', the batsman is called a 'hitter' and the bowler 'twists' rather than 'spins' the ball. In the *MCC Laws of Cricket* (1800) the 'bail' is singular, there are four balls to an over, and betting rules are included. (Gambling was part of cricket culture from very early – in 1646 a case came to court because the losing side in a game of cricket had refused to pay the wager of twelve candles to the winners.) Betting was done on the basis of how many runs a batsman would score; it featured as the eleventh of the MCC laws in *The Cricketers' Pocket Companion* (1826) and lasted until the 1880s. In *Instructions for Playing the Noble Game of Cricket* (1816) the batsman is the 'striker', and runs are 'notches'. In the 1859 match at the Elysian Fields, Hoboken, between an English eleven and a United States twenty-two, 'Hayward contrived to run out', rather than to 'get himself run out'.

The involvement of the eighteenth-century plutocracy meant large amounts of money being won and lost (£500 on eighteenth-century games at Hambledon). Richard Holt proposes that cricket was the first team game 'in which the upper classes were expected to exert themselves without the aid of a horse'. It is more likely that it was the first team game in which the upper classes were involved at all. The control of the landscape by the wealthy after the enclosure acts of the eighteenth century may give some idea of how a game involving so much space came to involve the rich, the poor and the rural middle classes. There is a traditional view that cricket was a great mixer of classes, largely based on anecdotal evidence of farm labourers having the temerity to bowl out peers of the realm in eighteenth-century matches. The reality is that the structure of rural society was rigid enough for the poor or the tenant farmers not to be a threat to the gentry; each knew their place. The rich owned the land, played the game, required the services of the poor and the tenant farmers, and put up the prize money. If we look at the people who wrote the rules of the game, aristocratic titles abound.

The first known rules were drawn up by the Duke of Richmond in 1727. The first score-sheet dates from 1769, with the first century (though 'century' was not recorded till 1864) scored by a member of a team captained by the Duke of Dorset. The rules of cricket were set by the Duke of Dorset and Sir Horace Mann and a committee of noblemen and gentlemen in 1774 (including the lbw rule and the width of the bat). The MCC, founded as a members' club in 1787 for the leading noblemen and gentlemen playing cricket, published its revised *Laws of Cricket* in 1788; until 1993 it was deemed the ultimate authority on the game.

If we think of the aspects of cricket that seem quintessential to the game, several of them turn out to be late developments. Until about 1910 overs were of four balls, and to get six runs the ball had to be hit out of the ground. There is an idea that the flattish areas of Surrey and Kent particularly favour cricket, yet until 1875 Lord's Cricket Ground was by no means flat. One player was killed by a ball that bounced up off a stone, and sheep were used to keep the grass short until 1899.

Of all major team games, cricket seems to attract the most philosophical interpretations. Cricket is seen as a conception of time, a way of understanding time, especially the changing speed of time. Cricket is about the 'give and take' of life. Cricket is about patience, about building, about the relationship between the individual and the state, or about the capacity to be a hero, perseverance, hope, tension. 'It's not cricket' is documented very clearly from 1867 (*The Cricketer's Companion*), and was probably used before then. There was, however, a period in which the game was absolutely 'not cricket'. Between about 1800 and 1840 the financial incentives to players and open betting at games meant that corruption was rife; some players were seen to be making a lot of money, sometimes by betting against themselves as players, and the popularity of the game fell. Following a clean-up, professional cricketers were employed by the clubs during the nineteenth century, their role being to make up the numbers in a match, and to bowl and field when the members wanted some practice. The game maintained a sense of 'gentlemanly conduct' precisely because until the 1960s it was controlled by the wealthy classes, for whom the 'win' mattered less than the 'play'. In this cricket mirrored other sports, where the construction of the elaborate rituals of fair play provided controls on aggression, on partisanship, on

Cricket terms

Call: to 'call' a player is to accuse him of cheating or fouling.

Declare: a team batting declares that they feel the opposition cannot reach the total number of runs they have, and invites them to try. 'Declaring' was initiated in 1889, after more than a century of four-innings matches.

For: in Britain the score is expressed as 10 (runs) for 1 (wicket), i.e. one man out. In Australia the same score would be 1 for 10. Thus 10 for 1 in England would be a typical England batting score after a couple of overs, while for Australia the same score would be a national disaster.

Innings: the duration of the batting side's time batting, or the time spent batting by an individual. Often used metaphorically, for example by Prime Minister Clement Attlee, who would sack cabinet ministers by saying, 'You've had a very good innings. Time to hang your bat up.'

Over: six balls, originally four; found in the 1755 *A Code of Laws of Cricket* – presumably an abbreviation of 'your turn is over'.

Stumped: the wicket-keeper removes the bails while holding the ball, while the batsman is out of his crease. In eighteenth-century records of matches the term 'PO' was used, thought to mean 'put out'; no doubt the batsman was.

delight at success and humiliation at failure. Professional cricket and professional cricketers remained at a lower status than amateur county cricket and cricketers. As much as anything, the timing of matches indicated this control: while other spectator sports had moved to allow for the income brought in by spectators, wealthy sponsors allowed cricket to be played as a leisure activity by the better-off. The introduction of evening cricket played under floodlights to allow working people to spectate without taking time off work came as a shock to the culture of cricket.

Croquet

The word *croquet* is used in some modern French dialects to mean 'hockey stick', and it comes from a French word meaning 'bent stick or crook'. Croquet's rise and fall were dramatic: introduced from

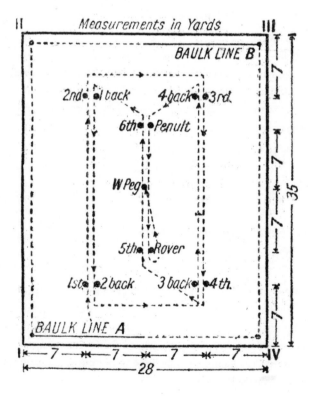

Ireland in 1852, it all but disappeared thirty years later. Cassell's *Book of Sports and Pastimes* (1907) states:

> Never probably has there been a game so universally
> and thoroughly popular in Great Britain as croquet,
> and never was a popularity so rapidly achieved or so
> soon undermined and thrown into the shade when
> its zenith had once been reached.

The Wimbledon All England Croquet Club was founded in 1868, but nine years later it was renamed the Wimbledon All England Croquet and Lawn-Tennis Club. 'Croquet' was dropped from the name of the club in 1882, but restored in 1899 – 'for sentimental reasons' according to the club's website – though placed after tennis. The phrase used to describe ending a croquet match, 'pegging out', has a metaphorical use outside the game.

Cross-country running

'Paperchase' or 'hare and hounds' was a frequent form of cross-country running event in the nineteenth and early twentieth centuries, involving one or two runners setting off and leaving a trail of paper shreds to be followed by the rest of the runners, who set off after a designated time, the 'hounds' (followers) trying to catch the 'hares' (leaders). The game is reflected in the fact that many running clubs are called 'Harriers'.

Cross-country running had developed from betting in the seventeenth century, with wealthy gentlemen requiring footmen to run beside their carriages and horses. Betting on contests between 'running footmen' led to their being hired for this specialist skill, and then making a profession out of challenge matches as 'pedestrians'. Amateur running contests emerged in the early 1860s, initially as training for rowers, but then as a club activity, with the first amateur club, the Mincing Lane Athletic Club, being founded in 1863; Mincing Lane was at that time a major commodity-dealing area in the City of London, indicating the social status of the club's founders.

Curling

The 'roaring game' is the term often associated with curling, from the noise made by the stones as they travel. The name 'curling', documented from 1620, is similar to the Flemish *krullebol* (curl-bowl) played in a bowling alley, and there is also a link to a similar game, *bolspiel*. In curling a large match between districts has been called since the eighteenth century a 'bonspiel', which may be an earlier alteration or mishearing of 'bolspiel'. The game may have been brought from Flanders by fifteenth-century migrants to Scotland – a bowling game on ice with brushes appears in a painting by Pieter Breugel done in the early sixteenth century.

Curling has its own jargon: the target area is the 'house' with the 'cock' or 'tee' in the centre; the person releasing the 'stone' is the 'shooter', and it must be released before the 'hog line', which may come from *hoog*, the Dutch for 'high'. A game is made up of ten 'ends'. The ice course is the 'sheet' and is sprayed with water, which freezes into droplets called 'pebbles' that allow the stone to move; brushing them with the 'broom' makes them melt and slows the stone down.

Cycling

The early impetus in making a sport out of cycling was French, though an Englishman won the first race, in 1868, using a wooden bicycle with iron tyres. In the 1860s the Michaux family were making machines with the name *velocipède* ('fast foot'), but the word 'bicycle', from the Greek words for 'two' and 'wheel', was based on the pattern of the earlier 'tricycle' (three wheels) and is known from two United States patents from 1868. The word was adopted into French the following year as *bicyclette*, and it is often supposed that the word came from French. The confusion stems from the fact that a French engineer made improvements to an early velocipede and took the pattern to the United States in 1865. From *velo* comes the word 'velodrome' for a cycling arena. *Bell's Life in London & Sporting Chronicle* (1891) gave 'cycler' as well as 'cyclist', though this term was in use for only a few years.

Between 1880 and 1914 the bicycle was an agent of major social change, bringing easy and cheap access to the countryside and gentle exercise to many who would otherwise have remained mostly stuck in cities and towns with no physical activity other than walking. It also highlighted the unsuitability of women's dress for exercise, and opened up, through the use of bloomers, the possibility of women wearing trouser-type clothing for sport. This in turn had an effect on women's views of themselves – the adoption of lighter, less

Cycling terms

Frequent coverage of the Tour de France and its offshoots, and some success in Olympic cycling events, have made people more aware of the terminology of cycling, which derives from several languages.

Danseuse: a cyclist when standing on the pedals and rocking from side to side.

Echelon: a diagonal line of riders, each one using the slipstream of the rider in front; from the French word meaning 'ladder'.

Keirin: a Japanese word combining two words from Middle Chinese, meaning 'compete' and 'wheel'; a keirin is a race led by a pace-setting motorcyclist, who peels away before the last lap.

Lanterne rouge: the last one of the trailing group of riders in a race, carrying an imaginary red light like the last truck in a train.

Madison: originating at Madison Square Gardens (known as the 'wooden saucer'), a madison is a long-distance race for two teams of riders, who take turns to sprint.

Peloton: the main pack of riders in a race – a French word meaning a 'small ball' or a 'small group of soldiers'; it is related to the word 'platoon'.

restricting clothing and more public physical activity is generally held to have played a large part in female emancipation. Alternative views suggest that cycling was something of an isolated case, and that in the case of women's sports it was the sport that changed to accommodate the restrictions imposed by women's clothes and expectations of behaviour.

Darts

Darts was not recorded as a sport until 1901, though forms of the sport must have been around much earlier. A 'dart' was a short spear, or any stick-based projectile, the word coming from Old French in the fourteenth century. Proposed precursors for darts are contests in which crossbow bolts were shot at the base of a barrel, and a game called 'puff and dart' that involved small darts being shot out of a blowpipe, a common sport in pubs in the mid-nineteenth century.

In 1996 the Sports Council withdrew support for darts on the grounds that it was not physical enough, but Sport England in 2005 re-recognised it as a sport. What told in darts' favour was not the activity itself, but the fact that players can walk several miles between the 'oche' (the line from which players throw) and the board during the course of a tournament.

Discus

A Greek word meaning 'disc', discus was known as one of the sports in the ancient Olympics. The area from which the discus is thrown was known formerly as the 'balbis', but this word has disappeared from English, except in the field of geometry. It describes a line that is terminated at both ends by another line – in discus-throwing, the balbis is a rectangle missing one side; another balbis occurs in the shape of rugby goalposts.

Eventing

The origins of showjumping lie in military training of animals ('dressage' means 'training' in French), and it has been a spectator sport since 1860, and since 1952 a sport in which men and women compete on an equal basis. While 'showjumping' is documented from 1929, 'eventing' dates from 1965; one-day, two-day or three-day 'events' are more formally known as 'horse trials', the sense being that the horse is being tested. The origins of 'dressage' lie in the Renaissance – there was an academy of riding in Naples in 1532. The military training of horses grew in popularity in France during the seventeenth century, from where it spread to Britain.

Fencing

The vocabulary of fencing is derived mostly from French, with some words from Italian ('ballestra', 'deviamenti' and 'passata sotto'). In an echo of boxing, the word 'fence' is related to 'defence': in Manyng's *Chronicle of England* (1338) 'fens' was used to mean the 'action of defending'. The first use of the word to mean 'to use a sword defensively or aggressively' appears in Shakespeare's *The Merry Wives of Windsor* (1598). The names of two of the swords used in fencing, the épée (which has retained the accents) and the sabre ('saber' in the United States), come from French; 'épée' is a late-nineteenth-century adoption of a French word for 'sword', and 'sabre' is an unexplained alteration of the French word *sable*. 'Foil' is less clear: the foil is a sword with a blunted tip, and it has been suggested that this is related to an Old English word meaning 'to trample down or tread', which exists as the surname Fuller, originally 'a person who treads cloth to knit the fibres together'. Alternatively, a foil in this case may refer to the doubtful idea of fighting as 'self-defence', where your sword exists mainly as a means of 'foiling' your opponent's attacks. It may also come from a Middle English adoption from French, the word 'foin', meaning a 'thrust with a pointed weapon', ultimately from the Latin *fuscina*, the trident used by some Roman gladiators. Samuel Johnson's 1755 *Dictionary* proposes that it comes from the French *fouiller*, meaning to 'search', possibly in the sense of 'probing your opponent's defences'. Webster's *Dictionary* (1852) prefers a derivation from the Welsh *fwyl*, meaning a 'driving, impulsion or stroke'.

The top third of a fencing blade is called the foible, meaning 'weak', the blade being thinnest and weakest at this point; the strongest part, the lower third, is the forte, meaning 'strong'.

Fencing has been an Olympic sport since the founding of the modern games; during the 1924 games two competitors lost their self-control and fought for a couple of minutes in earnest, until one of them drew blood.

Fives

Often thought of as having originated at Eton College in the nineteenth century, fives was a common medieval game, its name deriving from the use of the hand, i.e. the five fingers ('bunch of fives' has long been a slang expression for the fist). Fives was also called 'hand-tennis' and simply 'ball-play'. Strutt, writing in 1801, before the public-school remaking of the game, proposed that the name comes from there being five players on each side, making it possibly a kind of volleyball. This confusion may come from the simplified form of tennis, called in French *longue paume* or *jeu de paume* ('game

of the hand'), in which a ball was hit across a net or available barrier using the hands. A further confusing development was the use of the 'fives bat' for a variation that did not use the hands – fives bats were still available for sale in Bussey's *Winter Sports Catalogue* for 1894.

The two main varieties of the game, Eton fives and Rugby fives, are named after the schools where the varieties developed, the main difference being that the Eton fives court has a step and single buttress on one side of the court, reproducing the features of part of the wall of Eton College chapel, where the game was played.

Football

Football has become the pre-eminent sport of the Western world, and, as trans-national investment pours more and more money into major clubs, seeing their potential for advertising and merchandising as virtually limitless, it looks likely to spread to those few parts of the world not currently besotted. For well over a hundred years people have marvelled at the attraction of football: this from the *Badminton Library of Sports and Pastimes* (1889):

Such is the simple game which has now been brought
to such an extraordinary pitch of skill that none but
those who have seen can well appreciate, and which
is so well appreciated by those who have seen it, that
it is no rare thing for ten or twelve thousand
spectators to watch and follow a match with interest.

Several proposals have been made for explaining why football should be so convenient for bringing together big business, mass following and technology new and old behind a game that is apparently simple and basic. Desmond Morris believed sport to be a 'safe' diversion from violence, filling the gap left by the decline in hunting activities after the development of agriculture. Football ritualises this 'false hunting' in the way that players 'attack' goals and 'shoot'; the goalkeeper in this scenario is the cornered beast, presumably because a fair proportion of strikers instinctively kick the ball at the keeper.

Though the game was first recorded in Britain in the early fifteenth century, it seems improbable that kicking something roughly the size and shape of a defeated enemy's head had not been around for some time before that. Some have claimed that the Latin *harpastum* meant a variety of football. One proposal (in 1721) was that the god Pan learned the game from Apollo.

By the sixteenth century *calcio* was well established in Italy, and 'campball' or 'camping' was common in East Anglia. Both of these involved a considerable amount of fighting, had more or less designated areas (more delineated in Italy, less in England), and were centred on the idea of getting a ball past the opposing team to a designated 'goal'. 'Campball' may be derived from the Old English word *cempa*, meaning a 'warrior', or *campian*, meaning to 'fight', or from *champ* meaning 'field' (see 'Champion') – the fact that it was later called 'fighting camp' may lend weight to the idea of a derivation from *cempa*. One recorded campball or 'camping' match in the eighteenth century involved three hundred men from Suffolk playing three hundred from Norfolk. This sounds very much like the Shrovetide football match at Ashbourne in Derbyshire, which reputedly has been played since the twelfth century – again a large number of players are involved, and rough handling occurs, though rules do prohibit the ball being carried by motor vehicles. Other annual matches were played at Bromfield in Cumbria, Derby, Chester, Kingston, Corfe, and Inverness, where all-female matches took place.

Naturally, such all-in fights were viewed with alarm by town authorities, who tried to ban them. One of the earliest written references to football is from when it was banned by the Scottish Parliament in 1424. John Stow records the mayhem caused by apprentices playing football in Elizabethan London. Richard Mulcaster is often credited with the first published documentation of 'footeball' in his educational work *Positions wherein those Primitive Circumstances are Examined, which are Necessarie for the Training up of Children* (1581). Mulcaster supported football's benefits and proposed smaller teams, introducing 'sides' and 'parties' (teams), 'standings' (positions), 'judges over the parties' (referees) and 'trayning maisters' (coaches).

Puritanism, both in Britain and North America, in the sixteenth and seventeenth centuries suppressed the game. Philip Stubbs in his *Anatomie of Abuses* (1573) condemned 'prophane exercises upon the sabboth day', including 'bowling, tennisse-playing, football playing, and such other devilish pastimes'. By the middle of the seventeenth century it was illegal to play football in Boston. But the game survived, often in the streets rather than in the 'football closes', as they were called at Hitchin and Baldock. By the early eighteenth century a rural football match could be an occasion for general celebration and merry-making: *A Match at Foot-ball, or The Irish Champions* (1721) involves maids dancing beforehand, other sports, and prizes:

> And now both Bands in close Embraces met
> Now Foot to Foot, and Breast to Breast was set.
> Now all impatient grapple round the Ball
> And Heaps on Heaps in wild Disorder fell.

This seems to be more a description of a rugby match than a football match; the match involves some kicking, but mostly it is carrying and throwing. Indeed, it is worth questioning why football is called 'football', for there is no evidence of any rules before the nineteenth century that ban handling the ball.

In medieval Scone in Perthshire there was a variation of the game that has puzzled historians; the rules state that every man in the parish was required to play, and that nobody during the course of play was allowed to kick the ball. This supports the views of a number of sports historians that the key point about football was not that it was played with the feet, but that it was played on foot. There is much to support this idea: the tradition that the game has always been a commoners' game (the famous mention of football in Shakespeare is the term in *King Lear*, 'a base football player'), and that for the wealthy sport out of doors meant hunting, until the development of cricket in the late seventeenth century; the vast numbers involved (compared to polo, which is played on horseback by eight players on a pitch nine times the size of a football pitch); and the words of William Fitzstephen writing in 1174 in London. In a description of a Shrove Tuesday football match he writes:

> All the youth of the city go to a flat patch of ground
> … for the famous game of ball. The students of each
> school have their own ball; the workers of each guild
> are also seen carrying their own ball. The older
> citizens, fathers, wealthy citizens come on horseback
> to watch the younger men competing.

Then Fitzstephen goes on to say the spectators enjoy watching and participate vicariously. The key points here are that the people who *play* are students and guild workers, while the people who *watch* are more important and come explicitly on horseback; what the young men do is described as *certamina*, meaning 'contests'. The first sentence in Latin reads *Post prandium exit in campos omnis iuventus urbis ad lusum pilae celebrem*; literally 'After eating, all the youth of the city celebrates the game of ball.' *Celebrem* here gives the indication that this was a regular occurrence; *lusum pilae*, the phrase translated as 'game of ball', is vague, and occurs in a number of Latin texts of the period, where it could be a version of football, tennis, fives or volleyball. Other contemporary texts indicate that *lusum pilae* was the term used for ball-games played around Easter or on May Day, inside or outside churches, by priests (E. K. Chambers, *The Medieval Stage*, 1923).

In the fifteenth century a monk at Caunton in Nottinghamshire wrote about football as it was played locally:

> The game at which they had met for common
> recreation is called by some the foot-ball-game. It is
> one in which young men, in country sport, propel a
> huge ball not by throwing it into the air but by
> striking it and rolling it along the ground and that
> not with their hands but with their feet. A game, I
> say, abominable enough, and, in my judgement,
> more common, undignified, and worthless than any
> other kind of game, rarely ending but with some loss,
> accident or disadvantage to the players themselves.

This is medieval football as we expect it, authoritarian disapprobation included, but now with the specification that it is played by kicking rather than handling.

As the game developed round the country, local variations emerged, probably dependent on terrain, available resources, and local imagination (at Ashbourne the ball is 'goaled' by hitting it three times on a designated stone). Montague Shearman, writing the athletics and football volume of the *Badminton Sports Library* in 1889, indicates that the method of propulsion of the ball, kicking, punching, carrying or striking, depended almost entirely on the size and composition of the ball available.

Between the mid-eighteenth century and the 1860s there was a marked decline in popular football. Street football games began to disappear, the working public were more interested in pedestrianism, and the wealthy in boxing and horse-racing. Where football is recorded, as in the *Everyday Book* (1830), it resembled the traditional 'fighting' game; in this case it was played every Sunday at Islington by Irish workers, and 'some fine specimens of wrestling are sometimes exhibited'. The development of the game in the nineteenth century led to the major split into two codes, and then three, all of which claim the word 'football'. Changes in educational structures in the early nineteenth century led to the teaching at public (i.e. fee-paying) schools being the province of the teachers, while the boys were responsible for organising their own sports. In this environment 'fighting' football thrived, even when it was banned – probably because it was banned. Each school developed its own codes, which included preferences for dribbling, catching and holding, and occasionally running with the ball, as at Rugby, whose style was adopted by some other schools. Rugby was chief among the schools that by the 1830s were seeing themselves as producers of the commanders of the empire, with a strong sense of discipline, which extended to the running of games. In this environment, which came to be known as 'muscular Christianity', a core theme was the sublimation of the individual to the needs of the team; team games implied competition, and competition implied rules.

From the 1840s Rugby, Eton and Harrow codified the rules in various ways, stipulating such ideas as eleven players per side, running or not running with the ball in hand, and whether it was acceptable to kick an opponent's shins. In 1846 some former public-school pupils at Cambridge tried to agree on a set of rules for playing a game of football; they failed, but persistence led to the earliest surviving set of generally acceptable rules, known as the Cambridge Rules (1848), which was accepted by the first football club, in Sheffield in 1857.

In 1863 the representatives of fourteen clubs met to determine the rules of what they called the Football Association; dominated by former Rugby School pupils, the meeting went on for weeks and included a meeting with players from Cambridge University; the sticking point was whether the game should be dominated by carrying the ball or dribbling with the feet. When it became clear that the dribbling version was going to prevail and that hacking would be outlawed, the Rugby contingent withdrew, one member saying that the proposed game 'savours far more of the feelings of those who like their pipes or grog or schnapps more than the manly game of football'. The Football Association published the new laws in December 1863, and Association Football became separate from Rugby Football. J. C. Thring summarised the sets of rules in a booklet called *The Winter Game* (1863), which included 'the simplest game', with a field shaped like an oval with the two ends cut off, and including some features from rugby (a 'pack', 'hot' or 'bully', which was essentially a scrum), but with the ball having to be kicked into the goal; 'the second game', in which players in front of the ball were 'off-side'; 'the Cambridge Football rules', in which 'shinning' (kicking shins) was forbidden; and the Association rules, in which teams changed sides after a goal was 'won'. Until the initiation of the FA Cup in 1871, football maintained a strong amateur ethos, amateur clubs winning until 1883, but never after that; northern professional clubs, in which players were recompensed for time off work, proved too strong and, effectively, professional.

There were still many differences between the game in the 1860s and now. The ball could still be caught and brought to ground; teams changed ends after a goal was scored; if the ball crossed a line other than the goal line, the first person to get to it claimed the re-entry kick; forward passing was forbidden, so tactics involved getting the ball to the best dribbler and supporting his advance on goal (so early formations usually comprised a goalkeeper, two defenders and eight forwards).

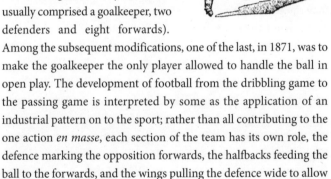

Among the subsequent modifications, one of the last, in 1871, was to make the goalkeeper the only player allowed to handle the ball in open play. The development of football from the dribbling game to the passing game is interpreted by some as the application of an industrial pattern on to the sport; rather than all contributing to the one action *en masse*, each section of the team has its own role, the defence marking the opposition forwards, the halfbacks feeding the ball to the forwards, and the wings pulling the defence wide to allow space for the centre forwards.

The concept of 'ownership' is strong within football: the question of who owns the name, and who owns the game. In areas of the north of England where rugby league is strongly supported, 'football' means rugby league; in rugby-playing boys' schools it means rugby union. But given that association football was taken over by the educated elite in the nineteenth century, then taken up by the working classes at the end of the century, more or less abandoned to a violent underclass in the 1970s, and then reclaimed by big business in the

1980s, the question of who owns the game is very much a class issue, and thus at the heart of what is meant by the word 'football'.

Strutt in 1801 described the game as 'formerly much in vogue among the common people of England, though of late years it seems to have fallen into disrepute and is but little practised'. At this time the social distinction was clear: games in the park of Trinity College, Dublin, in 1780 were played between pensioners or commoners (poorer students) and not the wealthy fellow-commoners.

Between 1875 and 1890 the game quickly lost its public-school association, partly because many of the schools retained their own individual codes. But at this time it was never a wholly working-class sport: a report in the *New York Times* of 1882 noted that in England many young 'business-men' (i.e. men employed in businesses rather than shops or factories, etc.) were playing the sport. At the beginning of the twentieth century records show that new clubs were likely to be formed by skilled workers, and photographs indicate these as the most frequent spectators at matches. Clerks with steady incomes were particularly active in starting professional clubs and were attractive to sponsors (Hargreaves in *Sport, Power and Culture*, 1986).

Over the course of the second half of the twentieth century spectator numbers declined, football supporting attracted violent hooligans (not a new phenomenon), and numbers fell further. Hargreaves proposes that one aspect of the distinctive rise in the 1950s of working-class youth culture was the way this group associated itself with football, so that it became less identified with adult working-class culture and more with the tensions and extreme subordinations of frustrated young men. Another theory explaining the rise of football hooliganism in the 1970s proposes that it arose from resentment at the separation of football from its traditional working-class audience; a similar sentiment can be seen in the proliferation from this period of fanzines with a strong anti-middle-class position. After the Hillsborough disaster of 1989, when the caging in of fans to deter violent pitch invasions contributed to the deaths of ninety-six people, the Football Association published *The Future of Football*, a report that included the desire to attract middle-class customers.

One result of this was a further backlash seen in fanzines. In August 1994 *Red Devil*, the Manchester United fanzine, reviewed Nick Hornby's book on his own experience of supporting Arsenal Football Club, *Fever Pitch*:

> Bear in mind that Hornby is an Oxbridge educated
> football fan who has an obsession with Arsenal, and
> as such cannot be regarded as the genuine article …
> the diary of a stamp-collector rather than a look at
> life on the terraces from a genuine supporter.

In the interests of fair play, *The Gooner* (Arsenal's fanzine) in 2004 complained about the way people were being priced out of football:

> There are countless kids across North London who
> would love the opportunity to go to Highbury
> occasionally who wouldn't be able to, even if the
> opportunity arose, simply because they are priced
> out of the market.

(Priced out, in the memorable words of Roy Keane in 2000, by 'the prawn sandwich brigade'.)

The complaints about the social mobility of football throw into relief how well established are the constituencies for most sports, and the importance of football both financially and socially. Bill Shankly, manager of Liverpool Football Club in the 1960s and 1970s, said: 'Some people think football's a matter of life and death, but I can assure you it's more important than that' (there are variations in the wording). Many undertakers sell coffins emblazoned with club colours, so he may have been right. Wind-up radios give a maximum charge of forty-five minutes and are popular in Africa, where they allow groups of people to listen to one half of a match before three minutes of frantic recharging.

What is clear is that both parts of the word, 'foot' and 'ball', derive from Germanic sources, Old English *fot* and a common Germanic word, not documented in Old English, but found in Old High German as *bol*. One of Britain's most pervasive exports, football is *le football* in French, *futbol* in Spanish, *futebol* in Portuguese, *fussball* in German, *voetball* in Dutch, *futboll* in Swedish, *futbol* in Russian, *futball* in Hungarian, and *futbol* in Turkish.

Golf

As is often the case with sports, our knowledge of early golf comes from legal documents – except that we cannot be sure: the game referred to is *pilam ludendo altercantes* (playing ball alternately), which two boys played in 1277, one of them unfortunately dying a few days after being hit by the ball. From 1363 there were several references to *cambuca* or *cambuta*, a game played with sticks and balls, often taken to be the precursor of golf. James II banned golf in Scotland in 1457 in favour of archery.

A Privy Seal document from Scotland dated 1502 refers to 'William Mayne, bower, clubmaker and speormaker', indicating that by then there was already enough golf played to support equipment makers and keep them in business. Thereafter there are continuous references to golf in Scotland, Mary Queen of Scots playing it suspiciously soon after the death of her husband Darnley, the Marquis of Montrose using 'bonker clubs, an irone club and twa play clubis of my awin', and a reference in 1691 to 'ane play club, ane scraper, and ane tin fac'd club', and one a few years later concerning 'standing and holding the club to hit the ball well'.

The path to the origin of the word 'golf' itself is strewn with red herrings, such as the word 'gowff', supposedly Scottish for 'to hit hard', connected to the Scottish pronunciation omitting the 'l' – Entick's *New Spelling Dictionary* (*c*.1780) gives the spelling 'goff'. A Flemish origin is often proposed, and certainly golf was played on land and on ice in the Low Countries in the late medieval period, as shown by the so-called 'Golf Book', a book of hours (prayers for particular times of the day) produced in Bruges in the 1540s, which shows people apparently playing golf, with clubs, balls and holes. The game was called *kolven*. But it was already called 'golfe' in England by 1513. The Dutch word *kolf*, from the Danish *holbe*, and the German *Kolbe*, meaning 'club', refers to the club, not the game, and the game *kolven* postdates the first use of 'golf' in English or Scottish.

In a period before standardisation, courses and scores varied considerably. In 1825 James Calvert won the gold medal of the Montrose Golf Club, with a score of 107 on the seventeen-hole course. 'The Montrose golf course possesses a great variety of hazards and requires very great skill in the players, to extricate themselves out of them' (*Caledonian Mercury*, 30 April 1825).

In *Hints on the Game of Golf* (1886), H. H. Hutchinson talks about 'addressing yourself to the ball'; the phrase had been around for about twenty years as the more familiar 'address the ball', but 'addressing yourself to the ball' somehow implies more gravitas. In the *Laws of Golf* adopted by the Royal and Ancient Golf Club of St Andrews in 1891:

> the reckoning of the strokes is kept by the terms
> 'the odd' [now 'one over'], 'two more', 'three more',
> and so on. The reckoning of the holes is kept by the
> terms – so many 'holes up', – or 'all even' – and – so
> many 'to play'.

In the current game, when playing 'matchplay' (scoring by holes won rather than strokes taken), when a player is five holes in front with five holes left to play, and thus cannot lose, the term 'dormy five' is used. 'Dormy' or 'dormie' has been used since the 1880s and means that the player could effectively not lose even if he or she went to sleep.

Gymnastics

Gymnastics derives from the Greek terms *gymnos*, meaning 'naked', and *gymnazein*, meaning to 'train naked' and thus to 'train'. The related words were adopted into English gradually, 'gymnastic' recorded in 1574, 'gymnastic' (as a kind of exercise) in 1581,

'gymnast' in 1594, 'gymnasium' in 1598, and 'gymnastics' in 1652. Gymnastic societies were formed in Germany and Bohemia in the early nineteenth century, and were then exported to Britain and the United States, and in countries speaking Germanic languages 'gymnasium' came to mean a 'school' or 'academy'. Television reporting of gymnastics competitions currently often refers to 'tumbling', or a gymnast will be referred to as a good 'tumbler'; it is an example of how experts dumb down as an act of familiarity, in the same way that a football commentator will talk about a striker having a 'poke' at goal, or a cricketer will be said to 'go fishing' when he speculatively pokes his bat out at a ball.

Handball

Handball is both a foul in football (the most outrageous, generating an instant response) and a game in its own right. There are an estimated forty-five variations of handball played currently, and it is one of the oldest known games; as *jeu de paume* and *palo della mano* it is a strong contender to be the ancestor of volleyball and fives as well as tennis, but the modern game was popularised in Germany as *torball* and in Scandinavia, particularly in Denmark as *håndbold*, in the nineteenth century; it was introduced to the United States in the 1880s.

In the 1863 *Laws* of the Football Association, what we now call 'handball' was then called 'knocking on', which is now the term for knocking the ball forwards with the hands in rugby football.

Hockey

We have evidence for a game that looks like hockey being played two and a half thousand years ago, from a stone relief on an Athens wall. Hockey in Britain developed from shinty, hurling and bandy, the name possibly deriving from an Old French word for a shepherd's crook, *hoquet*, though the use of the word 'hawkey' in Suffolk for 'bandy' is a possible influence. There is a curious instance of the word 'hockie' to describe sticks used in a game in Galway in 1527, but after that there is no record of the word until 1785. There is a story that the sport was named after Colonel John Hockey, who developed the game among the garrison of Fort Edward, Nova Scotia, in the eighteenth century; if anything, it was a form of ice-hockey that was developed here around 1800. Hockey was codified at Eton and other public schools, with a club set up at Blackheath in London in 1861, rules agreed between London clubs in 1875, and a Hockey Association in 1886.

Between 1887 and 1900 the hockey stick was redesigned to give the 'club end', which caused a divergence in the name for the implement. In 1902 Slazenger sold 'hockey clubs and bandy sticks', while Tydesley and Holland, in Manchester, and Wisden & Co in London sold 'hockey sticks'.

Hurling

Modern hurling, as played in Ireland, is a team game played with club-shaped sticks and a 2½-inch ball, but there have been other variants. In Cornwall, according to the 1830 *Everyday Book*, a ball was used which had a silver coating displaying the text 'Fair play is good play'; in this variant the ball was 'hurled' (thrown). According to Strutt in 1801, the use of a bat or club in Cornish hurling did not become common until the sixteenth century, implying that the sport had been around for some time before then. Richard Carew's *Survey of Cornwall* (1603) contains a detailed description of 'hurling to goales', which seems much like modern American football, with blocks and marking and a prohibition on forward passing; specific roles for players included 'foreward', 'rereward' and two 'wings'. This hurling was distinguished from 'hurling over countrie', in which the field of play could cover 4 miles, and the goals could be buildings or trees. A similar version of what tends to be thought of as 'medieval football' was the Welsh *knappian* or *cnappan*, though one report indicates that this could be extremely violent, involving men on horseback armed with clubs. Irish hurling, similar to Scottish shinty, was reorganised in 1884 by the Gaelic Athletic Association as an act of promoting Irish culture, a strong example of sport as a group-identity builder. The stick used is a 'hurley' (*caman* in Irish), and the ball is a 'slitter' (*sliothar* in Irish).

'Hurl' is similar to words in other Germanic languages that mean to 'throw violently' or 'rush forcibly', though it is not recorded in English before about 1200.

Ice-hockey

One of the key terms in ice-hockey, the 'puck', derives from Irish, and James Creighton, who set up the first game in Canada, was from Halifax, an area strongly influenced by Irish immigration. Creighton himself was an 'ice-hurley' player. The first match, at Montreal's Victoria skating rink in 1875, resulted in a 2:1 score to the winners – but two 'games', not 'goals'. It ended with 'shins and heads battered, [and] benches smashed', in keeping with later manifestations of the sport; there had been thirty players on each side. Cassell's *Book of Sports and Pastimes* in 1907 described an early game as 'a general free for all without rules or goals, a wild glorious almost maddening excitement'.

However, it is likely that there had been some form of ice-hockey before this, probably in Holland, where skating had long been part of outdoor culture. An engraving by Romein de Hooghe (1645–1708) shows a skater holding a curved stick with a wedge-shaped end, and, nearby, balls and a short pillar protruding from the ice.

Some of the terms in ice-hockey appear to be deliberate attempts to avoid using terms from football; thus 'goaltender' or 'net-tender' is preferred to 'goalkeeper' (shortened in Canada to 'goaler' rather than 'goalie'), 'pipe' to 'goalpost', 'defenseman' to 'back', 'allowing' a goal to 'letting a goal in'. Notably, too, the game has three periods of play and the rink is divided into three sections.

Jai alai

Said to be the world's fastest ball sport, jai alai came from the Basque country and supposedly had its origins in a ball-game played against the enclosing outer walls of churches, a link to Eton fives. The ball is hurled with tremendous force against a wall, using a long basket strapped to the player's hand. The name *jai alai* means 'merry festival' in Basque.

Jogging

It is sometimes claimed that jogging is the most natural human sport. Humans evolved to run over the savannah, not so much in short sprints as in long following runs at a relentless pace, to wear down and catch animals wounded in the hunt, as demonstrated by the palaeontologist Richard Leakey when he ran down an antelope by maintaining a slow but continuous pace. 'Jogging' in this sense has been used since the 1960s, but previously meant to 'walk or run with a jolting action'.

Joust

The Old French word *juster*, and later *jouster*, meant 'to come together', 'meet', 'approach', and from this developed the meaning in English, about 1300, of 'to join in battle' or 'encounter, engage'; from this came the sense of fighting against someone. There is an earlier quotation (*c*.1250), given by the *OED*, in which the sense is to 'ally oneself to', apparently the opposite of to 'fight against'. The older spelling in English was 'just', but it changed to 'joust' under French influence, the change in pronunciation following. To 'joust' meant to 'engage in a tournament'; 'tilt' was the word specifically to describe two men on horseback charging at each other with lances. 'Tilt' comes from an Old English word *tealt*, meaning 'unsteady', and meant 'to upset or overthrow'; it is the same word as when something 'tilts' before falling over.

Judo

The decreasing interest in wrestling at the end of the nineteenth century was held to be one of the reasons for the importation of Chinese and Japanese martial arts and self-defence disciplines. Of these, several names have become well known: 'judo', from Japanese words meaning 'gentleness' and 'way', since 1889; 'karate' ('empty hand', in use in English since the 1950s); and 'kendo' ('hard way'), from the 1970s.

Judo was previously known as 'ju-jitsu' or 'jujutsa', an umbrella term in use well into the later twentieth century but little used now, taken from the Japanese *jujutsu*, from the Chinese words for 'gentleness' and 'science'.

Knurr and spell

Also called 'longbadding' in Lancashire, knurr and spell was for a long time a popular and widespread sport, particularly in the north of England – Joseph Strutt in 1833 called it 'Northern Spell'. The origin of the name is 'knorr', a word meaning a 'knot of wood', with 'spill', an Old Norse word meaning 'game'. The game involved hitting a small ball (the knurr) as far as possible with a long-handled mallet, sometimes called the 'pommel'. In some areas the ball is suspended in a sling from a gallows-type contraption; in other areas it is released from a trap, called the 'spell' (which connects it to an old game called 'trap-ball'). In South Yorkshire the ball rested on a brick, and the game was called 'nipsy'. A professional sport in the nineteenth century, knurr and spell matches attracted large numbers of spectators as players contested for prizes of, for example, £10 or £25 as advertised in *Bell's Life* in 1861.

Lacrosse

Lacrosse is known to have been played before the first contact period between indigenous North American people and Europeans, but was first documented by Jesuit missionaries in the St Lawrence area about 1630. The game as observed by Europeans involved as many as a thousand participants on each side, with goals miles apart, and is thus not dissimilar to the British pre-1800s version of football, as evidenced by its local names: *dehunyshigwa'es* in Onondaga ('men hit a round thing'); *da-nah-wah'uwsdi* in Eastern Cherokee ('little war'); *tewaarathon* in Mohawk ('little brother of war'); *kabocha-toli* in Choctaw ('stick-ball'); *baaga-dowe* in Ojibwe ('hip bumping'). The last of these was anglicised as 'baggatiway' in a description in 1736, but 'by the French in Canada it is named *jeu de la crosse*', reputedly from the stick carried by the players being in the shape of a bishop's crozier. When 'lacrosse' was adopted into American English in 1718 from Canadian French, the word *crosse* meant a 'hooked stick', and the stick is still called a 'cross' or a 'crosse' (crosser meant 'cricket' according to Cotgrave in 1611). Lacrosse positions are now 'defence', 'midfield', 'attack' and 'goalie', though in Cassell's *Book of Sports and Pastimes* (1907) they were given as 'goalkeeper', 'point', 'cover point', 'third man', 'defence fields, centre and attack fields', and 'third, second and first home'.

Long jump

The Badminton Library (1865) uses 'long jump', while *Bell's Life* magazine (1876) uses 'wide jump'. The *OED* has quotations for 'long jump' from 1882 and 'broad jump' from 1889. British schools' physical training manuals in the 1930s use 'long jump', while Jack Kerouac uses 'running broad jump' in *On the Road* (1951), an American version that had been in use since at least 1911 (The Badminton Library – *Athletics*). The *New York Times* of 11 March 1928 used 'wide jump', while their last use of 'running broad jump' was in a report dated 9 May 1965. After that date the *New York Times* used 'broad jump' twice only, both times in obituaries of athletes who had won titles in the 1920s. The final mention, in 1976, is of 'the broad jump (now called the long jump)'.

Given that 'wide jump' and 'broad jump' were terms also used for distance jumping with a pole ('pole jump') the potential for confusion is wide (or broad, or long).

Marathon

After the Battle of Marathon (490 BC) one of the Greek combatants, Pheidippides, was sent as a messenger to Athens to announce the victory over the Persians. He ran the entire distance (now commemorated as the 26 miles 385 yards of the modern marathon, in use since 1908), said the word *nenikékamen* ('we have won') to the senate, collapsed and died. There are variations as to the runner's name, whether he, or someone else, ran both ways, and doubts as to whether the event took place at all; of greater importance at the time was the fact that the entire victorious Athenian army had to march back to Athens the same day to protect the city from expected naval attacks. The distance run at the first modern Olympiad, in 1896, was 24 miles 1,496 yards, from Marathon to Athens. The plain of Marathon was named after the plant *marathron*, meaning 'fennel'.

Long foot-races were regular pedestrian events before the start of the modern Olympics, though they were not referred to as 'marathons'. For example, Celia Fiennes, the late-seventeenth-century traveller, wrote about seeing a 22-mile race, lasting two and a half hours, which took place at Windsor; this would equate to just under three hours for a modern marathon. Even after the start of the modern Olympics, *The Observer* newspaper in 1909 referred to 'a marathon race of 15 miles'.

Motorsport

The *Brooklands Gazette* was first published in 1924. The magazine was renamed *Motor Sport* the following year and is still published. It has seen probably the longest sports journalism career, that of Bill Boddy, whose first article was published in *Motor Sport* in 1930, and who was still writing when this book was published. 'Motorsport' undoubtedly comes from the title of the magazine. Is there a hint of the compilers of the *OED* feeling bewildered by motorsport? As examples of usage, their entries give firstly the later title and subtitle of the *Brooklands Gazette* ('the organ of motor and motor cycle sport'), then a comment on motor sport in the United States being 'apt to be

more of a circus performance ... than to be of practical value', and finally the quotation: 'I must admit I'm no motorsport fan and know next to nothing about Grand Prix.' Motorsport indeed has both fans and those who wonder why it is classed as a sport at all. The Latin word *motor* meant a 'person who moves or shakes something'.

Netball

Netball was a development from women's basketball (there were several versions, one called 'basquette'), based on such circumstances as a misunderstanding of a drawing of the basketball court's lines as dividing the area into three non-crossable zones. This zoning was subsequently adopted into the rules for women's basketball, along with a shooting circle. The rules were developed following Martina Bergman-Österburg's introduction of one form of women's basketball at her women's physical training college in 1893, and were issued under the auspices of the Ling Association in 1901.

Pall mall

Pall mall was a game that involved using a wooden mallet to strike a ball through a metal hoop suspended at the end of a long alley. Via Middle French, the name came from Italian *pallamaglio* or *palla a maglio*, from *palla*, meaning 'ball', and *maglio*, meaning 'hammer'. Popular in seventeenth-century England, it gave its name to the London street.

Pedestrianism

Pedestrianism is an example of how the identity of a sport can achieve vast popularity and then diminish and disappear totally. The term covered a number of activities, over a period of three hundred years.

In 1660 Samuel Pepys was writing about foot-races arranged between the servants of the wealthy, and these developed to include foot-races between the wealthy themselves. Men with an ability to run fast over distances would quickly find employment, and in the eighteenth century footmen were being employed and groomed specifically for their running skills; wagers earned their employers large sums of money, and this provided an incentive for the runners to leave employment and turn professional. The sport continued to grow through the eighteenth century, and the term 'pedestrianism', first recorded in the early nineteenth century, came to encompass other activities, so that by the 1870s it included throwing races (two people competing to reach one mile in the smallest number of throws of a given object), rabbit-coursing, ratting, cycling and quoits. Foot-racing, the most important aspect of pedestrianism, included both walking and running, with competitions between 'peds' and against the clock.

Basic foot-racing provides a simple opportunity for betting, and Shakespeare has Falstaff in *Henry IV Part 1* challenge Poins to a race for £1,000. £10,000 changed hands after a time/distance trial at Newmarket in 1788. Organisers would put up prize money, while backers would add to this if they made big gains. Examples of the prize money on offer are the £100 won by 'Captain' Barclay at the age of fifteen in 1794 (he is reputed to have won the equivalent of half a million pounds in his career), and a thousand guineas for a mile race in 1825. Regular challenge matches held round the country every week offered money to the winner – *Bell's Monthly Magazine of Sports and Pastimes* advertised thirty-four races to be held between 9 and 30 June 1860, for prizes up to £25, occasionally with watches being offered as well. Money governed the sport in the United States too, from the offer of $1,000 made in 1835 to anyone who could run 10 miles in under an hour; at a time when $250 was a reasonable annual income, prize money of $25 meant a good incentive for a healthy young man, and the sport grew accordingly. In 1833 Joseph Strutt wrote: 'foot-races seldom happen but for the purpose of betting, and the racers are generally paid for their performances.'

The feats of pedestrians were various and well-recorded. Walter Thom's *Pedestrianism* (1813) contains six and a half pages of data, listing names, dates, places, times and distances from between 1762 and 1812. These included such feats as:

> Mr Dowler, a publican at Towcester,
> Northamptonshire, walked five hundred miles in
> seven successive days, for a bet of one hundred
> guineas. He started on the 3rd of November 1808, and
> finished on the 9th, at three o'clock in the afternoon.

Others include Levi Whitehead, of Bramham (4 miles on Bramham Moor in 19 minutes); and James Farrer, for a wager of 200 guineas, ran against time on Knutsford racecourse, doing 4 miles in 20 minutes 57 seconds.

Captain Barclay's feats did much to increase the popularity of pedestrianism as a spectator sport. Newspapers reported on his progress and training, and thousands watched his 'thousand miles in a thousand hours' walk in 1809, achieved in forty-two days. During this performance his training, sleeping pattern and diet were minutely recorded, and he may be regarded as one of the first sporting celebrities. But oddities also provided the sport with the potential for entertainment, and these can be found from the seventeenth century until the nineteenth. After the Restoration in 1660 races are recorded between disabled runners (Charles II watched a race between two men who each had a wooden leg), and in the eighteenth century there were such instances as a seventy-five-year-old man running 4½ miles round Queen Square in London, a fish-hawker who ran 7 miles with a 56-pound basket of fish on his head in 45 minutes, and a man rolling a coach wheel round a platform for a distance of 8 miles in an hour.

Women were not excluded from these races; 'smock races' refers to the prizes, and by transference to the people who competed. Voltaire witnessed a race between women while he was in exile in England between 1726 and 1729.

By the mid-nineteenth century individual pedestrians were famous enough to have nicknames or performing names, which added to their individual appeal to supporters. These included the American Deer (Billy Jackson), the Lame Chicken (J. Davies), the North Star (Tom Maxfield), the Suffolk Stag (George Frost), the Gateshead Clipper (John White), and the Crowcatcher (William Lang). These names sit curiously beside that of Deerfoot, a North American runner also known as Louis Bennett, who ran several competitive races in the 1860s. His 6-mile race in 1861 was seen by over six thousand people.

By the mid-nineteenth century pedestrianism was undoubtedly the most popular working-class sport. When the Suffolk Stag won the 10-mile championship at Manchester in 1852, thousands of prints of the race were sold. In New York, in October 1844, extensive advertising brought thousands more spectators to the Hoboken Beacon racecourse than could be accommodated, and rioting broke out. With numbers and involvement like this, amateur interest in the sport, growing from the public schools through the universities, began to establish its own presence. The Highways Act in 1835 banned pedestrianism from the roads, so it moved on to running tracks, many of which were built next to pubs, giving their owners opportunities for enormous profits, but leading both to a more formal organisation of the sport, and to the possibility of financial control being concentrated in the hands of the victualling trade. There was a boom in amateur pedestrianism in the 1840s, but splits in the sport were becoming apparent. By 1838 the status of pedestrianism can be seen in the fact that six Birmingham medical students announced a race but declined to give their real names, preferring instead 'Sprightly', 'Vulcan', 'Neversweat', 'Rustic', and so on. In 1850 the first athletics meeting was held at Exeter College, Oxford, and this kind of event spread through the public schools and universities in the 1850s; in 1862 the first cup for amateurs only was presented at the Hackney Wick running track. Amateur 'athletics' began to distance itself from professional 'pedestrianism', and by 1880 the foundation of the Amateur Athletics Association and a number of betting scandals were leading the latter into a decline.

In the United States the word 'pedestrianism' was less used, other than for reporting pedestrian events abroad, such as a race run in Sydney in 1853. However, occasional events in the United States were reported. In October 1855 the *New York Times* ran an exuberant story about the walker Curtis, praising his 'great triumph of physical endurance and moral resolution, and it contributes to the annals of pedestrianism as the record of the most perfect possible display of skill in that noble art'. Curtis had walked 960 half-miles in 960 half-hours over three weeks.

Until 1838 pedestrian events were listed in *Bell's Life* under the 'Ring' heading, but then pedestrianism was given its own heading, under which were included all the track and field events in use that are now part of athletics. 'Pedestrian' events, meetings and records were being widely reported in newspapers such as *The Guardian* and *The Observer* in the early twentieth century, but the last time the word was used as a banner in *The Times* was on 27 January 1954. Professional pedestrianism survived into the twentieth century, but more as a supplementary income for good runners; the prestige records and reported achievements went to the amateurs.

Pedestrianism brought to the world of sport the first accurately measured running tracks (at the Honourable Artillery Company Ground and Lord's Cricket Ground), the first accurate timings (six watches were sealed in a box for one of Captain Barclay's races), the first records, and the first setting of distances for running, which lasted until well into the twentieth century.

Pole vault

The supposed origin of pole vaulting lies in the use of poles to cross water. In the early nineteenth century Thomas Bewick made a delightful vignette of a man who has got himself stuck at the top of his pole suspended over a pond (delightful for the viewer, but not for the model). In the 1880s the sport was distinct from 'practical pole jumping', 'broad jumping' or 'wide jumping', which was a practice for crossing water in the fenlands that developed into a local sport, to do with achieving distance more than height.

The first recorded 'pole jumping' competition was in 1812, but by the end of the nineteenth century athletes were still making a vertical descent on to unpadded ground. The term 'vaulting' came into use after the 1880s, derived from the French word *volte*, meaning 'jump', but 'pole jump' remained in use until the First World War.

Polo

Though polo was probably first played in China or Japan a thousand years ago, Europeans first came into contact with it in the north-east of India in the nineteenth century, after the game had been developed in Persia. Balti Tibetan has *polo*, Lhasa Tibetan has *pulu*, and Lhodra Tibetan has *puli*, all of which describe the wooden ball used in the game. The game was first documented in English in 1835, having been observed in the state of Muneepoor; it was described in *Pemberton's Report on the Eastern Frontier of British India* as 'hockey, which is played by every male of the country capable of sitting on a horse'. The sport was brought to Britain in 1869, and within a few years matches were drawing huge crowds. By 1876 polo had arrived in the United States; it was an Olympic sport between 1900 and 1936, Argentina winning the last gold medals. Though full-sized, the horses used in polo are called 'ponies'; the use of this word has been documented from 1872 (*OED*).

Quintain

From a simple jousting practice in which the horseman had to hit a target with a weapon, usually a lance, while galloping past, 'quintain' became a number of bizarre variations. One was to simultaneously hit the target at one end of a beam and avoid the weight that swung round from the other end; another was tilting at a target while standing in a boat being rowed, and another was using the leg as a lance. From being a knightly exercise and a practice for jousting, quintain became a popular rural sport in the seventeenth and eighteenth centuries, especially at weddings. Charles Hoole notes its popularity in 1757: 'At this day tilting, or the quintain, is used, where a hoop is struck at with a Truncheon, instead of the races, which are grown out of use.' No doubt variations of the target evolved, depending on what materials or junk was available. The origin of the word is equally bizarre: the Latin *quintana* was the name given to a secondary street in the layout of a Roman military camp, which became the name of the market traditionally held there; the idea of a small street developed into a 'run-up to a target' and then to the 'target' itself. Alternatively, the *Gentleman's Magazine* for 1783 proposes that the fifth gate in the camp, called the *Quintana*, was where soldiers trained in the use of the javelin against a target. Joseph Strutt in the 1833 edition of *The Sports and Pastimes of the People of England* suggested that the name came from the sport's inventor, 'Dr Quinctus or Quintas, but who he was, or when he lived, is not ascertained'.

Quoits

Few sports have disappeared from view so much as quoiting, which in its heyday supported several professionals and tournaments. In the 1830s quoiting, largely a working-class activity, was being formed into clubs and competition structures, with large numbers of spectators. David Weir made £900 between 1839 and 1844, and

Robert Walkinshaw won £800 over seven years up to 1868. The quoiter aims a 'shoe' at a 'hob'; this was no game for rustic pensioners, though it was popular in working-men's clubs in the late nineteenth century. The quoit was a 16-pound iron ring to be flung 22 yards. By the 1940s it had become an indoor game, with rubber rings thrown at hooks on a vertical board. The word appears as Anglo-Norman French *coyte* in a thirteenth-century glossary as a translation of the Latin *discus*, which gives a good idea of the sport's antecedents.

Racing

The word 'racing' now is automatically associated with horses, a connection that can be traced to the late seventeenth century. Previously, 'running' horses was the term more commonly used, and this usage can be found in the tenth century. However, from the fifteenth century a 'horse-race' was a fast ride on a horse, from an established sense of 'race', meaning a 'fast rush'. The first sense of 'race' as competitive is documented to 1513 (*OED*). The word was originally Scandinavian, referring to a quick movement or a rush of water.

Horse-racing became the first major spectator sport in the United States, with up to seventy thousand spectators present at the race between Eclipse (from the North) and Sir Henry (from the South) at the Long Island Union Course in 1823. At a 4-mile race in 1842 between the Northern champion, Fashion, and the

Southern, Boston, overcrowding led to a riot, again with seventy thousand people attending.

In Britain horse-racing has a long history (it is mentioned in *Beowulf*, written down in the eleventh century) and has inevitably been associated with those wealthy enough to own horses, being known as 'the sport of kings'. Indeed, many monarchs were supporters of horse-racing, and from the eighteenth century there were attempts to exclude the poorer classes. The government's reaction to races without restrictions (spectators sometimes joined in along the course) was in 1740 to place a minimum prize level, suppressing the smaller meetings that attracted too many workers and too much low-level betting and crime. Newmarket was specifically set up for the aristocracy, with the racecourses finishing miles apart, so they could only reasonably be reached on horseback and by carriage. Horse-racing continues to be held throughout the week, with no preponderance for weekends, except for the Grand National and four of the five 'Classics', including the Epsom Derby.

Relay

In thirteenth-century French *relayer* meant to release a fresh set of hounds in a hunt, as the previous set of hounds had tired. From this developed the usage of an arrangement of fresh horses at stages along a journey; thus the word was adopted for a job requiring operatives being replaced in turns, and then a race with a number of stages, each taken by a fresh runner, which dates from the end of the nineteenth century.

Road or moor bowling

Moor bowling was a familiar sport in nineteenth-century Northumberland, where the contest was to see who could reach an agreed distance in the smallest number of throws of an object of a determined weight. The game has largely disappeared in Britain but is still played in Ireland. An earlier version of the game was played by distance rather than number of throws, the winner being the one who covered a greater distance with the given number of throws, usually twenty. A match in Ireland is still called a 'score', from the Irish word *scor*, meaning 'twenty'.

Rounders

Curiously, given that rounders occupies an undesirable position as being the unwanted ancestor of baseball, the first recorded documentation of the word is in 1828 (*OED*), considerably later than baseball. Rounders does share many things with baseball – both have 'batters' and 'catchers', but rounders has a 'bowler' or 'feeder' instead of a 'pitcher'.

Rowing

'To row' is known from about 950 as the Old English word *rowan*. As a competitive sport for crews, rowing is documented from 1778, when two boats, *Chatham* and *Invincible*, rowed against each other for £60. Thomas Doggett, a theatre manager, had previously instituted a race for a coat and badge, for watermen on the Thames; the race has been held every year since 1715. However, 'rowing' as a competitive sport is now distinguished from 'sculling' by each crew member having one oar only; scullers use two oars. 'Shells', boats without keels, were developed in the United States in the 1860s.

'Row', as the 'act of rowing', is known in the United States from 1832, particularly when talking about non-race rowing, while 'crew' is the more usual word to describe the sport. This term appears to have taken over from 'rowing' around 1940, though it does not appear in the 1940 *Dictionary of American English* (University of Chicago). However, the *Dictionary of American Slang* (1960) states that the 'crewcut' came from 'college crewmen who have favoured such cuts for years'.

Rugby

The long road to the game now called 'rugby' is perhaps most meaningfully joined in the early nineteenth century, when football was played at various public schools, each one with its own code. For example, at Charterhouse School the game was played in the courtyard of the old monastery, with its hard paving slabs, which encouraged a kicking and dribbling game rather than body-tackling. At Westminster, Eton, Harrow, Winchester and Shrewsbury dribbling, catching and holding the ball were the standard, while Rugby encouraged hacking (shin-kicking), catching and, from the 1820s, running with the ball, a practice that was taken up by Marlborough and Cheltenham. The educational reforms at Rugby around this time included a hierarchical disciplinary system run by the boys, which led to the ideas of team spirit and discipline in sports. This environment produced rule-making in sports, particularly team games, an idea that

was taken up by other schools, each developing its own codes. From 1846 we see the first documented codification of football, from Rugby School, with 'running in', leading to a 'touch down'.

In 1846 two former Shrewsbury pupils at Cambridge tried to set up a club with some former Eton pupils, but the codes were felt to be irreconcilable. In 1846 a further attempt, with former Shrewsbury, Eton, Harrow, Rugby and Winchester pupils was more successful, but the rules have been lost, though a set of rules from 1856 were found in the archives of Shrewsbury School. The rules allow dribbling, catching and stopping the ball but not running with it, and the old activities of hacking (kicking an opponent's shins) and tripping were abandoned. In 1855 members of Sheffield Cricket Club played football during the winter months, and this led in 1857 to the founding of Sheffield Football Club, with rules that favoured dribbling. The attempts to reconcile the different codes around this time include arrangements to play the first half of a match by the home team's code, and the second half by that of the visitors. In 1862 a further set of rules, issuing from Uppingham School, banned running with the ball, but allowed players to catch and stop the ball with hands before placing it at their feet. By this time former public school and university men had formed clubs up and down the country, and in 1863 another codification meeting was attended by members of fourteen London-based clubs including three Blackheath clubs that were dominated by former Rugby School pupils. Around the same time there was a meeting at Cambridge to update the rules, again between a group of former pupils of public schools including Rugby. What transpired from these meetings was a split between those who favoured running with the ball and hacking, and those who favoured dribbling. A few of the rules that were allowed by the new Football Association were soon dropped; these included no forward passing, and players being allowed to catch the ball and claim a free kick. At this point those clubs that maintained the running and hacking code went their own way, though many of the public schools retained their own codes; following pressure from Richmond and Blackheath clubs, both dominated by former Rugby School pupils, the Rugby Football Union was set up in 1871. Hacking and tripping were both abolished, though until 1881 Rugby School allowed five minutes of shin-kicking at the end of a game – it was actually an old English sport in its own right, called 'purring', and featured in the seventeenth-century Cotswold Olimpick Games, where it is still done.

Rugby from 1871 allowed twenty players on each side, and the scrummage became central to play, with the players upright rather than pushing shoulder against shoulder with heads down; when the ball emerged, the fly-half would run with it until tackled, whereupon there would be another scrum. Changes to the rules included fifteen-player teams (1875), releasing the ball when tackled (1878), and by the end of the 1880s passing became widespread. A *New York Times* report on rugby in 1882 uses the terms 'collaring', 'punting', 'handing off' and 'scrimmages', though 'scrummage' was the accepted term at Rugby and generally after about 1880. An 1890 *Guide to Football* defines terms in use, including 'punt out', 'punt on', and a 'fair catch' – in which a 'player makes a mark with his heel at the point where he made the catch' – now 'making your mark'.

The shape of the ball, according to one source, derives from the rubber bicycle inner tube, available from about 1889, but there is a reference to the ball 'pointing towards the goal' in *Tom Brown's Schooldays*, written in 1857, and rubber bladders were available in the 1870s. Nineteenth-century balls were larger and more rounded, and sometimes loose lacings were used as an aid for carrying, the shape and size of the ball being codified in 1892.

In Ireland the elitist origin of rugby meant that the game survived partition in 1922, the Irish Rugby Union having been formed in 1879, its members drawn largely from higher education and clubs of former pupils. Similarly, in Scotland the Scottish Football Union was formed by six public-school clubs in 1873; they declined to give their organisation the name of an English public school until 1924.

Rugby league

The establishment of the Northern Rugby Football Union in 1895 was based on fair payment for players for 'broken time', time that would have to be taken off from work, for which employers would not pay. The acceptance of full professionalism did not occur till 1898, and then with the stipulation that players should also have another job, presumably as they did not want to be seen to be moving into the rather discredited world of professional sports. This rule was abolished in 1905, at the same time as a league format was set up. Various other changes reflected the nature of professionalism: a report on players' injuries between 1890 and 1893 had shown dozens of major injuries, some fatal. The response was to remove the scrum after a tackle and replace it with passing back between the legs. This change meant that owners of clubs lost less money through having to pay injured and unproductive players, who soon began demanding more money than the small payments officially made under Northern Union rules. The name 'Rugby League' was adopted in 1922.

The All Blacks' rugby union tour of England in 1905 revealed to the New Zealanders the size of the crowds attending professional matches, and the Northern Union code was exported to New Zealand. At roughly the same time, a 'broken time' dispute in Australia led to the establishment of a professional code there.

Shinty

'Shinty' derives from the Gaelic word *sinteag*, meaning to 'leap', and is first mentioned as having been played in the Western Isles in the eighteenth century. Shinty is similar to hurling, and probably came to Scotland from Ireland: the modern Gaelic name for shinty, *camanachd*, is similar to the Irish for the version of 'hurling' played in the northern area of Ireland, *camánacht*. 'Shindy', a variation of 'shinty', is the source of 'shindig', meaning a 'wild dance or party'.

Shot put

'Putting the shot' looks like what you do when you 'put' the shot, but the actual usages of the word are less simple than at first appears. The event uses the spelling 'shot put' or occasionally 'shot putt', and the *OED* records the action as 'putted the shot' (1938) and 'threw a shot put' (1989), as well as 'put the shot'.

'Putting' involves not allowing the hand back farther than the elbow. The sport was earlier known as 'casting the stone', stones being replaced by cannon shot in the fifteenth century; the term 'putting the weight' was also used in the late nineteenth century. Walker's *Critical Pronouncing Dictionary* (1791) has the entry for 'puttingstone: In some parts of Scotland, stones are laid at the gates of great houses, which they call Putting-stones, for trials of strength.'

Shuffleboard

Shuffleboard, the game in which a disc is sent along a marked target with a stick, used to be 'shovelboard' and before that 'shove-board'. There is no explanation for the change beyond that 'shovelboard' is slightly easier to say than 'shove-board'. The table-top version, 'shove-ha'penny', was previously known as 'shove-groat'.

Singlestick

Singlestick was a form of combat sport similar to fencing, and used as training for sabre skills, using a wooden stick or cudgel. The addition of a wicker basket-hilt to the stick in the seventeenth century allowed the stick to be used more like a sabre or 'backsword', and 'singlesticking' or 'cudgel-play' became a common sport in the eighteenth century. The convention of using the stick not as a thrusting weapon led to a succession of conventions as to what constituted a fair target. Singlestick was an Olympic sport at St Louis in 1904. 'Cudgel' developed from the Old English *cycgel* and *kicgel*.

Skating

R. Jones in his *Treatise on Skating* (1772) wrote that 'it is remarkable that learners throw their arms about carelessly, or in a manner, as if they were catching at something to prevent their falling', manifesting a degree of sympathy often seen in those who know how to do something. Some of the postures that Jones describes – the 'flying Mercury' (as seen in medical logos), the 'fencing position' (now the 'lunge'), the 'salutation', the 'serpentine' – are still recognisable, though they were replaced in the 1860s by clearly defined movements called 'One Foot Eights', 'Threes to a Centre', 'Rockers', 'Brackets', 'Loop change Loops' and 'Bracket change Brackets'.

Televised competitive ice-skating has made people familiar with terms such as the 'Axel jump' (a spinning jump, named after its inventor, Axel Paulsen, who performed it in 1882), the 'Biellmann spin' (holding one shoe behind and above the head, after Denise Biellmann, who used it with great success in the 1970s), and the 'Salchow' (a spinning jump invented by Uriel Salchow in 1909).

Cassell's 1907 *Book of Sports and Pastimes* includes 'dancing on ice', with known dance figures, and 'waltz', which is now called 'ice dancing', and retains the same figures.

Skiing

The Norwegian word *ski* developed from the Old Norse *skith*, meaning a 'piece of wood', which in Old English was *shide*. An isolated use of the word (as plural 'skies') shows a misunderstanding, as the writer believed that people used them for wading through snow (*OED*). Competitive skiing often involves courses with 'moguls', bumps in the snow, which variously impede or injure the skier; 'mogul' comes from an Austrian-German word for a 'hillock', used in the fifteenth century to mean a 'chunk of bread'.

Snooker

In 1875 the junior officers of the Devonshire Regiment stationed at Jubbulpore in India tried several variations of billiards during the rainy season. One version, called 'pyramid', involved paying every time your opponent potted one of fifteen red balls laid out as a triangle. This and elements from other variants became the new game of 'snooker', the name being a slang term for the newest recruit at the Royal Military Academy in Woolwich. There are inevitably various versions of the exact circumstances of the first use of the word: one officer using it at another after a missed simple shot, an officer claiming that as it was a new game they were all 'snookers' at it, or that it was a 'snooker' of a game. However, the game was brought to Britain by a professional billiards player employed by the Maharaja of Jaipur.

Softball

'Softball' originated as an alternative form of baseball, which was taken up by women from the 1930s as women's baseball decreased in popularity from its heyday in the early twentieth century. The sport was originally an opportunity for baseball players to practise indoors during the winter but developed into a sport in its own right. The International Softball Federation has established the exact day, time, place and manner of the origin of the sport: Thanksgiving Day 1887, in Chicago, after the Yale–Harvard football match, with a rolled-up boxing glove and a stick.

Speedway

Harness racing, or 'trotting' as it was called from the later nineteenth century, was also known as 'speedway' in the early twentieth century, though this was an extension of the name of the track used for harness-horse racing. Now most race-tracks in the United States are called 'speedways'. Motorcycle racing on a dirt track, also called 'speedway', was imported into Britain from Australia in 1928.

Squash

There are distinct stories regarding the origin of squash. One variation is that it developed from the game of racquets, itself reputedly invented by inmates of the Fleet Prison at the beginning of the nineteenth century. It was taken up by Harrow School about 1820, though the line of contact has never been made clear, and players played with a ball that eventually burst. The punctured ball demanded more exertion by the players and was favoured for this reason. Another version states that at Harrow there were more boys wanting to play rackets than there was available space; accordingly a version with a larger and softer ball was devised for the younger boys. Slowing the game down (in terms of the speed of the ball, which thus travelled less) meant a smaller court, and more available space for courts. Another version proposed that the smaller boys at Harrow took over the Rugby fives courts, newly built in 1865, which were not being used, Eton fives being more popular. A squash court is still essentially the same in form and dimensions as a Rugby fives court.

Thus squash rackets, as it was still sometimes called in the 1970s, may be named from the ball that squashed on impact with the wall, or the courts that could be squashed in, or the young players who were squashed out. The *OED* favours the first of these, as the first recorded use of 'squash' was the name given to a ball.

Steeplechase

The apocryphal origin of the steeplechase is of a 4-mile horse-race run between two Irish gentlemen in 1752, using the steeple of a church as the finishing point and a guide during the course of the race. It would appear to be a natural development to use the same word for cross-country running, which had been common from the mid-seventeenth century as gentlemen set chosen servants to run against each other for betting purposes. In 1850, for a horse-race organised at Oxford University, a decision was made to replace the horses with undergraduate athletes, and by 1864 'steeplechasing' was an established event in university sports.

Stoolball

In 1909 the *Rules of Stoolball* were published, describing it as 'this genuine old Sussex game'. While it is similar to cricket in many regards, particularly in vocabulary, there are a few differences. The bowler bowls from a 'target', the bat is like a large table-tennis bat, the batsman (female in this case) must touch her wicket on starting her innings, and the wickets are 1 foot square, 4½ feet from the ground.

Stoolball is an uncomplicated game and was seen for a long time as a female counterpart to cricket (Strutt in 1833 described it as 'for women'), and more recently as a winter training game for cricketers. It is likely that the name derives from the use originally of a stool for a wicket, which connects with the use of the word 'cricket' to mean a 'stool'. Early references to stoolball show it being played in New England in 1621, lending some weight to its claim to be an ancestor of baseball. It was also occasionally claimed to have been one of the precursors of cricket. It had previously been called 'bittle-battle', 'bittle' being an alternative spelling for 'beetle', meaning a 'club', and was called 'stub-ball' in Wales. A game called 'stoolball', which developed in the enclosed spaces of prisoner-of-war camps in Second World War Germany, included aspects of rugby, basketball and the Eton wall game.

A Match at Stool-ball, a Song, the words by Mr Durfey (1715) shows a rural idyll:

> Come all great and small, short away to Stool-ball
> Down in a Vale on a Summer's Day
> All ye Lads and Lasses,

Met to be merry, a match for kisses, at stoolball play,

For cakes and Ale, and Sider and Perry,

Will & Tom, Hal, Dick and Hugh,

Kat, Doll, Sue, Bess, and Moll, with Madge
and Bridget,

And James and Nanny, but when plump Siss got the
ball in her Mutton fist, once fretted she'd hit it …

This clearly indicates that far from being a gender-segregated sport, stoolball at this time was that rare thing in sport, a gender-mixing opportunity; later stages of the lyrics show this aspect being pursued with some enthusiasm.

Stowball

Not to be confused with 'stoolball', 'stowball' was, according to Strutt in 1801, 'a species of goff', also called 'bandy-ball', though he never managed to see it played. This may have been a precursor of hockey, writers on old English sports describing it as having been played in the sixteenth and seventeenth centuries; contemporary sources also called it 'stopball' and 'stob-ball'.

Swimming

The eleventh-century *Exeter Book* describes the 'skills of men', one of which is *syndig*, from the Old English *sund*, meaning to 'swim'. In the twelfth century it was one of the seven knightly skills, along with archery, hawking, riding, chess, verse-writing and boxing, according to the Spaniard Peter Alphonsi. By the 1370s this had become 'swymmen and dyven', and by 1408 'swymmynge'.

Challenge matches and exhibition swims provided a living for a number of professionals. Much of this involved novelties, such as that suggested in Captain Stevens's *System of Swimming* (1845), in which a swimmer, floating on his back and holding up a small sail, could cross the Channel. Stevens says, perhaps resigned to the limitations placed on the spirit of adventure, 'the packet-boat is, however, still preferable.' Other advice was more sensible: Benjamin Franklin advised beginners to walk down into the water backwards and to throw an egg (which will sink) into the water between them and the shore – diving down to reach the egg would tell them that the water would buoy them up. For Stevens, 'the best of teachers [was] the frog, of whom I would advise all new beginners to take lessons.'

The first municipal swimming baths of modern times were those built in Liverpool in 1828. Is it a swimming 'bath' or a 'pool'? In 1952 the National Union of Teachers' *Curriculum of the Secondary School* called for schools to have a swimming 'bath', but now we would associate 'baths' with municipal structures rather than sites for leisure. Perhaps 'pool' carries some reference to a natural environment, which is left behind in the obviously constructed 'baths'. 'Baths', or even 'bath', may have a slight connotation of education or wealth – it is used in educational texts on fitness and recreation in the period 1920–40, but also appears earlier in, for example, *Baily's Magazine of Sports and Pastimes* for November 1904, where swimmers are described as swimming 'over a hundred and fifty yards in a bath'.

Table tennis

Table tennis supposedly evolved from post-dinner parties where, in imitation of lawn tennis, a row of books served for a net and books for rackets, with the broken-off top of a champagne cork as a ball. The name 'pingpong' is similar to other nonsense or imitative game or toy names of the period, such as 'yoyo' or 'tiddlywinks' (it was also early on known as 'wiff-waff', and other names used were 'Pom-Pom',

'Pim-Pam' and 'Neto'). Its popularity led to a number of firms developing and manufacturing sets of equipment, with their own rules. An early version sold at Hamleys in London was called 'Gossima', while Jacques & Son patented their version as 'Pingpong'. Table tennis and Pingpong differed in the kinds of bat or racket used (Pingpong preferred a 'battledore', originally with a longer handle and a face of gut or parchment), and in the kinds of service allowed. In 1901 the champagne corks were replaced by celluloid balls, and bats began to be faced with rubber. The Table Tennis Association and the Pingpong Association came into conflict in the early years of the twentieth century, the Table Tennis Association stating that the change of the name to table tennis was not unwelcome, 'as many felt that the alliterative appellation was slangy, and had a tendency to bring a really good game into ridicule'; in 1903 the two associations merged and in 1922 became the Table Lawn Tennis Association, with a pamphlet describing the game as 'lawn tennis played on portable miniature hard courts'. The name 'Pingpong', though dismissed so comprehensively, survived: *Competitive Sports in Schools and Colleges* (New York, 1951) mentions both 'Pingpong' and 'net Table Tennis'.

Tennis

There are two strands of thought concerning the origin of the name of the game 'tennis', which arrived in England about the beginning of the fifteenth century, though the appearance of the word 'raket' in Chaucer's *Troilus and Criseyde* of 1385 suggests an earlier date. One states that there was a record of some kind of call being made on serving (in 'real tennis', the version played in a court similar to the outside of a monastery, called 'court tennis' in the United States), and in French this could have been *tenez*, meaning 'take that'. Alternatively, and bearing in mind that the French game was called *jeu de paume*, meaning 'game of the open hand', there were Italian versions of the game called *racchetta*, *paletta* and, in Florence, *tenes*. It appeared in Middle English as 'tenetz'. The political and trade situation at the time would make France a more likely candidate than Italy for lexical influence. The record of a bill for 'lost balls' in the accounts of Henry VII would indicate that the game was sometimes played out of doors – the Privy Purse expenses for the period record it as 'tenes'. The use of the term 'court tennis' and the use of 'court' for the field of play in tennis show lawn tennis's ancestry.

In 1873 Major Walter C. Wingfield invented a new game, compounded of badminton, real tennis and squash rackets, to which he gave the names 'lawn tennis' and the more wonderful 'sphairistike'. Original courts were hourglass-shaped, and the net drooped in the middle. 'Sphairistike' meant 'skill at playing ball' and spawned a slang diminutive, 'sticke' or 'sticky'. Naturally the invention, and Wingfield's right to take out a patent in 1874, were disputed – a Major Gem claimed to have played a similar game with a Spanish friend, based on the Spanish game *pelota*; the rules were eventually resolved by the MCC in 1875. *The Madagascar Times* was still debating the question in 1885:

> the game itself cannot altogether be called a new one as it was known in slightly different form and under a totally different designation for many years prior to its universal adoption.

The popularity of the game led to followers of the enclosed-court version calling that 'real tennis', and for twenty years or more publications showed their author's preference by the use of 'tennis' to mean 'lawn tennis' or 'real tennis'. This is some indication of how tennis became a forum for displays of class distinction: real tennis had regularly been a sport played by all classes, with all forms of equipment and resources, though authorities had often tried to ban the poor from playing it. Tennis became an elite sport in the United States, a byword for the middle-class house party in England, and parodied in the 'Tennis anyone?' or 'Anyone for tennis?' attitude of the Edwardian daft young man (actually recorded from no earlier than 1953 – *OED*).

Tip cat

'Tip cat', or just 'cat', was another variation of knurr and spell. The 'cat' was an oval-shaped piece of wood, which when laid on the ground and hit would fly up in the air, to be hit again as far as possible. The striker then had to calculate how many times its own length the 'cat' had gone. 'Cat' is a common European word in various forms, though its origin beyond Europe is unknown.

Trap-ball

'Trap-ball' is a southern variation of knurr and spell; it is recorded from the fourteenth century, the 'trap' being the apparatus that sent the ball into the air. This use of the word 'trap' dates back to the sixteenth century and is incongruous – a 'trap' otherwise is designed to 'catch' something, not send it up into the air – a rare incidence of a word having two apparently opposite meanings.

Triple jump

Health and Physical Education for Schools in India (1934) gave instructions for doing the 'hop, step and jump', now known as the 'triple jump', a term that was already in use in the United States in 1896 (*New York Times*). Curiously, the *OED* gives the first recorded use of 'triple jump' as recently as 1964, which may be so in Britain, as the McWhirters' *Get to Your Marks* (1951) has 'hop, step and jump'. Early Olympics included the triple jump from a standing start, and it was one of the events at the mythical Irish Tailteann Games, supposedly dating from 1829 BC.

Tug-of-war

The tug-of-war originated in inter-regimental contests in the British army in India in the mid-nineteenth century. An Olympic sport between 1900 and 1920, it was contested by clubs rather than national teams. Thus in the 1908 Olympics the tug-of-war medals were won

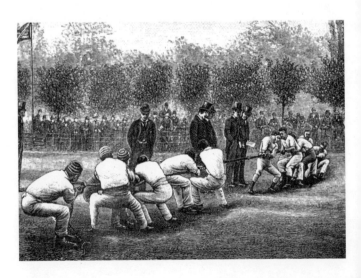

by the City of London Police, the Liverpool Police and the Metropolitan Police 'K' Division. 'Tug' comes from the Old English *téon* or *téohan*, meaning to 'draw or lead'.

Volleyball

Strutt in 1833 relates the story of a game of 'fives' played in 1591 before Queen Elizabeth I; it was probably called 'fives' because there were five players on each side. From the fact that it was played by hitting a ball over a net in a 'square greene courte', the game described sounds like volleyball. Around the same time *faustbol* was being played in Germany, a game which translates into English as 'fistball'. A game looking very like volleyball is seen in Hoole's translation of Comenius' *Orbis Sensualium Pictus* (1757), in which 'a Windball being filled with Air by means of a Ventil is tossed to and fro with the Fist in the open Air'. Modern volleyball, developed in Springfield College, Massachusetts, in 1896, was originally called 'mintonette'.

Water polo

'Aquatic handball matches' were held in 1876 by the Bournemouth Premier Rowing Club – one of several attempts to match field team sports to swimming; the London Swimming Association had in 1870 initiated 'football in the water'. The London Water Polo League was formed in 1889, a year after discussions had settled on the name of the sport. According to some reports, early versions of the game involved players balancing on floating barrels and using paddles to propel themselves and strike the ball – if so, this was presumably the reason for the selection of the name 'polo', however bizarre the spectacle. Other descriptions of the early form of the game suggest violence rather than pantomime, the game being called 'water rugby' in Scotland, and allowing players to be held under water until they released the ball.

Wrestling

'Wrestle' has had a number of variants, including 'warsle' in the North and Scotland, and 'wraxle' in Dorset and the West; it comes from the Old English *wræstlian*, and in the United States the form 'wrastle' is common. *Baily's Monthly Magazine of Sports and Pastimes* for January 1836 gives also 'the back-hold wrostle of the North of England (much science was displayed on both sides)'. Carew, writing about customs and pastimes in 1600, described wrestling in which an avoided fall was called a 'foyle'.

One of the world's oldest and most widely practised sports, wrestling has had many forms, incorporating varying degrees and ratios of skill and violence. As a frequent and popular sport, wrestling flourished in country fairs and as an entertainment in wealthy places

of amusement, and it survived the strictures placed on prizefighting. The entertainment potential, which comes from its basic nature of physical conflict without the obvious violence and bludgeoning of boxing, has allowed wrestling to become at various times more of an amusement than a sport. 'Free-style wrestling', imported to Britain from the United States in the 1930s, gave free range to aspects of drama, with 'good guy, bad guy' contests, villains, victims and assaulted referees, most of this being scripted. In *Mass Observation's Bolton Working-Class Life in the 1930s*, Mrs K. Carr stated that at a wrestling match she liked to see 'plenty of action such as throwing out of the ring, slamming on the mat, and a bit of punching'. For Roland Barthes, amateur wrestling was 'drama, ritualised and exaggerated', a performing of basic situations:

> A hold, that is, any figure which allows one to immobilize the adversary indefinitely and to have him at one's mercy, has precisely the function of preparing in a conventional, and therefore intelligible, fashion the spectacle of suffering, of methodically establishing the conditions of suffering.

Betting

Betting lies close to the heart of sport, and few sports have not been involved with betting from their early history. The first documented cricket match in England, in 1700 (the first documented anywhere was on 6 May 1676 – by the crew of a British ship anchored off the coast of Syria), records the bets placed by the players and may have been recorded precisely for that reason. The first laws of cricket (1727) were laid down to ensure a fair basis for betting. When eleven members of the Nottingham Club played twenty-two members of the Sheffield Club at cricket in 1800 (and the use of 'members' tells us that they were amateurs), the stakes were 200 guineas. In horse-racing, rules were necessary for the running of competitive races, which were primarily for betting – low prize money in the eighteenth century both depended on and increased owners' dependence on betting. The games and sports included in Hoyle's *Games Improved* (1779) included instructions for running betting 'on equal or advantageous terms', giving the odds for each stage of a game. At the beginning of the nineteenth century competition golf outside club contests had to be arranged privately and involved heavy betting, and when Agnes Beckwith, aged fourteen, swam the 5 miles from London Bridge to

Greenwich in 1875 there was a vast amount of betting. In the United States in 1824 the crew of a British ship challenged the Whitehall Aquatic Club to a race, with stakes of $1,000. Possibly the most notorious bet was when the Duke of Cumberland bet on Jack Broughton, the prizefighter, to beat Jack Slack in 1750, losing £10,000.

Bets had to be made on the basis of known hazards, form, and knowledge of fairness, so betting can be seen as having a direct influence on the concept of fair play. Organised betting, in the hands of bookmakers (people who recorded bets in a book), ran into trouble when the odds offered did not reflect probability, and when there were doubts about matches being thrown or competitors being bribed or 'nobbled' (the word is found from about 1850; 'fixing' is first found in attempts to corrupt juries, from 1790, in the United States). Amateur sensibilities officially condemned betting – the Amateur Athletics Association rules for 1880 stated that 'All open betting must be put down.'

Betting as an integral part of sport affects many cultures: Cashmore in *Making Sense of Sports* (2001) gives the example of a Mississippi Choctaw sport to which betting was integral, until white settlers joined in the betting and brought in extraneous corrupting influences, with the result that gambling and betting were banned, and the sport faded away.

In the 1880s betting papers sold 300,000 copies daily, and betting was for many people their primary experience of sport. There was betting on professional athletics, pigeon-racing, bowls, billiards, snooker, fishing, quoiting, in fact on every sport except cricket. Off-course betting was illegal till 1960, but in 1951 it was estimated that 44 per cent of the adult population bet on horses. There was a certain 'science' to some of this, and even today informed betting on horses is supposed to give the best chance of making money through betting. But to discourage public libraries from becoming study centres for betting, librarians pasted paper over the racing news in newspapers.

People who encouraged dogs to bite bears or bulls in the practice of baiting were said to be 'abetting'; the words 'bait', 'bite' and 'abet' are thus strongly connected. From Norse *bita*, meaning 'to bite', came *beita*, meaning 'to cause to bite', which developed into Old French *abeter*. These may be the origin of the word 'bet', found first in a document from about 1460 (*OED*). 'Gamble', found from the eighteenth century, may come from 'game', and 'wager', found from the early fourteenth century, is from Anglo-Norman French *wageure*, meaning a 'pledge' – it is related to 'wage' in the sense of a 'pledge or money given for services'.

Betting slang (early)

Balsam: money.

Battler: a racecourse better making small bets.

Corsey betting: reckless betting, from the French *corsé*, meaning 'tough'.

Dump: deliberately lose a match or race (American).

Hocus: to bribe a horse-owner (1859).

Levant: to renege on a betting debt.

Post: to pay a betting debt (Hotten, *Slang Dictionary*, 1865).

Post a pony: to lay down the stakes for a bet (Hotten, *Slang Dictionary*, 1865).

Square: deliberately lose a match or contest (1889), or nobble a contestant (1859).

Throw: deliberately lose a match or race (from 1868).

Betting terms

Accumulator: when the better or punter designates a selection in a number of races and bets on the first one, the winnings from the first race become the stakes for the second, and so on; from 1889 (*OED*).

Bettor: American term for someone placing a bet, a 'better' or 'punter' in British English.

Each way: the punter makes two wagers – first for the selected horse to win, then for it to come second or third, the return being decided on by odds given by the bookmaker; from 1869 (*OED*).

Evens: when there is an equal chance a competitor will win or not.

Form: a horse's past performance as an indicator of how it is likely to do in a race; from 1760 (*OED*).

Going: the state of the ground of a course at any time, specified as 'firm', 'heavy' or 'soft'; used in this way since the 1880s.

Hedging: a bet placed by a bookmaker after accepting heavy bets on one horse, the wager being made to offset losses if the horse wins; from the sense of to 'make secure', from about 1670.

Legs: 'blacklegs' originally, men who collected the money owed to bookmakers at Newmarket, so called from the mud they collected on their legs.

Odds: the bookmaker's view of the chances the competitor will win; from the sense of 'odd' as 'uneven', therefore that there is a difference between one thing and another. 'The odds' was in use in this way in the early seventeenth century.

Place: second place in a race; nineteenth-century, gradually being specified as 'second place'.

Pool-betting: the total amount bet on a horse to do better than third place.

Show: third place in a race; American, from 1903, in the expression 'win, place, or show' (*OED*).

Spot-betting: betting on an incident in an event, for example how many runs a certain batsman will make.

Spot-fixing: fixing an event in a contest to make money by spot-betting.

Spread betting: the pay-out is based on the accuracy of the prediction made, rather than an absolute result.

Tic-tac: the code of signals by which on-course bookmakers' employees (tic-tac men) signal the changing odds before a race; from 1899, and derived from the sound made by telegraph machines, therefore to do with the codified transfer of information.

Tip: the selection chosen by experts (or 'tipsters'); in Hotten, 1865.

Tote: the body that runs pool-betting on racecourses.

Tout: to sell or give betting advice, or someone who does this; originally someone who spied on horses as they practised to get an idea of their condition; from about 1810.

Turf accountant: delightful term for a bookmaker, dating from 1915 (*OED*).

Gambling. Theoretically 'gambling' is distinct from 'betting' in that the former is to do with chance, while the second may include the use of applicable knowledge; bearing in mind that a 'tout' was originally someone employed to spy on horses in practice, information was not always easy to come by. But a stronger difference lies in the usage: 'gambling' tends to be used when the person is involved in the activity, and 'betting' for when a spectator risks money on the outcome. The words 'gambling', 'gambler' and 'gamble' appear in that chronological order in the eighteenth century and probably come from a dialect version of the word 'game'. Given the importance of horses in the pre-industrial era, and the amounts of money bet on them in racing, 'gambling' is a less appropriate word than 'betting' for what took place, though some 'gambling' undoubtedly occurred as well.

Pools. Football pools, which appeared in newspapers from the 1900s but were declared illegal in 1928, became enormously popular in the 1930s, especially in Liverpool, where the Littlewoods pools venture started. Because it could be claimed that playing the pools involves skill in predicting results, it was possible to escape betting legislation. In 1934–5 £20 million was gambled on football pools, a figure that doubled within two years.

'Pool' comes originally from *poule*, used in French card games from the mid-seventeenth century to mean the 'collective pot of money staked', with the application to betting emerging in the mid-nineteenth century.

Stakes. The 'stakes' were originally the prize money hung in bags on the stakes that supported the ropes round a prizefighting ring. This money was the 'stake money' – a nice story, but the *OED* points out that unfortunately the earliest known reference, from 1540, is for the 'stakes and settynges that be sette within the dyce borde, whiche lye on lyttel heapes', while the first reference to putting anything hazarded on to a stake dates from 1592. But this leaves the etymology of 'stakes' undecided. Hotten's *Slang Dictionary* (1865) and Smythe Palmer's *Folk Etymology* (1882) offer no suggestions, but Partridge (*Origins*, 1959) suggests a figurative development from the idea of a stake put in the ground as a support or a mark.

In boxing and pedestrian contests the referee was usually also the 'stakeholder', the person who held the stakes. The first 'sweepstakes', where the winner takes all stake money betted, confuses the issue further, as its first documented usage is from 1495, when it was used as the name of a naval ship. The *OED* states that 'sweepstake' was often used as a name for a ship between the fifteenth and seventeenth centuries. The inference here is that the ship would sweep away any opposition.

Tattersall's. Richard Tattersall was a nineteenth-century racehorse ('bloodstock') auctioneer, who opened a betting room at Hyde Park Corner in 1815, which functioned as a club and quickly became the chief centre for race-betting in Britain, allowing members to bet against each other. It was a subscription-only service; Tattersall controlled the membership but allowed outsiders to bet via

intermediaries. The Australian Tattersall's dates from 1881. Tattersall's was where bookmakers might leave for inspection their books in which they had noted bets and odds, so that people could see that betting had been above-board.

Totalisator (Tote). The totalisator was a machine devised to calculate multiple betting. It was invented by George Julius, in response to a request to organise a foolproof way of calculating 'pari-mutuel' betting (meaning 'mutual stake'); this is where all the money bet on a horse-race is divided among all those who backed the winner – it was devised in nineteenth-century France and was long-winded and often faulty. The first machine was sold to Ellerslie racecourse in New Zealand in 1913 and proved a success, so that totalisators were still in use in the mid-1980s.

Clothing

Blazer. One story proposes that the first 'blazers' were bright red, worn by the members of the boat club of St John's College, Cambridge, in 1889. The *OED* documents blazers from 1880, and the word has a more likely basis in the meaning of 'to blaze', as 'to announce' or 'give news of', which would make a connection to the phrase 'blaze a trail'. An alternative idea is that blazers show the coat of arms of a club or college and are thus 'emblazoned' with the identifying information.

Boot. It is uncertain where the word 'boot' originated; it appeared in Middle English in the fourteenth century and was for long specifically applied to footwear extending above the ankle, as did football and rugby boots until the 1970s. This long association explains the retention of the word, though the tops of football and rugby boots now lie below the ankle.

THE SHUREKIK.
New Design, 5/4, 6/11, 7/6, 8/6.
Postage, 6d.

Cap. In *Boxiana*, published between 1812 and 1829, Pierce Egan mentions the 'champion's cap'; it is unclear whether this refers to an actual cap or a metaphorical one – pictures of prizefighters from this period do not show them wearing caps. *The New York Times* in 1882, reporting on American football, noted that caps were worn at the beginning of the match, and films from around 1900 show English rugby players running out to play wearing them; presumably the nature of play would lead to them being quickly lost after play started. However, *Cassell's Book of Sports and Pastimes* in 1882 shows caps being worn in association football matches. The official adoption of the practice of awarding caps for playing in international matches dates to 1886 for football, and the Australian cricket team's 'baggy green' cap dates from the beginning of the twentieth century – the word 'baggy' having originated in Australia.

Clothing. The progress of sport over the past four hundred years can be read as a progress of the specialisation of clothing, from the usual daywear to exclusive performance-enhancing gear, via some curious bypasses. The amateur movement of the Victorian period used the idea of clothes specifically for sports as one of many ways of distinguishing itself from the professional sports, which tended to be done in stripped-down versions of day clothes. The advent of a wider range of team sports also brought more use of distinguishing strips, as teams moved on from the wearing of different coloured sashes or ribbons.

Clothing was used to handicap runners in the seventeenth century; Samuel Pepys watched the Duke of Monmouth win a race in his boots against barefoot competitors. In the eighteenth century some running was naked, as it had been at the Olympics. Early-nineteenth-century swimming was segregated, as had been the case for sea-bathing; thus for indoor swimming men usually went naked. Gender segregation for sports at American colleges created a situation where at Yale swimmers in the university pool were required to swim naked until 1969, when women undergraduates were admitted.

Early-nineteenth-century sports were done in day clothes with the coat removed (but often not the hat). Captain Barclay's 'walking dress', in which he performed extraordinary feats of speed and endurance, consisted of breeches and stockings, pumps with a rosette, a tight coat with no tails but wide flapping lapels, a shirt with stock, and a beaver hat. He carried a large spotted handkerchief. *Physical Culture* (1886) shows boys doing exercises in vest, breeches, stockings and pumps, while girls wore dresses with pleats and a large bow, a bodice and blouse, stockings and pumps, frequently it seems undertaking a change of dress between exercises. By 1879, only two years after the first Wimbledon tennis championship, there were tennis fashions for women. By some it is considered that cycling, with its bloomers for women, liberated women's sporting clothes, while others believe that this was a one-off, as it had no effect on women's clothes for other sports or outside the sporting world.

In C. B. Fry's *The Book of Cricket* (1899) the Lancashire bowler A. Hallam is shown wearing a formal shirt with a rigid starched front. At this time, and earlier, it was considered normal to wear a tie as a belt, possibly as an indication of club colours. The clothes of amateur sport tended to be almost heraldic – blazers, caps and scarves that followed the pattern of schools and universities; one of the best-known set of sporting colours (outside of football) is the red and yellow of the MCC tie. 'Corks', shoes with cork soles that gave some spring, were thought to be good for running in around the turn of the nineteenth century. At the same time 'spikes' were adopted by many runners. By 1950 athletes were wearing cotton or wool 'sweat pants' in the United States, and 'tracksuits' in Britain ('sweaters' were originally for horses, used in the nineteenth century to make them sweat, which was felt to be good preparation for a race).

In the twenty-first century sports clothing has massively influenced fashion, so that 'sportswear' can mean 'sports clothes' or 'sports fashion', though professional sporting fabrics and designs are likely to cost several times the price of a high-street replica football shirt.

Costume (swimming). Athletic clothing, or rather the absence of it, reputedly began in the Greek Olympics when the runner Orsippus was found to have gained an advantage after dropping his loincloth. Wearing a costume became statutory in London baths after 1860, and a requirement for the Amateur Swimming Association from 1890, but before 1800 much bathing (segregated) was naked. Men's costumes were known as 'drawers' (they were 'drawn' on), and women's as 'gowns'. 'Costume' became the general word for both sexes around the end of the nineteenth century.

Gloves. During the tour of North America by an English cricket team in 1859, the batsmen wore 'gauntlets', not 'gloves', and a wicket-keeper's gloves are still occasionally referred to as 'gauntlets', or are described as having a 'gauntlet profile' because the cuff extends over the wrist. This refers back to the gauntlet's history as part of a suit of armour and unsurprisingly shows the word to be of French origin, as are almost all English words to do with medieval chivalry and knightly codes. Gauntlets are used in lacrosse, the sport having a name of French origin. 'Glove', being less grand, equally unsurprisingly comes from an Old English word. 'Mitt', used in baseball, comes from a post-Conquest Anglo-Norman French word for a 'glove'.

Boxing gloves, though used for practice during the days of prizefighting in the eighteenth and nineteenth centuries, were not used in professional fights. 'Mufflers', as they were known, were used by the boxer Jack Broughton in the first half of the eighteenth century as protection for the hands, and it is generally thought that this was the main role of boxing gloves. But in the later eighteenth century Daniel Mendoza set up an academy for training boxers, and such was the popularity of the sport among the wealthy that it was natural for young enthusiasts to want to have a go at sparring. Gloves in this situation were mostly necessary to avoid damage to the young gentlemen's features. The compulsory use of gloves, as laid down in the Marquess of Queensberry's rules (1867), and the legal definition of non-glove boxing as 'assault occasioning actual bodily harm' following a court case in 1882, separated 'boxing' from 'bare-fist fighting'. However, there is an argument that bare-fist fighting caused pain to the fist, a pain that meant pugilists learned to use restraint, avoidance and accurate placing of blows, while gloved boxing encourages repeated blows to the large target of the head, leading to eventual brain damage. Elliot Gorn, in *The Manly Art: Bareknuckle Prizefighting in America* (1986), argues that padded gloves, along with the Queensberry Rules, did not make championship fights of the 1890s less prolonged or brutal, but more amenable to commercial promotion, as they became more spectacular. The statistics are interesting: in 150 years of bare-fist fighting in Britain before 1885 only two fatalities were recorded; it is estimated that worldwide since 1880 1,300 boxers have died as a direct result of the sport.

Wicket-keeping gauntlets do not always provide sufficient protection, particularly when facing fast bowling. Alan Knott, England wicket-keeper between 1967 and 1981, reputedly placed strips of Plasticine or even steaks inside his gloves for extra padding.

Goggles. To 'goggle', meaning to 'turn the eyes from side to side', became a common word in the sixteenth century, also with the meaning of 'to look obliquely, or squint'. The first constructed goggles, made in the early eighteenth century, were made to correct a squint, and the word was later applied to various kinds of eye protection, including the opaque versions with a tiny slit to protect the eye against Arctic glare.

Gymslip. The invention of the gymslip is credited to Martina Bergman-Österberg, who, after training in the Swedish school of Ling gymnastics, was appointed to the London School Board in 1881. She developed several innovations in the training of female PE teachers and PE for girls, including the gymslip and netball. The use of 'slip' for a light dress dates from the eighteenth century.

Helmet. The word 'helmet' was adopted from the French during the fifteenth century. 'Helmet' may look as if it is a diminutive form of 'helm', but 'helm' existed in its own right as an Old English and later Middle English word before becoming obsolete, being used now only as a poetic or archaic term.

Jersey. The Tour de France was founded in 1902 by Henri Desgrange, the editor of the French newspaper *L'Auto*. When in 1919 the lead cyclist agreed to wear a distinctively coloured jersey so that spectators would know who was winning, yellow was chosen, being the colour of the paper *L'Auto* was printed on. The yellow jersey is called in French *le maillot jaune*. Knitting has a long history on the Channel Island of Jersey, but worsted stockings from Jersey were common before the first use of the word, in the mid-nineteenth century, to describe clothing for the upper body.

Jock strap. A United States patent dated 1897, taken out by Charles F. Bennett, was for a 'combined jock-strap and suspensory', presumably a truss of some kind. 'Jock' was a slang word for genitals, both male and female, and probably had nothing to do with the use of 'jock' to mean 'sportsman', which was an abbreviation of 'jockey' originally used for young horse-riders.

Kit. A kit was originally a wooden barrel, from the Dutch word *kitte*, and by the late eighteenth century it was applied to a soldier's equipment and clothing. The use of 'kit' to describe clothing dates from the 1960s.

Leotard. Jules Léotard (1842–70) was a French trapeze artist, the first person to complete a somersault in mid-air from one trapeze to another, and the inspiration for the 1867 song 'The Daring Young Man on the Flying Trapeze'. Léotard's usual attire was a tight-fitting full-length costume, then called a *maillot*. His skill and fame ensured that his name was immortalised in the name of the costume used by gymnasts and dancers.

Pads. Early cricketing pads, called 'leg guards' and worn by batsmen and wicket-keepers, were made of cotton wadding wrapped over a support of canes, held together by strips of canvas. The first documentation of the word in a cricketing context dates to 1843 (*OED*), when pads were becoming essential cricket equipment, though by then they had been in use for about ten years. The word 'pad' is known from the mid-sixteenth century, but there is no idea where it came from.

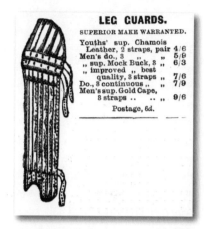

Plimsoll. The plimsoll shoe was developed in the 1830s by the Liverpool Rubber Company as footwear for the beach, and acquired the name 'plimsoll' (not 'plimsole') from the line where the moulded rubber sole met the canvas upper. This resembled the famous Plimsoll Line, which was applied to the outside of a ship's hull to indicate safe levels of loading. Either the resemblance was visual, or the effect was – if water came above the line, the wearer's foot would be soaked.

Shinguards. Alternately known as 'shinpads', they were recorded from the 1880s, but invented in 1874 by S. W. Widdowson, who cut down a pair of cricket pads; he had a career in swimming, athletics and rowing as well as football and cricket. They were originally worn on the outside of the stockings; the move to wearing them inside came in the 1890s.

Shirt. The use of the word 'shirt' for upper-body clothing for sport, eventually replacing 'jersey', dates from around 1890. The *Rules of Hockey*, published in 1887, describe the clothing to be worn as 'knickerbockers, stockings and shirt', while a price list of sports equipment from 1895 (*OED*) offers cricket and football shirts. 'Shirt' derives from the same source as an Old Norse word that developed in Old English into 'skirt'; the sense that bound together these and other similar words in Germanic languages is the idea of a short garment.

Shorts. In 1936 in the United States a 'trunk short' was a name for what in Britain are now called 'pants' or 'briefs'. However, the word 'shorts' had been used for short trousers since the early nineteenth century, and the expression 'football shorts' is documented from 1913 (*OED*). 'Shorts' superseded 'knickerbockers', which during the nineteenth century had been the usual word for sports trousers stretching to just above or below the knee. 'Knickerbockers', from which emerged the word 'knickers', came from the name of some early Dutch settlers in North America, the image of the loose-fitting breeches deriving from Cruikshank's illustrations to Washington Irving's *History of New York* (1809); and the first formal baseball club in the United States, founded in 1845, was the Knickerbocker Baseball Club. Though the word 'knickers' is retained in the States, particularly for baseball, by the 1960s it had become rare to find British football teams being described as wearing 'stockings, knickers and jerseys'; the word was used for the last time in *The Guardian* in 1958, and in *The Times* in 1963, but these were isolated examples.

Socks. From 1876 A. G. Spalding began to supply sports equipment and clothing, including baseball jerseys and knickerbockers. As these were of a uniform pattern, there remained only the pattern and colour of socks by which clubs could distinguish themselves from the opposition. Boston Red Sox and Chicago White Sox are the two best-known teams that retain this in their names.

Strip. The *OED* suggests that a player's strip is possibly what he or she strips down to; the first documented use given is dated 1974. Leigh and Woodhouse in *The Football Lexicon* (2004) suggest that in this

usage 'strip' is being replaced by 'kit'. Perhaps
'strip' means the clothing that identifies the
team, while the 'kit' also includes any
other equipment – boots, gloves, bat, etc.

Trainers. The Gola Trainer was marketed
in 1968, but it was not until the early 1980s
that 'trainer' took over from other expressions
(sports shoe, tennis shoe) as the generic term
for a soft sports-type shoe. In the United
States 'sneaker' is the term used.

Trunks. Swimming 'trunks' developed
in the United States in the late
nineteenth century as a thigh-length close-fitting garment, though
the first documentation (*OED*), from 1883, describes Captain
Matthew Webb's fatal attempt to swim through the rapids below
Niagara Falls, for which he wore the same red silk trunks that he wore
when completing the first observed Channel swim in 1875. 'Trunk-
hose' had previously been short breeches worn over tights,
documented from the sixteenth century; but it is uncertain what
meaning of 'trunk' this was based on.

Another word that was applied to a swimming costume is 'togs',
which came to Britain from Australia and New Zealand. It probably
derived from the use of this word as a slang expression for clothes,
which appeared about 1800. This in turn had come from the word
'togman' or 'togeman', a sixteenth-century slang or cant word for a
loose coat. An eyewitness account of the first athletics meeting, in
1850 in Oxford, describes athletes in their 'toggery'.

Other Australian expressions for swimming costume are
'bathers', 'swimmers', 'cozzies' (from 'costume') and the expressive
'budgie-smuggler'.

Competition

Battle-royal. A 'battle-royal' was a name for an event in a medieval tournament in which the two sides in a melée were commanded by a 'king', though this title may have been purely for the event. The pattern was taken by cock-fights, in which a number of cocks were set to fight until only one was left alive. Taken up by World Championship Wrestling in 1991 for professional wrestlers, the event may involve twenty wrestlers fighting until only one is left in the ring. Although this mixture of barbarity and showmanship has little claim to be thought of as sport, a similar activity – 'last man standing', or British bulldog (the name is documented from 1950 by the *OED*, which describes it as a children's game) – is used regularly as training for team contact sports such as rugby.

Bout. 'Bout' comes from the old past participle form of the verb to 'bow', 'bought', meaning 'having been bent'; 'bought' was also spelt 'bout' in the sixteenth century and came to mean a 'circuit'. From this the word came to mean a 'round' at any form of physical activity, similar to a 'turn'. 'Bout' as specifically applied to a timed boxing match is first found in Shakespeare.

Challenge. 'Challenge' arrived in English in the early fourteenth century as *calenge* or *chalange*, from a French development from the Latin *calumnia* (English 'calumny'), meaning a 'false accusation'. The first meaning of 'challenge' in English was an 'accusation' or 'reproach'. In the pre-amateur days of sport, most contests were either professional challenges – invitations to participate – or direct one-to-one challenges between pedestrians, boxers, horse-owners, and so on, set up either by themselves or by their backers. *Bell's Life in London and Sporting Chronicle* in the nineteenth century was full of challenges such as:

> Black Jack of Bedington wishes to run Ross of Newcastle or Anderson (the Hillgate Wedge) or Anderson of Tudhoe, 120 yards, for £10 or £15 a side; or he will take four yards start, and run Sutton of Kenton the like distance and sum. His money is ready at G. Smith, Victoria Inn, Seaton De'aval. First come first served.

> William Watkin of Longton informs his brother pedestrians that he has declined running altogether, and that, therefore, it will be useless to challenge him. 7th December, 1845.

Championship. The earliest documentation of 'championship', meaning a series of contests, is 1825, with the more conversational 'title' being first recorded in 1922. The change from *The Championship decided, or the Battle on Hungerford Downs*, published in 1822, to 'the Championship meeting', when the 'Championship of Croquet' is decided (*OED*, 1874), shows the meaning developing from the 'question of who is champion' to the 'contest to decide who is the champion'.

Club names. In the context of sport, language is integral to the building of identity – the identity of the sport and that of the group that supports both the sport and those who play it. The names of clubs may emerge from industries that the players work for or which sponsor the team, from geographical areas, from former schools, or from affiliation to a church or similar organisation. Nicknames, however, tend to emerge from the supporters and display curious traits. Those imposed from above or achieved by compromise tend to be less successful than those that emerge from grass-roots level, which may survive long after any active connection has been lost. Or they may be curiously incongruous, or reflect topical changes, such as when Chelsea Football Club supporters started referring to the club as 'Chelsky' after it was bought by a Russian. The former political/sectarian affiliation of Celtic Football Club is shown in the name 'the Bhoys', supposedly from a late-nineteenth-century postcard that referred to the club as the 'bould bhoys', a phonetic transcription of an Irish accent rendering of 'bold boys'.

In the nineteenth century, during the period when many sports clubs were founded, there was no feeling that clubs' names should refer to their location. Saracens was founded in 1876 and merged with Crusaders two years later; Wasps RFC was founded in 1867; Hampstead Football Club was founded in 1866 but by 1870 had changed to Harlequins. Hotspur had been a North London cricket club before it was associated with Tottenham Football Club. As part of the rebranding of the Rugby League in 1995 Leeds adopted the name 'Rhinos'. Leeds had always been the 'Loiners' (the term for a native of Leeds), and at first there was some antipathy, but the name seems to have been gradually accepted. West Ham Football Club fans prefer 'Irons' to 'Hammers'; though hammers appear on the club crest, the club was originally the Thames Ironworks Football Club. A deeper sort of ownership seems to be involved, one to do with lifelong and inescapable affiliation. Self-deprecation, pessimism or defiance may lie behind the adoption of apparently diminishing names, like 'the Shrimpers' for Southend United, and the adoption of the taunt 'Gooners' by Arsenal fans, or the Brooklyn Dodgers, also originally an insult, implying Manhattan residents' disdain for Brooklyn 'trolley-dodgers'. The 'Old Firm' was at first a satirical reference to the pairing of the two Glasgow clubs, Rangers and Celtic, whose money-spinning derbies were the most lucrative in Scottish football. Odd occurrences may provide curious names: West Bromwich Albion, known as the 'Baggies', derived their name from the bags holding the gate receipts that were paraded round the ground on match days. Club names, and in particular nicknames, imposed by owners or management often jar, implying that the most important criterion is that a nickname must emerge from those most permanently associated with the club, the fans. This must be especially the case when a club's players do not come from the area, or the same country, and may be employed for a season before moving on.

When an entire game decides to rebrand itself, things may go spectacularly wrong. In 1999 the National League for Sunday Cricket decided to adopt or invent new names for the counties participating, with Durham becoming the Durham Dynamos, Derbyshire becoming the Derbyshire Scorpions, and so on. *The Guardian* described this as 'nonsense', the Sunday League 'lurching further from tradition', and 'only Kent escaping a suffix and only until one is contrived' (6 March 1999). Kent eventually became the Kent Spitfires. Middlesex took the name 'Crusaders', but in response to complaints from Muslim and Jewish fans changed to Middlesex Panthers in 2009. While Kent may have some historical link to Spitfires, Middlesex and Derbyshire can have little connection to panthers or scorpions, but then footballers playing for clubs in those counties may come from Chile, China or the Ivory Coast. But then in 1860, according to *Baily's Monthly Magazine of Sports and Pastimes*, the active cricket clubs had included the Surrey Giants and the Surrey Lions. A delicate series of relationships underlies the names of Trinidad cricket clubs described by C. L. R. James, where according to Richard Holt:

> The Queen's Park club took white officials and a handful of the most distinguished 'coloured' families but no blacks. Shamrock catered for the Irish Catholics and other whites plus some middle-class coloureds … then came Maple, a brown skinned team, which ranked itself above Shannon, who were made up of the better-educated blacks. Finally there was Stingo, the leading black working-class team.

'Stingo' was a slang word for 'energy', drawn from a name for a strong kind of beer.

In the United States nicknames were adopted beside geographical information for sports clubs early on; in the 1860s baseball clubs were called the New York Mutuals (from a volunteer fire-brigade), the Brooklyn Eckfords (from a shipbuilding firm), the Liberty Club of New Brunswick, and the Union Club of Morrisania. The earliest of them all was the New York Knickerbocker Club, followed by the Brooklyn Excelsior Club. Richard Holt shows how in the 1890s very local affiliations and nicknames were used in the names of rugby clubs in the Pontypool area, with amongst others the Tranch Rovers, Garn and Varteg Pride, Talywain Red Stars, Panteg Harlequins. In the late nineteenth century, as association football came to be adopted by the urban working classes, clubs grew up that kept the names of the streets from which their players came, for example Gibraltar Street Rovers in Blackburn. Affiliation to a particular church or pub might be commemorated in a name – Everton was originally St Domingo.

COMPETITION

Perhaps the most surprising feature of club names is the frustration of the expectation that they should somehow be intimidating to the opposition. 'Daggers' for Dagenham and Redbridge Football Club sounds strong and 'up for it'; the Essex Eagles (cricket), Sheffield Sharks (basketball) and Calgary Flames (ice-hockey) are all 'power-names'. But what lies behind the selection of a name like the Pontynewynydd Lilies of the Valley (rugby, 1890s), and how does a club nickname like 'the Canaries' (Norwich City Football Club) intimidate the opposition?

Cockmain. Cock-fighting, with its potential for pub sponsorship and heavy betting, was a popular activity among the wealthy in both Britain and North America in the eighteenth century. A tournament was called a 'main' or 'cockmain'. The Old English *mægn* meant 'power or strength' and became 'main', surviving in the phrase 'might and main'; so a 'cockmain' may have been a 'show of strength'.

> COCKING.—OLDHAM.—A main of cocks came off in the new pit near Oldham, between Henry Booth and S. Smith, for £50 the main, which was won by Booth obtaining 6 out of 10, and Smith 4. Henry Booth will make a match with Old Chorley of Bolton, one or two days, at any convenient pit, for his own sum.

Derby. There is a theory that the word 'derby' comes from Stanley Park in Liverpool. Lying between the grounds of two rival football clubs, Liverpool and Everton, the park, which opened in 1870, was named after Lord Stanley, sixteenth Earl of Derby. The use of the word 'derby' to mean a 'match between two local rivals' is dated by the *OED* as late as 1914, and specifically to a Liverpool versus Everton match, so there is some plausibility in this explanation. But a match between two local rivals is often referred to as a 'local derby', which is saying the same thing twice. This may be to distinguish it from the Derby horse-race, or may be to emphasise the local nature of the rivalry.

The twelfth Earl of Derby won the toss of a coin that decided that a horse-race for three-year-old fillies, first held in 1780, would be named after him rather than Sir Charles Bunbury, senior steward of the Jockey Club. The race held annually is thus called 'the Derby'.

Yet another contender is the Shrovetide football match that has been played between two parts of the town of Ashbourne in Derbyshire since the twelfth century. The match retains some of the delights of early versions of football – the goals are 3 miles apart, any number can play, and participants are asked to avoid the use of 'unnecessary violence'.

Fixture. A fixed date for a race meeting has been called a 'fixture' since about 1825, but around this time there were two forms for the word; it had originally been a 'fixure' – it developed into 'fixture' by analogy with 'mixture', probably because it is easier to pronounce. 'Fixure' and 'fixture' are both recorded from around 1600 (*OED*), and it is odd that the more difficult to pronounce form stayed in use for so long; it seems to have died out about the time of the first use of 'fixture' to mean a sporting date.

Formula 1. The Fédération Internationale de l'Automobile defined in 1946 the standard regulations for motor-racing, setting out a range of formulas based on the construction of the cars. Formula One is for the highest performance cars, followed by Formula 2 (currently in abeyance), Formula 3 and Formula 3000. There were several attempts to define formulas for safe racing from 1907 up to 1939, which after 1946 were largely based on the need to limit the cylinder capacity of the engine. The first time the word 'formula' was used in the context of the restrictions on car construction was in 1927.

Grand Prix. Though motor-racing began in France in 1894, the first Grand Prix race was held at Pau in 1901, followed by the regular

Grand Prix races arranged by the Automobile Club de France, beginning in 1906. These were held on a circuit at Le Mans, there having been several fatalities during the 1903 road race from Paris to Madrid. The name 'Grand Prix' (meaning 'big prize') has been attached to a horse-race held in Paris since 1863.

Gymkhana. A 'gymkhana' was a 'sports arena' in Marathi and Hindi; the word is an anglicisation of *gend-khana*, meaning 'ball-house', with the proposition that the first syllable was altered to 'gym' by association with 'gymnasium'. The Mumbai Gymkhana, established in 1875, is used for indoor and outdoor sports all year round. Around 1900 the term 'gymkhana meeting', which was applied to any kind of sports meeting (the *OED* cites a 'bicycle gymkhana'), began to take on the specialised association with pony-racing.

Home and away. 'Home' in the sense of the host ground being the venue for a sporting contest dates to the beginning of the nineteenth century, when an arrangement for two matches, each one played at a home venue, was called 'home and home'. Newspapers from around the end of the nineteenth century show the emergence in football, rugby and water polo of 'away' matches and 'away form', though 'away' goals were not noted until 1966. An edition of the MCC *Laws of Cricket* published in 1800 describes the visiting team as 'the party who goes from home'.

Ivy League. In October 1933 the *New York Herald Tribune* used the phrase 'ivy colleges' to describe eight American universities, and two years later the same newspaper coined the phrase 'Ivy League'. In 1945 the 'Ivy Group Agreement' affirmed a common purpose for the administration of inter-collegiate football, which nine years later included all sports played between the colleges. The original application to football (American football) is a key point. Gorn and

Goldstein state that in the early twentieth century 'college alumni associations were founded to help control and promote college athletics, which for the most part meant football...' Particularly within the Ivy League colleges, 'far more than academic achievement, the experience and culture of football linked different generations of American leaders in a collegiate socialization process that helped provide cohesion for the children of the American upper classes.'

There is a story that the original group of four colleges, Yale, Columbia, Harvard and Princeton, were called the IV League, pronounced 'eye-vee'. This, and the question of whether it was football or rowing that provided the major forum of athletic competition that bound the colleges together, is much disputed.

League. In 1888 the Football League was initiated between twelve clubs from the North and the Midlands, playing what was described as 'a sort of American tournament for the League Championship'; the existing system of FA Cup matches and one-off friendlies did not provide a regular source of income to pay the professional players' wages. The pattern was already established by the South London Football League in 1885 for London schools. The expression 'American tournament' was first used in Britain in 1878 (*OED*), to describe a system for professional billiards players to arrange matches. The word 'league' comes via French and Italian from the Latin word *legare*, meaning to 'tie'.

Match. The word 'match' has been used for a sporting contest since the early sixteenth century and derives from an earlier sense of matching adversaries. The earliest documentation of 'match' is from about 1440 (*OED*), 'This was a mache un-mete' ('this was an uneven match'), showing that the sense of 'match' here was 'to match people equally or unequally'. In the sixteenth century, too, there was no specification that a 'match' had to match only two contestants: in 1545 Sir Roger Ascham wrote: 'To make matches to assemble archers togyther, to contende who shall shoote best, and winne the game...' In the eighteenth and nineteenth centuries, when individually arranged contests were set up, this would be described as 'the match being made'; when it happened, it 'came off'. The sense of an arranged contest between a pair of players survives in golf in 'matchplay', where the results of a contest between teams are decided by the results of the matches between pairs or fours of players. Team sports were played in 'matches' from the early eighteenth century – the *OED* gives examples of 'a match at cricket' from 1700, and a 'football match' from 1711. The exact usage took a while to settle: where we would now say only 'a cricket match', *Bell's Life in London* for July 1828 had 'a cricket match', 'a match of cricket' and 'a match at cricket' in the same report.

SKITTLES.—A match has been made between B. Sexton of Norwich and the Unknown, for £20 a side. £10 a side has been staked in the hands of Mr T. Chandler, of the Red Lion, Blackman-street, Boro', the remaining £10 a side to be made on Wednesday evening next, at Mr Stevens's, Clarendon Arms, Wyndham-road, Camberwell New-road, when the place of playing will be named.

Olympic Games. Athletics meetings have been called 'games' in English since at least the end of the fourteenth century. Major games have generally limited themselves to athletics events, though there have been some exceptions. The first post-classical Olympic Games held in Greece took place in 1859; it included chariot races, and agricultural and industrial shows, including prizewinning exhibits in agricultural machinery and soap-making.

The nineteenth century was the heyday for the founding of major games. The Much Wenlock Olympian Games ran from 1850 to 1914; the Liverpool Olympics ran annually from 1862 to 1871, and there were National Olympian Games at Crystal Palace in 1866 and at Birmingham in 1867. The Morpeth Olympic Games ran from 1881 to 1958, providing competition for professional pedestrians and wrestlers. The mother of all these was the Cotswold Olimpick Games, brought together by Robert Dover in 1612, a collection of traditional sports, including shin-kicking, but graced with some of the King's clothes, which Dover had managed to get 'purposely to grace him and consequently the solemnity of the Games'. A few decades on, a collection of poems by writers such as Ben Jonson further raised the status of the games:

> The Cotswold with the Olimpick vies
> In manly games and goodly exercise.

The Victorian Scottish romantic revival led to an increased interest in Highland Games, not only in Scotland, but also in North America, where up to twenty thousand spectators watched the New York Caledonian Games.

The spirit of the Olympic Games steers a delicate course between amateurism and ultimate achievement, the prizes being the theoretical ones of taking part and the rather more tangible and remunerative ones of winning. Thus in 2009 the reduction in funding for cycling training in Britain was perceived as a cause for complaint by a medal-winner, who described the possibility of the 2012 games becoming the 'have-a-go Olympics'. Though the word 'chivalry' has been dropped from the Olympic oath, athletes still swear to participate 'in the true spirit of sportsmanship, for the glory of sport and the honour of our teams'. The very success of the Olympics compromises the idea of success for athletes; as Simon Barnes points out (*The Meaning of Sport*, 2006), for those who participate in the sports for which the Olympic Games is the only real public stage, they have a chance of glory once every four years.

Paralympics. The Paralympics emerged from the National Spinal Injuries Unit at Stoke Mandeville Hospital, Buckinghamshire, which used sports for rehabilitation of wounded servicemen and women. They were adopted for the 1948 London Olympics as 'The International Wheelchair Games', becoming the 'Paralympics' in 1960; according to the International Paralympic Committee they are games that run parallel to the Olympics.

Play-off. In baseball a 'play-off' is one of a series of games at the end of the season to decide the league champions (from 1932), while in association football it is one game of a knockout contest to decide which team is promoted to the division above. The first use of 'play-off' as a contest to resolve an undecided contest dates from 1895 (*OED*), though a similar usage existed earlier, for example a report of a pedestrian race in 1845 (*Bell's Life in London and Sporting Chronicle*) that describes a 'race-off' after a 'dead heat'. A similar idea is the 'repêchage' in Olympic competition, in which runners-up in heats are allowed a second chance to qualify for the finals by competing against each other; 'repêchage' means 'fishing out, rescuing'.

Regatta. The first mentioned regatta in Britain was in 1768, though no racing was involved. The word comes from the Italian, first found in Genoa and Naples, and later in Venice.

Rubber. A 'rubber' essentially means a 'heat' or 'leg'. Used in the sixteenth century to mean the decider of a group of an odd number of games, it developed in the late eighteenth century to mean a set of games, and a sufficient number of people to play.

Seed. Adrian Beard in *The Language of Sport* (1998) suggests that the origin of 'seeding' in knockout competitions comes from the advisability of planting seeds at a certain distance apart, an explanation supported by Andrew Delahunty in *Talking Balls* (2006). The term 'seeding' was first used in the United States in 1898, but for a long time it was treated as not quite a 'proper' word: most of the quotations given in the *OED* up to the 1920s have the word in inverted commas. *The Times* on 23 June 1924 made explicit its discomfort by stating that the word did not appear in the *Oxford Dictionary*, and this was an indication of 'how little seeding accords with British notions'. By 1936 it was securely included in H. C. Wyld's *The Universal English Dictionary*.

Tournament. 'Tournament' derives from the Old French *torneiement* (medieval Latin *tornamentum*, which influenced later English spellings), from *torneier*, meaning 'to joust'. In Middle English this became the verb 'tourney', meaning 'to take part in a tournament'. Literally, the Old French verb *torner* meant 'to turn', which might imply that the word came from what the mounted combatants did at the end of a run at each other (a joust). Joseph Strutt in *The Sports and Pastimes of the People of England* (1801) proposed that 'tournoy' implied 'running in turns'.

However, the first documentation of the word in the *OED* gives 'in ioustes and in tornemens', which may imply that these were not

the same thing. The first 'tornemens' were mock battles between groups of armed men; growing cultures of chivalry changed these from military training of large groups to individual ritualised combats. *Tournez* in the fourteenth century carried the meaning of 'an act of valour', and the sense of 'responding to a challenge' is seen in the phrase 'to take or have a turn at'. The wheeling or sequential sense of 'turn' may have been combined with this in the application of a tournament for a number of fights in sequence, the sense which from the mid-eighteenth century developed into the modern meaning of the word.

World Series. For a sport mostly played in one country, the baseball term 'World Series' may seem presumptuous, arrogant even. But according to one story, the annual play-off games between the champions of the National League and the American Association was once sponsored by the *New York World* newspaper, and the name derives from the sponsor. Evidence for this story is hard to come by, and a more likely explanation of the name is the aspirations for the game as proposed by another sponsor, Spalding, who called the 1886 games between St Louis and Chicago 'the World's Championship'. Spalding's vision for the future encompassed baseball spreading to Australia and Britain, from where teams, naturally with Spalding equipment, would challenge American teams for the championship. 'The World's Championship' became 'the World's Championship Series', and then 'the World's Series', and finally 'the World Series', at different dates between 1917 and 1964 in various publications. *The New York World* never sponsored the play-offs and never claimed any association with the title.

Equipment

Arrow. 'Arrow' was the usual word used in English after about 1000, but previously there had been two different words: *flo*, found for example in a ninth-century text by King Alfred, and used in Scots dialect till the sixteenth century; and *stræl*, which disappeared about 1200 (*OED*). The two less common Old English forms *earh* and *arwe* derive from a word for 'bow' and probably mean essentially 'the thing that goes with the bow' (there may be several reasons why we now say 'bow and arrow' rather than 'arrow and bow', but there is still a sense that the arrow 'belongs' to the bow).

Bail. The *Laws of Cricket* published by the MCC in 1800 refer to 'the bail', singular rather than plural – at this time the wicket consisted of two uprights and a cross-piece. As soon as three stumps were introduced, in the 1830s, two bails were needed. One suggestion is that the word was adopted in the sixteenth century from the French *bail*, meaning the horizontal part of a gate, but the first documented use in English describes a crossbar that a hawk could perch on without damaging its tail (*OED*). 'Bail' also meant the 'handle of a kettle', which when made of wood would have been similar in shape to a single bail.

Ball. If there is one thing beyond the human body that is integral to sport it must be the ball. Ball play is seen in 4,000-year-old Egyptian paintings, and Homer tells of how Nausicaa and her friends played ball while waiting for the palace washing to dry.

If 'ball' as a game usually means throwing it from one person to another, in baseball the 'ball' becomes the centre of the whole game, the metonym by which it is understood. Don DeLillo builds a novel, *Underworld* (1997), around the ball used at the Giants–Dodgers Pennant game in 1951. American ball sports become concentrated in baseball: the club becomes the 'ball club', the match the 'ballgame', and the stadium the 'ballpark'. The ball itself, which every spectator in the stands wants to catch, is:

> this five-ounce sphere of cork, rubber, yarn,
> horsehide and spiral stitching, a souvenir baseball, a
> priceless thing somehow, a thing that seems to
> recapitulate the whole history of the game every time
> it is thrown or hit or touched.

Celluloid balls made table tennis; rubber tubing helped perfect the oval ball that made rugby pre-eminently a running and carrying game; and the dimples caused accidentally on early modern golf balls by use were applied deliberately when it was found that they made the balls fly straighter. The famous early golf balls ('featheries') were made by stuffing a leather pouch with enough boiled feathers to fill a top-hat. The cloth that stuffed early tennis balls came from Tunis and may have been an origin for the name of the game.

In the earliest known laws of cricket (published in 1752, but reputedly written down eight years previously), the ball is referred to as 'she'; the text is supposedly being dictated by an old countryman, but the use of some vocabulary makes it clear that this is not consistent. However, it somehow rings true.

Variations of 'ball' are common in Germanic languages, not documented in Old English, but found in Old High German as *bal*, in Old Danish as *bold*, and Old Swedish as *balder* or *baller*. In the early nineteenth century balls did not 'bounce'; they 'hopped'.

Barbell. The *Manual of Physical Exercises* for Manchester schools (1906) recommended several exercises using the 'barbell' or the 'wand'. The 'barbell' is a rod with weights on either end, while the 'wand' is without weights; the *OED* lists 'barbell' as 'a steel bar weighted with a ball of iron at each end, used as a dumb-bell', very much along the lines of what would have been lifted by a circus strongman. 'Bar-bell' and 'wand' came into use in the late nineteenth century.

Bat. There was probably an Indo-European root-word that sounded like 'bhut', which developed into the Latin *battuere*, meaning 'to beat', and the Gaulish *anda-bata*, meaning 'a gladiator'. These arrived late in Old English as *batt* and later *batte*, meaning 'a mace or club', found in Layamon's *Brut*, a history of Britain composed around 1200.

In falconry, a bird hitting down with its wings is said to be 'batting' (it is similar to the expression 'to bat an eyelid'), and 'to bat' does not necessarily mean 'to hit with a bat'. The original rules of basketball, from 1891, state that 'the ball may be batted in any direction with one or both hands.'

Cotgrave's 1611 French–English *Dictionary* translated *crosse* as 'a cricket-staff, or the crooked-staff wherewith boys play at cricket'. This makes sense given the shape of early cricket bats, curved at the end, and broadening down from the handle, though it may be wondered why the word 'club' was not used; this was the term for the not dissimilarly shaped implement used for golf in the sixteenth century. In 1706 Phillips's *New World of English Words* (the sixth edition, the first having been published in 1658) defines a 'bat' as 'a kind of club to strike a ball with, at the Play call'd Cricket'. Yet fifty years later Johnson (*Dictionary*, 1755) did not refer at all to cricket in his definition of 'bat'.

In the mid-nineteenth century both 'bat' and 'club' were used to describe the implement used in baseball (the description of baseball in *Captain Crawley's Handbook of Outdoor Games*, 1878, describes the baseball bat as 'like a light Indian club'); but by 1870 'bat' alone was used.

Table tennis uses a 'bat' or a 'racket', as did early lawn tennis. The Table Tennis Association in 1901 preferred 'raquet', while the *Official Laws of Pingpong* (1902) specify a 'battledore'; the 1922 rules authorised by the Table Lawn Tennis Association used 'bat'; 'bat' was used by Chester Barnes, the United Kingdom champion, in his *Table Tennis* (1979), but the *Laws of Table Tennis* (2004–5) use 'racket'. *The Sports Book* (Dorling Kindersley, 2007) prefers 'bat'.

If this is confusing, a 'bat' is used in the game of 'racquets'.

Bobsleigh. The sport of bobsleighing grew from the Cresta Run in St Moritz, the result of imagination and the construction of a natural ice run with embankments by Caspar Badrutt, a local hotelier, in the 1870s. Using sleds in different ways, tourists developed the luge (feet-first, 'luge' from the name of a small Swiss sled) and the skeleton (head-first), as well as the bobsleigh. Bobsleighs were originally two sleds fastened together, first used in North America for hauling logs.

Sled, sledge or sleigh? 'Sleigh' is from Dutch *slee*, itself short for *slede*, and is originally Dutch American; 'sled' came from Middle Flemish or Middle Low German *sledde* into British English in the fourteenth century; and 'sledge' is from Middle Dutch *sleedse*. Of the three, 'sleigh' is perhaps the most likely to be associated with snow, and 'sled' the least, but this will differ from region to region and writer to writer: *The Complete Book of the Olympics* (1984) by David Wallechinsky uses 'bobsled'.

Bow. Similar to many other Germanic language words for 'bow', this word has its roots in words meaning 'bend'. An early alarm call in military camps was 'bills and bows!' (*OED*).

Caber. The 'caber' is a wooden pole about 20 feet long and weighing 100 to 150 pounds, which is 'tossed' by holding it upright with the hands clasped underneath, running, and with a jump throwing it upwards with the intention that it turns 180 degrees and lands upright. 'Caber' comes from the Gaelic *cabar*, meaning 'pole, spar or rafter'.

Canoe. Definitions vary as to what constitutes a 'canoe' – open or closed, curved prow and stern or flat-pointed – but the paddle seems to be the key and is for the *OED* what defines a canoe. The word has entered English in two forms, first as 'canoa', the Spanish transcription of the Haitian word as encountered by Columbus. This form existed in English until the eighteenth century, alongside another form,

'canow', as well as the variants 'caano', 'cano', 'canno', 'canoo', 'cannoe' and 'canoe'. According to Nuttall's *Pronouncing Dictionary of the English Language* (1879) and Walker's *Pronouncing Dictionary* (1791), the pronunciation was as now, though in the earlier book the spellings 'canoa' and 'canoe' were given. Given the range of spellings available it is perhaps strange that 'canoo' did not prevail.

Catamaran. The Tamil words *katta*, meaning 'a tie or bond', and *maram*, meaning 'wood', make up this word, which was adopted into English as 'catamaran' in the mid-seventeenth century. *Hobson-Jobson's Anglo-Indian Dictionary* (1886) gives other anglicisations as 'cutmurram' and 'cutmural', which look like folk etymologies, and also cites an Italian text of 1583 that puts the word into an Italian form as *gatamerono*. The first documentation (*OED*) is in 1697, but in 1662 a 'double-bottomed ship' had been designed by Sir William Petty and tested successfully by the Royal Society. In what was effectively the first ocean-going yacht race, *The Experiment*, as it was called, beat the official 'pacquett-boat' from Holyhead to Dublin by fifteen hours.

Catgut. Were tennis rackets ever strung with the intestines from cats? If so, it would have been an experiment at best. 'Catgut' is the cord made from twisted animal intestines, usually sheep or goats, but occasionally pigs, horses, goats or donkeys. There are a number of stories surrounding the origin of the word: it was originally 'cattlegut'; it was a development from 'kitgut', 'kit' being an old word for a 'violin'; or because it was used to string fiddles, which sound like caterwauling; or from catgut makers, who wanted to preserve the mystery of their craft, using the unlucky association with cats to keep prying eyes away. For the *OED* the name derives exactly from cats' guts, whether they were used or not. Partridge (*Origins*, 1959) puts it down to 'folklore'.

Chequered flag. One suggestion is that the chequered flag was originally a tablecloth, waved at the end of a day's racing to signal the start of a large meal; another traces the first chequered flag to cycle races in nineteenth-century France. The spellings 'cheker'd' and 'chekkered' preceded 'chequered', which is a medieval French importation.

Club. Golf has been using 'clubs' since at least the fifteenth century; an early-sixteenth-century book of hours in the British Library shows Flemish men clearly playing golf with clubs that are only slightly less bent at the hitting point than modern clubs. A mid-fifteenth-century English–Latin glossary gives the word 'clubbe' for *pedum*, usually a 'shepherd's crook'. The word probably came from a Scandinavian source and was used to describe a weapon from around 1200.

Ditchfield's *Old English Sports* (1891) points out that the word 'bandy' was used for a golf club, and also a hockey stick and a cricket bat. In 1902 in London Slazenger sold 'hockey clubs and bandy sticks', while Tydesley & Hollbrook in Manchester and Wisden & Co in London sold 'hockey sticks'; in 1883 the Duke of Clarence played hockey with a 'club'. Considering that sixteenth-century golf clubs, eighteenth-century cricket bats and nineteenth-century hockey sticks all look remarkably similar, and conceivably share a common ancestor, it is reasonable to suggest that the divergence of the names of the implements is an example of the creation of the culture of specific games, the idea of enthusiasts wanting to differentiate 'their' game from others by means of language.

Cue. The probability that billiards is largely French in origin is strengthened by the word 'cue', *queue* in French, meaning 'tail'. Early prints and drawings show people using what was called a 'mace', thick at one end and fine at the other, to push rather than strike the ball (the flattening of one side of the thick end still allows this). At the end of the seventeenth century people began to use the 'cue' end of the 'mace' for a more controllable strike. Though the word 'cue' is recorded in English from the mid-eighteenth century, 'stick' was more commonly used until around 1800.

Dinghy. The Hindi word *dengi* is proposed by *Hobson-Jobson* as coming from the Sanskrit *drona*, meaning a 'trough'; the earliest forms in English were 'dinga' and 'dingu', with 'dinghee' coming later. The spelling with 'h', to indicate that the 'g' is hard, appeared in the nineteenth century. The word is now used to describe the smaller sizes of boats used in competitions.

Dumb-bell. A dumb-bell was originally exactly a dumb bell, an exercise apparatus dating from the early eighteenth century with a mechanism for pulling a vertical rope with a weight attached, but no bell. It was also used to train bellringers. During the course of the century the name became applied to other kinds of weight-training equipment. In 1902 the *Model Course of Physical Training* published by the Board of Education pointed out that:

> the value of dumb-bells is not in their weight but in
> their having to be gripped. Disused carbines are
> entirely unsuitable for use in Elementary Schools.

'Dumb' and 'bell' were both Old English words, deriving from Germanic forms.

Golf balls. The first golf balls were made of wood and were superseded by 'featheries' – comprising a core of compressed goose feathers pushed into a hand-sewn leather bag. 'Gutties', made from gutta-percha after 1848, were smooth, but failed to fly very far, and had to be reshaped after play. The application of a pattern into the surface reduced air friction and allowed the ball to travel much further; the pattern led to these balls being called 'brambles', from their resemblance to blackberries. From 1898 the rubber ball, with a solid rubber core and rubber thread surrounded by gutta-percha, replaced brambles, with the dimpled surface being introduced in 1908 ('dimple' has been recorded in English from about 1400 and may come from the Old High German word for a 'whirlpool'). Current golf balls have between 330 and five hundred dimples, which reduce drag and allow a dimpled ball to travel twice as far as a smooth one.

Golf clubs. The names of golf clubs, apart from 'driver' and 'putter', are now mostly superseded by numbers, which is an inevitable if sad product of standardisation. Clubs forged by hand deserved individual names, and they do not correspond to the items in modern matching club sets; made individually, each was different. Correspondences, where they work, do so on the basis of the jobs the clubs do, though a well-equipped golfer at the beginning of the twentieth century might have felt able to deal with any eventuality only if armed with up to twenty-five clubs.

The names of the clubs are mostly from Scottish dialect, in some cases from Gaelic.

Baffy: from Old French *baffe*, meaning a 'blow from the back of the hand'.

Brassie or *Brassey*: a wooden club with a brass base.

Cleek: a club with a straight, narrow face. The word is found in Scotland and northern England and was used for a long hook – Hoole's translation of Comenius' *Orbis Sensualium Pictus* (1757) shows a 'cleek-net', a net at the end of a pole. 'Cleek' may also refer to the wrought-iron head, rather than the entire club; the 'cleek-maker's mark' identifies who the maker was. The word is first documented from 1829 (*OED*).

Jigger: fifteenth-century French had a word *giguer*, meaning to 'jig' or 'dance'. A jigger is a short club used for approach shots where the ball has to be lifted a short way to the green.

Mashie: possibly a Scottish version of the French *masse*, meaning 'hammer', with the '-ie' diminutive.

Niblick: the short face of the club is said to be shown in the name, a corruption of Gaelic *neb laigh*, meaning 'broken nose'. Alternatively it is a diminutive of 'nib', meaning 'beak'. Known from the mid-nineteenth century.

Rake: a club with channels in its upper half, for playing a ball in sand or water.

Rutting iron: designed for lifting the ball out of ruts or holes in the course, or from beneath tree-roots.

Spoon: the concave surface of a club.

Gutta percha. The sap of a Malayan tree, written as *gâtah-pârcha* in the *Malay Dictionary* (1852), gutta percha was first used for golf balls from about 1850, replacing the 'featherie' that had been used previously (a leather ball densely filled with feathers), and the wooden balls that preceded them. The gutta percha, moulded while warm into a perfect sphere, created balls that were cheaper and lasted longer than featheries. Gutta percha was also the raw material for making gum shields for boxers, often made by the boxers themselves by warming a lump of the rubber in hot water and biting it into shape. Often gutta percha became very hard – the 1863 Laws of the Football Association forbade players to wear gutta percha on the soles of their boots.

Hurdle. The Badminton Library volume on athletics states clearly that hurdle races were run at Eton College in 1837 and 1838, but it is likely that this form of sprint format applied to a steeplechase-type event was around much earlier. The first inter-university athletics meeting, in 1864, had two hurdle races out of eight events. Hurdles for documented races in 1843 and 1866 were set at 3 feet 6 inches, the standard height of a sheaf of wheat, though hurdles were originally movable fences for penning sheep and other animals. As *hyrthil*, the word is documented from the early eighth century. Sprinting hurdles are still 3 feet 6 inches for men, and 2 feet 9 inches for women; for 400-metre races the heights are lower.

Indian clubs. In *Physical Culture* (Ontario, 1886) E. B. Houghton recommends the use of Indian clubs for girls only. Indian clubs, shaped like long-handled bowling pins, were introduced to Britain by soldiers stationed in India, where the clubs had long been used as training equipment by wrestlers. Gymnastics using Indian clubs featured in two Olympic Games, in 1904 and 1932. Other equipment

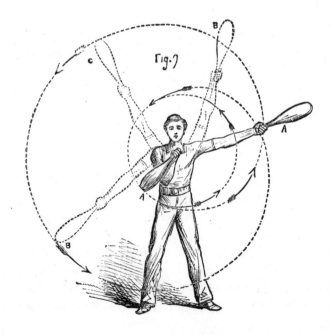

for gymnastics and training included the 'physical exerciser', an early name for the punchball, barbells, sceptres and wands (sticks with or without a lump at one end).

Javelin. It has been said that the first sport was spear-throwing, though it could be claimed that running must have preceded it, as the run-up to throwing a spear if nothing else. Throwing the javelin, the modern form of spear-throwing, featured in the 1859 Olympic Games but was an athletic event in the ancient Olympic Games from 708 BC. In 1780 javelin was adopted in athletic games in Scandinavia, at which the running throw was used. The word 'javelin', first found in English in the early sixteenth century, comes from a word for a casting, rather than jabbing, spear, found in Old Norman French as *gavelot*, Breton as *gavlod*, and Middle High German as *gabilôt*.

Kayak. 'Kayak' is a term used in all the languages of the indigenous peoples from Greenland to Alaska to describe a canoe made of a wooden framework with a covering of sealskin. First noted in English texts in the mid-seventeenth century, it has had a variety of spellings, including 'kajakka', 'kajak', 'kiack', 'kaiack', 'kajack' and 'kajac' (*OED*).

Mallet. The Anglo-Norman French word *maillet* or *malliet*, meaning 'hammer', was adopted in the Middle English period but was first used in the context of croquet in 1867. Mallets had been used previously in pall mall and polo.

Oar. Cassell's *Book of Sports and Pastimes* (1907) states that an oar is divided into the 'handle', the 'loom' and the 'blade' (called the 'spoon' if it is curved, a 'macon' blade if it is wide). 'Loom' here is a usage dating back to the end of the seventeenth century, coming from *lome*, a Middle English word meaning 'tool', and sometimes specifically applied to the part of the oar between the handle and the rowlock, or the handle itself.

Pistol. The founder of the modern Olympics, Baron de Coubertin, was a French pistol champion, so pistol-shooting was one of the sports in the first modern Olympics. 'Pistol', found from 1570, comes from the French *pistole*, and the German *pistole*, which came from the Czech *píštala*, meaning 'firearm'. 'Pistol' had an earlier form, 'pistolet', found from 1550, which may come from the Italian *postolese*, from the town of Pistoia in Italy, where guns were manufactured.

Puck. The puck, the disc used in ice-hockey, was documented in use in March 1875 (though possibly used much earlier), on this occasion being made from a sliced rubber ball. The word was a development from the Anglo-Irish 'to puck', used in hurling, meaning 'to hit', documented since the mid-nineteenth century. 'To puck' may be a development from the verb 'to poke', or may have been from the Irish *poc*, meaning 'poke or push'. Tim Considine in *The Language of Sport* (New York, 1982) describes early college games of ice-hockey in Canada, where the 'puck' could be anything that would slide along the ice, including a ball and a tin can. Later designs, made with the intention of rendering the puck more visible to spectators, included the Firepuck, fitted with light-reflective materials.

Racing car, sports car. A 'sports car', a term that dates from 1919, is not a car that is used for motorsport, for which a 'racing car' would be used. 'Racing car', to describe vehicles used in motorsport, dates from 1901 but was in use much earlier to describe small horse-drawn racing carriages.

Racket. 'Racket' or 'racquet'? The difference is sometimes just a style of spelling, sometimes a distinct meaning. 'Racquet' as a spelling variation came in after 1600, while 'raket' had been in use since the late fourteenth century. The first use of the word in English is to describe the game rather than the implement, and it is likely that the word for the implement came from the game, which was first played with the open hand, and thus may come ultimately from an Arabic word *rahat*, meaning 'palm of the hand', which became medieval Latin *rasceta*, Middle French *rascette*, and later *raquette* for hand-shaped implements including a tool like a paddle for scraping the underside of a boat. As an implement, it is not found in English before the mid-sixteenth century.

'Racket' is the usual spelling, both for the implement and the game 'rackets', from which squash developed, but 'raquet' is preferred in North America; the spelling 'raquets' has a certain cachet, which explains its use by a number of private-membership clubs. 'Racquet' enjoyed some popularity in the late-Victorian and Edwardian period, particularly in books aimed at the amateur market. Before then, dictionaries and books such as the *Annals of Gaming* (1775) give the spelling 'racket', and in post-1918 dictionaries 'racquet' tends to be preferred.

Rings. The pair of hanging rings used in gymnastics were until the 1960s called 'Roman rings' (now 'hanging rings'); the term was first used in nineteenth-century Germany. These were to be used statically and so were distinct from the 'flying rings', a string of pairs of rings, the athlete progressing along the line of them, swinging.

Scuba. Scuba – the name is an acronym of Self-Contained Underwater Breathing Apparatus – is defined as 'self-contained diving' and 'underwater swimming'. The term was first used in 1952, in the United States.

Shuttlecock. Also known as the 'shuttle' and 'bird', 'shuttlecock' has been the name of the game and the object hit since the sixteenth century. The word is made up of 'shuttle', meaning something that moves back and forth (though in Old English it originally meant a 'spear or arrow'), and 'cock', from the feathers that make the shuttlecock fly straight and slow. Sometimes 'shuttlecock' was changed to 'shuttlecork', an example of folk etymology, probably from the cork the feathers were pushed into. Smythe-Palmer suggests that the corruption is the other way round, that the original word was 'shuttlecork', but the first documentation of this is about a hundred years after the first 'shuttlecock'. For Webster in 1828 the word came from either 'cock' or 'cork'; he defined it as a 'cork stuck with fethers'. Olympic regulations state that a shuttlecock must have fourteen feathers.

Skate. Around the year 1660 the word 'skate' was adopted from the Dutch *schaats* as 'scate'; the fact that skates come in pairs and the need to differentiate between singular and plural meant that the 's' at the end of the Dutch word was misunderstood as a plural (in fact the plural of *schaats* is *schaatsen*). This mistake was not universal (there is a reference to 'scatses' from 1688 – *OED*), but a process of anglicisation or folk etymology. Pepys in 1662 spelt the word 'skeates', and there were spellings 'scates' and 'skaits' up to the early nineteenth century. The earlier history of the word shows confusion between skates and stilts. The Old French *escahsse* became *escase* in the north of France and meant a 'stilt'; this was adopted into English as 'scatch'

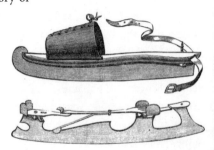

and Middle Dutch as *schaetse*, at which point its meaning changed to 'skate'. Jones's *Treatise on Skating* (1772) refers to 'irons' rather than 'blades', though steel blades had replaced bone ones in the mid-seventeenth century. Around the mid-seventeenth century the word 'scrick-shoes' was used, but is documented once only, in a pictorial philosophical dictionary (Hoole's translation of Comenius' *Orbis Sensualium Pictus*, 1757).

Skiff. Now a name given to a kind of racing yacht, a 'skiff' was at first specifically a sea-going boat. There are a number of possible sources for the word – the French *esquif*, the Italian *schifo*, and the Spanish and Portuguese *esquife*, all of which could have been adopted by sailors mixing with speakers of those languages.

Stumps. One theory proposes that when cricket was played in the thirteenth century it was possible to get a large enough expanse of clear ground only by cutting down trees, and that the stumps of these formed the first wickets. The first documentation of the word in a cricketing context is 1735 (*OED*), but nine years later the word was so well established that the *Laws of Cricket* stated that the stumps must be 22 inches long. The phrase 'to pull up stumps' refers to the use of the word to mean a 'stake', and this is a far more likely source for the word.

Target. A target was originally a small 'targe', an Old English word meaning 'shield', which was used for archery practice. The target was set on a 'butt', and the word 'butts' came to mean the area set aside for practising archery, and is retained in many place-names.

Trampoline. The 'trampoline' is named after two brothers, the Due Trampoline, who after their trapeze act would bounce energetically and acrobatically on their safety net – that at least is the generally accepted story, though there is no documented evidence for it. It is documented that George Nissen and Larry Griswold in 1936 invented a taut fabric apparatus for training acrobats and named it 'trampoline' after the Spanish word *trampolin*, meaning a 'diving board'. 'Trampoline' was used as the tradename of the product they developed, which was generically called a 'rebound tumbler'. Long before that, there was a report in *The Times* in 1799 of a performance in which an acrobat 'positively leaps over a large tilted wagon … and does not make use of a springboard or trampoline' (*OED*). Other quotations from the 1930s make it clear that the word was widely used and understood in Britain before it was trademarked in the United States.

Vaulting horse. Vaulting horses have been around since the late sixteenth century, with smaller ones called 'vaulting bucks'. The 'pommel horse', also known as the 'side horse' or 'pommelled horse', is documented from 1909 (*OED*), 'pommel' being an Anglo-Norman French word for a decorative knob.

Whistle. About 1878 rugby and football referees started to use whistles, having previously waved handkerchiefs to signal for play to stop. The word 'whistle' comes from the Old English *hwistlian*, meaning to 'make a shrill noise'.

Field of play

Astroturf. Astroturf was invented by Monsanto for use in the Houston Astrodome in 1965, hence its name.

Block hole. Possibly giving some support to the story that a cricket wicket at some time included a hole that the bat would have to be put into, the 'block hole' is described in *Games and Sports* (1837) as a hole in the middle of the popping crease. The expression is used now to describe the mark made by the batsman to show where to set the base of the bat (to know where it is in relationship to the stumps behind him). A ball bowled to this point is described as 'in' rather than 'on' the block hole.

Bullseye. There are several proposed origins for a bullseye. One suggestion is that it is the name for any prominent object, deriving from the glass knobs set in the decks of nineteenth-century ships, to concentrate the light and transmit it below deck; from this came the 'bullseye lantern', with its large convex glass lens to magnify the light from inside. Or a bull's eye is about the size of the centre of a target for shooting, large enough to be seen from a distance, but small enough to be very difficult to hit. Or a bullseye was a nickname for an eighteenth-century coin, a crown (5-shilling) piece. The *OED* gives the first documented use of the word meaning 'target' as 'a bull's eye of eight inches diameter' (1833), in a set of instructions for cavalry.

Bunker. A bunker was originally a Scottish word for a seat or bench, possibly related to 'bunk' and 'bank', which came to mean a 'seat made from a rise in the ground', and then a 'patch of sandy ground on a golf links, from which the turf has worn away'. The first recorded use is in 1824, in Scott's *Redgauntlet*.

Canvas. The 'canvas', as in 'on the canvas', has been associated with defeat in the boxing or wrestling ring since about 1910. The word comes from the Latin *cannabis*, meaning 'hemp', from which early coarse canvas was made.

Chicane. The series of sharp turns in a motor-racing track called a 'chicane' comes from the French word *chicaner*, which means to 'trick or cheat', and, according to Cotgrave's 1611 *Dictionary*, 'to write in a

very fast hand' (*OED*). Johnson's definition for to 'chicane' is 'to prolong a contest by tricks' (1755).

Dugout. The dugout, the shelter below ground level beside the pitch in football and baseball, seems an improbable invention; why would people who need to see the game clearly want to be below the level of the players? One answer lies in the dugout built by Aberdeen Football Club coach Donald Colman in the late 1920s, so that he could clearly observe the footwork of his players; the date suggests the adoption of a term from the First World War trenches. However, the first use of 'dugout' in this way comes from baseball in the United States in 1912 (*OED*).

Furlong. The ideal length of a ploughed field in medieval England was one eighth of a Roman mile, 220 yards being the measurement of how long (*lang* in Old English) the furrow (*furh* in Old English) was. The furlong is the distance by which horse-racing courses and winning margins are measured.

Goal. In a 1721 poem called *A Match at Foot-ball or The Irish Champions*, the preface describes the goal as 'form'd by sticking two Willow Twigs in the Ground, at a small Distance, and twisting the Tops, so that they seem a Gate'. Recognisable as basically the form of a goal in modern games, the small size of the football goal was maintained: in Joseph Strutt's *The Sports and Pastimes of the People of England* (1801) it was only 2 or 3 feet wide. Possibly as a result of the game being decided by one goal only, football at this time was often called 'goal', and this was the name of a game played in North America in the nineteenth century, presumably taken there by British migrants. There is some evidence for this form being used earlier in a literary context.

Historically there has been some dispute over the origin of the word. Its first documentation is in a sixteenth-century sporting context, as the finishing point of a race, and this usage was retained until the nineteenth century; pedestrianism reports in the 1870s used the word in this way. The metaphorical use is first documented in Shakespeare's *Pericles* in 1608 (*OED*).

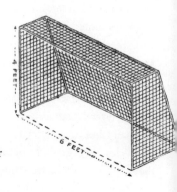

Dryden in 1697 used the word for both the start and the end of a race:

> Hast thou beheld, when from the goal they start,
> The youthful charioteers with heaving heart
> Rush to the race?

But this may be poetic licence.

It seems likely that the word is derived from an Old English word *galan* or *agalan*, meaning 'to impede or delay'; from this it came to mean an 'obstacle or barrier', and thus a 'boundary'. It is possible that this survived as a term in medieval games before being found in the 1530s, notably in a dictionary definition of the Latin word *meta*, as 'a but [target], or pricke [small target] to shote at, somtyme a marke or gowle in the felde, whereunto men or horses do runne'.

Links. Areas of sandy grassland next to the sea that are flat but unfertile provided several sites for golf courses in Scotland. The Old English word *hlinc*, meaning a 'ridge', developed into 'link', and a line of such areas made the ideal place to play golf. However, the first use of the word in a golf context is in 1861. The plural form, 'links' rather than 'link', has become singular; Fowler (1998) offers this advice: 'The word has the same form as a singular noun and as a plural one: *a suburban links; there are numerous links within easy reach of the city.*'

Net. The first compulsory use of nets in football, to settle disputes over whether the ball had gone between the posts, was in 1892. 'Net' is a very early Old English word and derives from an Indo-European root to do with knots and tying.

Pitch. Cricket has been played on pitches since the 1870s, and field games have used the term since the 1890s (in the United States the term is 'field', which was the former term in the United Kingdom); the pitch is a development from the use of the word to mean a place where someone is stationed for a given purpose. In turn, this comes from the use of 'to pitch' meaning 'to set in place', as in 'to pitch a tent'. There is, however, a much earlier expression, 'to pitch a wicket', meaning 'to set the stumps for a game of cricket', which was in use from the late seventeenth century (*OED*). In football the word 'park' is often used, and rugby players mostly call the playing area the 'park' or 'paddock', though in the South Midlands the term 'piece' has survived, this being the name of the playing area at Rugby School.

Pits. The Targa Florio endurance race in Sicily, which began in 1906, necessitated several stops for cars to be adjusted or repaired, the laps being 45 miles long. So that mechanics could get easy access to the wheels or underparts of the cars, pull-off areas were created beside the track, at a lower level than the road. The first use of 'pit' in this way was in 1912 (*OED*).

Pole position. In the first laid-out horse-racing courses, the 'pole' was what is now known as the 'rails', the rail running round the inside of the course. The horse that got to start the race next to this had a distinct advantage. 'Pole position' was thus the best position to be in. The expression is found first in 1851 (*OED*).

Popping crease. The *Rules of Cricket* printed in 1744 state that the popping crease must be 3 feet 10 inches from the wicket; current laws have moved it a further 2 inches, not much of a change in over two and a half centuries. 'Popping' in this case is derived from a use of the word 'pop' meaning to 'hit'. John Nyren's *Cricketers of My Time* (1833) gives another, less likely origin, which may have been the case but is not supported by other evidence:

> Between the stumps a hole was cut in the ground, large enough to contain the ball and the butt-end of the bat. In running a notch [a run], the striker was obliged to put his bat into this hole … the wicket-keeper … was obliged, when the ball was thrown in, to place it in this hole before the adversary could reach it with his bat.

Such a practice would have made it clear when a batsman was in or out, but, as Nyren says,

> many severe injuries of the hand were the consequence of this regulation; the present mode

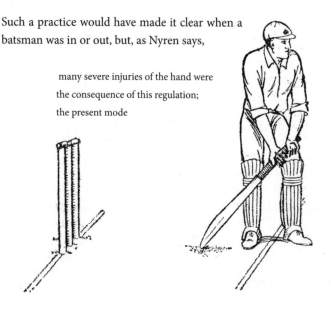

of touching the popping crease was therefore
substituted for it.

'Crease' means a 'line' but its origin is unknown.

Ring. In the period in the nineteenth century when boxing was illegal, prize-fights were informal, if enthusiastically supported, affairs. The organisers maintained the practice from earlier days of marking out the arena by making a ring round the combatants, sometimes with a rope held by the front row of spectators; this could easily be hidden or abandoned if necessary. 'The Ring' in the nineteenth century became a metaphor for the culture and news of boxing, particularly in sporting journals. The *Slang Dictionary* of 1865 noted that the term was also used for the world of horse-racing aficionados, with the term 'prize-ring' used to distinguish the boxing fraternity.

Rink. The first use of 'rink', adopted from the French word *renk*, meaning a space for jousting, was in the Scottish dialect, as a place for jousting and later racing, and then figuratively for a contest itself. Later, from the 1780s, 'rink' was used for the area of ice specified for curling, and later for ice-skating, and from the 1870s for roller-skating, when the craze in the United States gave rise to the term 'Rinkomania'.

The first refrigerated rink built in London was the Glaciarium, constructed in Covent Garden in 1844, with a skating area backed by a panorama of Lake Lucerne. Entry cost 1 shilling, with skating an extra shilling. The proprietor published bills announcing the spectacle 'on Thursday 25th of January, 1844, [of] the most extraordinary Thaw ever witnessed in this Country or any other'. 'Glaciarium' became a generic word for ice-rinks, as established in Melbourne in 1906 and Sydney in 1907. The quality of the ice has always been important – a notice in the *Sporting Gazette* of 15 April 1878 states that it used 'real ice – Gamgoe's patent, not natural'.

Rinks now are resurfaced by a 'Zamboni', a machine named after its inventor, Frank Zamboni.

From the 1860s 'rink' is recorded as a curling or bowls team, or the teams engaged in a game, and then the measured strip on a bowling green, and occasionally the entire green.

Scratch. The phrase 'up to scratch' derives from prizefighting. The 'scratch' was sometimes a line scratched in the turf in the middle of the ring, sometimes a square; if a boxer was unable at the beginning of the round to get to this line, or put his foot inside it, or if he could not stand after resting there for a count of thirty, he was surely beaten, not being 'up to scratch'. The word developed to mean the starting line of other kinds of contest – the *Birmingham Daily Post* of 7 December 1857 describes the runners in a pedestrian match of 'six-score yards' being 'brought to scratch'. At the end of the nineteenth century handicap races between boys of varying ages would be organised, with the younger runners being given a distance advantage; the older boys running the full distance were called 'scratch markers'.

Slalom. Slalom comes from the Norwegian words *sla* and *låm*, meaning 'sloping track'. The *OED* records the word from 1921.

Square. If an imaginary line is drawn between the two goals in a field sport (rugby, hockey, etc.) and another line set at right angles to that, any movement along the second line is 'square', thus allowing the wonder of a 'square ball', a ball passed along this line. The expression is recorded from 1967 (*OED*).

Tee. A golf tee was in the seventeenth century a 'teaz', a small pile of sand or earth rather than a peg. Though its origin is uncertain, Partridge ingeniously links it to 'taw', the 'shooting marble' in games of marbles, though only documented from 1709; but that might not be a problem, for children's game-words would not be the most documented. A further suggested connection is with the shape of the letter T, on which the ball might rest, but this does not square with the cone shape of the pile of earth.

Trip. The 'trip' in horse-racing is the length of the course. A successful horse 'steps up to the trip' or 'gets the trip', meaning it manages to maintain and increase its pace throughout the race. The expression dates from the 1950s.

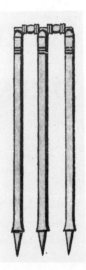

Wicket. 'Wicket' derives from an Anglo-Norman French word meaning a 'gate'. In cricket, the wicket is an active participant in the game, the word in this case referring to the ground between the two sets of stumps, as in the assessment by Keith Boyce, former head groundsman at Headingley:

> The wickets just after the War were very good. But during the 1950s the wickets started to go back. They lost pace, they lost bounce.

During the second half of the nineteenth century, wickets that absorbed too much water and became spongy were referred to as 'sticky wickets', as they slowed the ball down on the bounce and appeared to make it stick. Thus the word is capable of meaning: the set of stumps; the act of getting a batsman out (take a wicket); a batsman's period at the crease (synonymous with 'innings'); the passage of play between two batsmen being out; and the ground between the wickets.

Non-playing personnel

Caddie. Spelt 'caddy' in North America, and with the alternative British English spelling of 'cadie', the word derives ultimately from the French *cadet*, meaning 'head of a minor branch of a family'. 'Cadet' came to mean a 'younger brother', and the word came to be used as 'caddy' in Scotland, to mean a person looking for employment as a porter or messenger, and thus was appropriate for the specialised use as a carrier of golf clubs.

Coach. In one of the more improbable trajectories of a word derivation, 'coach' has travelled from a small town in Hungary. In nineteenth-century university slang a 'coach' or 'coacher' was someone who privately worked with a scholar, someone who might figuratively 'carry' his charge; this model was later transferred to an athletic coach, in the 1880s. A 'coach' as a means of transport derived ultimately from the town of Kocs in Hungary, renowned for its production of carriages, which came to be known as *Koczi szeter*, which became *coche* in French, and thus 'coach' in English by about 1550. In the early twentieth century the word 'coacher' was commonly used.

Manager. During the nineteenth century the 'manager' of a cricket team was the role we would now call 'captain' (*OED*); as the jobs of managing and captaining diverged, the 'managing captain' moved off the field. The word ultimately comes from the Latin word *manus*, meaning 'hand', so that 'managing' is connected to the idea of 'manipulating' and 'handling'. The use of the word 'gaffer' by team members to describe the manager is a manifestation of the different statuses within English of words from Old English origins and those adopted from Latin via French and other Romance languages. A manager or someone of a higher status within a club would be unlikely to refer to himself or herself as a 'gaffer' – the term would be employed only by players, ground staff, stewards, etc. – people nominally of a lower status within the club hierarchy. 'Gaffer' is an abbreviation of 'godfather', formed from two Old English words, while 'manager' was probably adopted from Italian, in the sixteenth century, in the sense of 'handling a horse' – thus linking it to 'manège', a space for training horses.

Mascot. Popularised by the performances of the operetta *La Mascotte* by Edmond Audran in 1880 and 1881, the word 'mascot' means a 'good-luck charm', deriving from earlier words meaning 'spell' and 'witch'. Football mascots began to appear before matches in the nineteenth century in the United States, both animals and costumed people; during the 1980s the appropriateness of some of these long-standing usages of aspects of indigenous cultures came into question. In the United Kingdom their problem has more recently been behavioural, with some mascots being removed from public view.

Referee. Literally a person to whom disputes were referred, the neutral referee's decisions in football matches (association and rugby) replaced decisions made by the captains of the two sides, or by referees appointed by each side. The change in rugby football was in stages: first the appointment of a neutral umpire off the pitch in 1881, and then the introduction of a referee on the pitch in 1885. Tennis maintains the hierarchy between 'umpire' and 'referee', with the umpire in charge of a match, and the referee in charge of the tournament.

In the 1880s referees were often supplied by the sporting papers that announced and reported on sporting contests.

Second. Prizefighters were attended by two assistants, a 'second' and a 'bottleman'; the bottleman held his water, while the second gave him support. *Fistiana, or the Oracle of the Ring* in 1848 described how a fighter would sit on his second's knee between rounds while being given water and a rub-down. Old English had no word to go between 'first' and 'third', but used the word 'other'. 'Second', ultimately from the Latin word *sequi*, meaning to 'follow', was quickly adopted into Middle English.

Umpire. The role of the umpire is described in the Middle English poem *Piers Plowman*, where Robyn the ropemaker is called upon to

act as the judge of the fairness of the exchange of a cloak for a hood. Robyn here is described as the *noumpere*, derived from the French *nonper* or *nomper*, meaning 'not paired, but separate'. The 'n' soon became detached from the word and shifted across: 'a numper' became 'an umper'. By the seventeenth century the word was in the form we have today. Samuel Johnson gave the derivation as from *un pere*, presumably someone who could give a judgement from a patriarchal position.

The first documentation of a sporting umpire dates to 1714 (*OED*): '... and in case they can't Decide such Differences, then they shall be referr'd solely to the Decision of the said Sir Thomas Parkyns as Umpire.' This makes clear that the umpire was not the first person to decide on fouls or awards. This would put the umpire in a position similar to that of the umpire in modern rugby, that of final authority rather than the person first appealed to. Neutral umpires were introduced to rugby in 1881, disputes previously having been settled by the captains of the teams or umpires appointed by them.

Passages of play

Ball. In the context of cricket, a 'ball' means a 'bowled ball', the passage of play between the ball leaving the bowler's hand and its being hit or missed by the batsman. In cricket, this usage dates from the eighteenth century. A 'no-ball' is an illegal delivery (from 1744, *OED*).

Break. The first use of 'break' for a continuous score in billiards or croquet dates to 1865 (*OED*), and from this it came to mean a run of good luck, or, in the phrase 'give me a break', to mean 'an opportunity' or 'a fair chance'. The word was used from the early twentieth century for the way the ball leaves a baseball bat.

Bully. Originally a term of endearment, as used by Shakespeare, 'bully' appears to have come from German and Dutch words meaning 'lover' or 'kinsman'. By the late seventeenth century the word had come to mean a 'swaggering fellow', and by the mid-eighteenth century a 'ruffian', or as Johnson has it (with a rare typographical mistake) 'a man who has only the apperance of courage'. The first sporting association comes in accounts of football at Eton School in 1865 (*OED*), where a bully was a free-for-all kind of scrum. Probably the 'bully-off' in hockey derives from the idea that once the ball is dropped, and three stick contacts have been exchanged, a free-for-all follows. 'Bullying' and 'a bully' appear in the rules of hockey published by the Hockey Association in 1886.

Bye. A variant spelling of 'by', a ball bowled in cricket that the batsman fails to hit, but nevertheless makes a run from, has been a 'bye' since the mid-eighteenth century. The word has also been used since the 1880s for a knockout tournament competitor whose opposite number has to pull out, and for the holes in a round of golf that are left unplayed at the end of a match, and since the 1840s for the end line of a field of play, beyond which the ball is 'out'. The sense of being 'apart' implicit in the word is similar to that in 'bypass', 'by the way', and 'highways and byways'.

Cannon. In the French version of billiards as played in the eighteenth century there were no pockets on the table, and points were scored solely by the cue ball hitting the other two balls, known as a 'carom'. This developed into 'canon' and then 'cannon'. The earliest version of 'carom' was *carambole*, which was the name of the red ball, the 'carom' stroke, or the game played in this version. *Carambole* was shortened to *carom* about 1820, a few years before 'cannon' appeared in English.

End. An 'end' is a set of arrows loosed in archery, or a set of stones sent in curling, or all the activity in a game of bowls in one direction of the green. This appears to be a transference from an earlier meaning of 'end' as a 'boundary' – formerly an 'end' in archery was a mark set to determine where the target or archers would stand.

Go! On the face of it, 'Go' would seem to be the obvious thing to say to start a race, but did anything precede it? We may be used to children's races beginning with 'Ready, steady, go', progressing to 'On your marks, get set, go', and then '(Up) to your marks, go'. But finding out when and under what circumstances these were adopted is not easy.

Health and Physical Education for Schools in India (1934) gives: 'On your marks, ready, go.' *Brewer's Dictionary of Phrase and Fable* notes 'Ready, steady, go' as a traditional children's start to a race, becoming more serious with 'Up to your marks'. 'On your marks' or 'Up to your marks' indicates that the athlete is to come forward to his or her starting point, and 'Get set' indicates that the starting pose should be assumed. The *OED* gives 'On your marks, get set, go' as dating from the 1930s, and 'Ready, steady, go' from only the 1960s. *Brewer's Dictionary of Modern Phrase and Fable* (2000) proposes that an earlier version of 'Ready, steady go' was 'One, two, three, go'. In *Bicycle Bob, or Who Will Win?*, a penny dreadful published in 1895, a cycle race is begun with the single word 'Now!'

Before being given the starting instructions, athletes (and horses) are 'under starter's orders'; since in horse-racing this involves the horse being in a restraining enclosure, 'under starter's orders' has been slang since about 1945 for 'having been arrested' (Partridge).

Haka. 'Haka' is a Maori word for 'dance'. The haka as a pre-match challenge was introduced by the 'New Zealand Natives' rugby union team on their tour of Australia in 1884, and again in 1888–9 during a tour of Britain. The *New Zealand Listener* remarked in 1957 that 'haka' was one of a group of terms that had been adopted into English and had acquired meanings different from those they had in their original languages, and thus could be thought of as 'New Zealandisms' (*OED*).

Heats. A 'heat' was originally an informal race run before a competitive one, to warm the horses up. After this a 'heat' became a preliminary race or a race in its own right, and there developed the format of a day's meeting in which the winning horse of the day was the first to win two heats. But a 'dead heat' has since 1796 been one in which two or more competitors finish simultaneously.

Howzat. Also spelt 'owzat' (and the name of a game that occupied many cricket-mad schoolboys through maths lessons), 'howzat' is a phonetic form of 'How's that?' shouted by bowler and fielders in a cricket match when they think the batsman is out. Incredibly, the first documentation of it in the *OED*, from 1921, is from the United States.

Lap. The 'lap' of a race is a comparatively late development from the idea of to 'overlap'. To 'lap', a Middle English use of the word meaning to 'lay things together, one partly over the other', developed into the sense of 'overlap' in the seventeenth century. The sense of one of the circuits or lengths of a race track is first recorded from 1861.

No-side. Not often heard now, 'no-side' is the term for the end of a game of rugby union. Its first documented use (*OED*) is in *Tom Brown's Schooldays* (1857).

Play. While cricket has a 'ball', baseball has a 'play', the action between the pitcher taking stance to pitch and the ball going dead. Its first recorded use was in 1868 (*OED*).

Rally. The first sporting rallies were in boxing, meaning an 'exchange of blows', and later a separate bout. Egan, describing the fight between Tom Molineaux and Tom Cribb in 1810, writes:

> Molineaux, immediately on setting to, commenced
> another rally, when the Champion [Cribb] put in a
> severe body-blow, but the Moor [Molineaux was
> black] treated it with indifference, and in return not
> only mill'd Cribb's head, but in closing threw him.

The expression was applied immediately to the new sport of lawn tennis in 1879, though rallies were also called 'rests'; the expression is still used in real tennis. 'Rally' is a development of the French *ralier*, meaning to 'come together', in which sense it is applied to a meeting of motor cars or other vehicles, which itself gave rise to the sport 'rally driving', originally (from 1911) a long motor race.

Scrum. The word 'skirmish', from the Italian *scaramuccia*, had a variant 'scrimish', which developed into 'scrimmage', meaning a 'fight', and, in variants of football, a tussle of strength, at first disordered, and then arranged formally. 'Scrummage' and 'scrimmage' developed in rugby football in the 1850s and 1860s, 'scrimmage' being taken up by American college football, and 'srummage' developing into 'scrum' in rugby union.

Serve. The natural progress of a tennis match between fairly equally matched partners is that 'game goes with serve'. The player who serves has the advantage, presumably of hitting the ball hard from a

static start. Tennis in the sixteenth century employed the services of a 'naqueter', a French term meaning a 'door attendant'. The job of the naqueter was 'to serve at tennis' (1532), and later (1611) 'to serve, or stop, a ball at tennis'. A 'naquet' was 'the boy that serves, or stops the ball after the first bound, to make a better chace, at tennis' (all *OED*). In other words, a servant served in order to get the game going in the most advantageous way to all. The first use of 'service' in tennis dates from the end of the sixteenth century.

Stymie. 'Stymie' is a Scottish dialect word meaning 'someone who does not see well', deriving from 'stime' or 'styme', meaning 'the smallest glimpse possible'. A stymie is thus what happens when there is an obstruction between the golf ball and the hole, either that the player cannot see the hole or neither figuratively can the ball.

Turnover. Used in rugby and American football for the accidental loss of possession of the ball, 'turnover' dates from 1969 (*OED*).

Places

Arena. Arena is used to mean both the business area of a sports ground, and figuratively a particular organised sport and all its ramifications, or sport as a whole. The Latin word *arena* meant 'sand', particularly the sand of an amphitheatre for gladiatorial or animal-baiting contests.

Ballpark. Baseball stadiums began to be called 'ballparks' around 1890, having been previously termed 'ball grounds', 'baseball grounds', 'ball fields' and 'baseball parks'. The term 'ballpark' is an indication of how much baseball had come to be the basic or obvious ball-game in the United States by this time.

Coliseum. The Coliseum, the amphitheatre in Rome built by the emperor Vespasian, took its name from the Colosseum, a massive statue of the emperor Nero, which stood nearby, and which came to be an alternative spelling for the stadium. Despite being the most famous venue in the ancient world for what were considered sports, the name has been seldom used for sporting arenas in the modern world, probably because of the association with the business of death for spectators' pleasure.

Grandstand. Though the word 'grand-stand' is not recorded in English until 1834, there were grandstands much earlier; it was agreed in 1615 that at Doncaster racecourse 'the stand and the stoopes shall be pulled up, and employed to some better purpose, and the race to be discontinued' (the 'stoopes' here were posts). Another word used in this situation was 'scaffold'. The BBC flagship sports programme *Grandstand* was first broadcast in October 1958; its highest audience number was for the 1966 World Cup final, with 27 million viewers. Linguistically, *Grandstand* was chiefly remarkable for the reading of the football scores, taken over by *Final Score* before Grandstand's demise in 2007; during the forty-nine year history of the programme the scores were read by two people, Len Martin and Tim Gudgin, whose voices have been two of the best-known in British broadcasting.

Pavilion. Originally an Old French word from the twelfth century describing a military tent, a 'pavilion' has been the tent or building used by cricketers since 1799, also used for changing, and for storing equipment for other sports. Early-nineteenth-century paintings of cricket matches show large tents with decorative fringing, which conform to the idea of a pavilion of earlier times, and the word was extended to the showy, sometimes temporary, wooden buildings in parks or open places (an extreme example is the Brighton Royal Pavilion). A 'pavilion' in heraldry was an elaborate form of mantling used particularly on royal coats of arms.

Stadium. The measure of horse-races in furlongs comes from the Greek word *stadion*, thought to have been a measure of about one eighth of a Roman mile. Stadiums or stadia (either is accepted as the plural form) were the buildings constructed around the race-tracks. The first stadium proposed in Britain in modern times, planned in 1834, was the English National Arena, the name now applied to the stadium on the site of the former Wembley Stadium.

Track. Though there was a purpose-built running track in London during the sixteenth century, the first permanent athletics tracks were set up following the Highways Act of 1835 and the removal of pedestrian events from public roads. Early enclosed athletics tracks were those owned by Mrs Betty Berry of the Snipe Inn, Audenshaw, the White Lion track at Hackney (1862), and the Bellevue Pleasure Gardens at Gorton, opened in 1841, and in 1847 called 'an emporium of pedestrianism'. By 1849 there were fifteen purpose-built running tracks, such as Emerson's at the Old Hat Inn, Ealing, which had a track of 160 yards.

Not all of these were attached to pubs, though the advantage to a publican of being able to bring in up to six thousand spectators would outweigh the expense of building spectator facilities. Garratt's Copenhagen Grounds in Manchester, Lillie Bridge in Chelsea and the market garden track in Chelsea owned by the Cheese brothers remained independent of the victualling trade. 'Running grounds' was an alternative term used in the late nineteenth century.

'Track' comes from a French word meaning the 'mark or trace left by something', so ultimately is derived from the Latin *trahere*, meaning to 'draw or drag'.

Players, roles and positions

Acrobat. In the fourteenth century we find a *disporter*, meaning 'an acrobat', and a hundred years later *disporteress*, 'a female acrobat'. 'Acrobat' is a relatively recent import, from French in about 1825, which used the Greek words *akros*, meaning 'highest', and *batos*, meaning 'going'. More advanced than the acrobats were the 'neurobats', from the Greek word for 'sinew', who were tightrope walkers; the word is now used mainly for medicines.

Also-ran. This gentle euphemism from horse-racing means 'loser'. The phrase was first used at the end of the nineteenth century.

Anchor man. This term for the strongest member of a team probably comes from the tug-of-war, where the person at the back with the rope wound round his torso is customarily the strongest puller. By the 1950s the term had been transferred to the strongest party in a relay team.

Athlete. The Greek word *athletes*, meaning 'one who contends for a prize', developed into the Latin *athleta*, and when first used in English, in the sixteenth century, the word 'athlete' was applied to competitors in Greek and Roman games in antiquity. By the early eighteenth century it was being applied to wrestlers, but Johnson did not include the word in his 1755 *Dictionary* (and contemporary writers noticed the omission). The sense of 'contending for a prize' remained in use for much of the nineteenth century, though the sense of a 'robust and fit person' is documented from 1827 (*OED*).

The word 'athletics' did not appear till the eighteenth century, and there is still a semantic difference between an 'athlete' and 'someone who participates in athletics'. However, the word 'athletic' has been used as a noun in place of 'athlete': *Baily's Monthly Magazine of Sports and Pastimes* for December 1858, announcing a wrestling tournament, requires that 'the athletics are to be in the ring ready for action'.

Bantamweight. In 1884 a new weight range was introduced into boxing competitions, for men up to 8 stone 4 pounds, called 'bantamweight' after the dwarf chickens first found in Java in the mid-eighteenth century. Currently bantamweight is 8 stone to 8 stone 6 pounds.

Batsman. In 1800 a batsman was sometimes called a 'hitter' (*Rules and Instructions for Playing the Game of Cricket*), though the usual term was, as now, 'batsman'. 'Batter' was sometimes used until the mid-nineteenth century and is still the term used in baseball. When the 'batsman' is facing the bowling he is the 'striker', and when 'backing up' he is the 'non-striker'. While the *Laws of Cricket* for 2010 still use the word 'batsman', the alternative, non-gendered 'batter' is being used more frequently.

Cox. The 'swain' or 'servant', often an officer, who was in charge of the small boat, the 'cock', that was used to ferry the captain and other officers to and from shore or other ships in the era before steam, was called the 'cockswain'. Shortened to 'coxswain', though the logical spelling should have been 'coxwain' since the spelling of 'x' equates to the sound 'ks', it became 'cox' in the mid-nineteenth century. Pepys in 1660 spelled it 'coxon', probably following navy pronunciation.

Defence. The arrangement of team-sport teams into 'backs', 'halves' and 'forwards' was more common than 'attack', 'midfield' and 'defence' before the 1970s, when it became fashionable to arrange football teams as 5-2-3 instead of the W formation. In the late Victorian period the defending players in a team were sometimes called the 'behind'. 'Mid-field' dates from 1901 (*OED*), only a few years after the first documentation of 'full-back' (1887) and 'centre-forward' (1891).

Field. The 'field' can be all the contestants in a race, or all except one. The first use of 'the field' to describe all the horses in a race except the favourite dates from 1742 (*OED*). Cricket has also used 'the field' to describe all the players in a match, and the side fielding, both from the mid-nineteenth century.

Fielder. The team fielding, or bowling, in cricket is disposed around the batsmen according to how the wicket-keeper and bowler feel they will best get the batsman out or prevent runs being scored. The field is divided into two halves, 'leg' or 'on', the side of the batsman's legs, and 'off', the side of the batsman's bat – terms that have been in use for over two hundred years. The names of the positions for the fielders, or 'fieldsmen', have hardly changed over two hundred years, and those that have are still recognisable. The *Cricketer's Pocket Companion* of

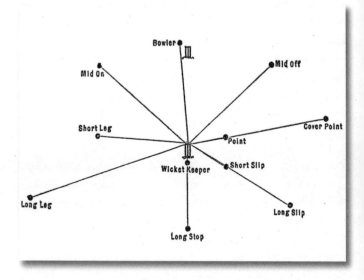

1826 has a 'first and second short slip', 'point', 'middle wicket off', 'leg or hip', 'long stop', 'long slip to cover the short slip', a fielder 'to cover point and middle wicket', 'longfield off-side' and 'longfield on-side'.

It is claimed that the 'slips' were positioned to benefit from or recover 'slips from the bat', but actually this quotation, from Nyren's *Cricket Tutor* (1833), goes on to state that this is the job of the 'long stop'. The slip's position was already set out by 1816 in W. Lambert's *Cricketer's Guide* (*OED*). The first slip is closest to the wicket-keeper; the second slip is positioned beside the first slip further from the wicket-keeper, and so on.

'Point' stood at the point of the bat, very close, effectively where the end of the bat would be if held out horizontally. The position is now further away from the batsman, but if positioned close would be called 'silly point'. 'Gully' occupies an area between the point and the slips, suggesting a channel running between them that the ball might run along. A fairly recent term, 'gully' is first documented in cricket from 1920 (*OED*) and comes from the word 'gullet'. 'Cover', 'mid-on' and 'mid-off' are abbreviated forms of the 1826 terms.

'Third man' was the reserve fielder on the off side, to get the ball if it was missed by the short slip and the long slip. 'Leg or hip' has become 'square leg', the fielder who stands on the leg side, 'square' to the line of the pitch, that is along a line at 90 degrees from the line of the pitch. He might be 'short' (close) or 'long' or 'deep' (further away). 'Square leg' dates from the 1870s.

Goalkeeper. The 'goalkeeper' was first documented in 1865 and noted in 1871 as being the only player in a football team allowed to handle the ball. The first documented use of 'goalie' is 1925, but the *OED* documents 'goalee' from four years earlier. The 'goal-tender', the expression used in ice-hockey and soccer in the United States, is now more commonly called 'goalie' in the USA and 'goaler' in Canada. 'Goal-tending' in basketball is interfering with the ball on its downward passage to the hoop and is foul play.

Greyhound. The first greyhound tracks were established in the United States in 1919 and in Britain (in Manchester) in 1926. There were dogs known as *grighunden* in Old English but the meaning of *grig* is unknown. Its alteration to 'grey' may be folk etymology.

Jockey. 'Jockey' is essentially a diminutive form of the name Jack, particularly common in Scotland and the North of England. Most jockeys were grooms in the employment of the people who owned the horses they rode, and the word was first applied specifically to professional horse-riders in the late seventeenth century.

Pitcher. Chadwick's *Dime Book of Baseball* (1867) has the 'pitcher' and the 'catcher', who together make up the 'battery', though the pitcher was the earliest of these terms to be used regularly, and 'battery' in its earliest uses applied to the pitcher alone. 'Battery' here was probably related to the idea of a group of guns directed on one area. A pitcher may be called a 'hurler'; the culture of pitching involves specific postures adopted before and during the process of 'delivering the pitch' (a phrase adopted by salesmen from the 1870s). In *By-laws and Rules of the Knickerbocker Base Ball Club* (1845) rule number eleven states that the ball 'must be pitched and not thrown for the bat'. 'Pitch' probably comes from an Old English word meaning 'to pierce', via Middle English *pichen*, meaning to 'thrust'; it is documented from 1773 as a word for bowling in cricket and is still used in cricket for where the ball first hits the pitch when bowled.

Professional. In seventeenth-century Paris a group of five professional tennis players (those who maintained the tennis courts and played against rich patrons as required) were licensed to play twice a week and advertise their activities in the same way that theatres did. In Britain horse-racing was probably the first sport to have professional sportsmen, as wealthy horse-owners paid jockeys retainers not to ride for other owners. The use of the word to describe a person paid for 'professing' an employment, that is 'declaring it publicly', has involved a certain moral contortion in British sporting history, to do with class, status, and views of the importance of winning, so that in cricket, for example, the concept of 'professional' was long euphemised as 'player'.

Professor. Nineteenth-century swimming teachers called themselves 'professors', and Jack Broughton, who in the early eighteenth century established the rules of boxing, was sometimes known as 'Professor Broughton'. During the nineteenth century the term was used to distinguish a professional from an amateur sportsman.

Rugby field positions. Rugby union and league field positions are dependent on the scrum.

Prop: two props are positioned on the outside of the hooker in the front row of the scrum, and tend to be players of large stature. The loose-head prop is on the side where the ball is put into the scrum, and the tight-head prop on the far side. They prop up the scrum.

Hooker: in the middle of the front row of the scrum, the hooker tries to hook the ball behind him using one of his feet. Recorded from 1905 (*OED*).

Lock: the two locks form the second row of the scrum, locking together the three players in the front row – they are 'second row' in rugby league. Previously 'lock-forward' or 'lock-man'. Recorded from 1906 (*OED*).

Flanker: taking up position in the scrum beside the locks, but ready to break away quickly, the flankers are 'blind-side' or 'open-side', and are also called 'wings'. The player on the blind side is on the opposite side of the field to which the opponents' backs are deployed and so cannot see quickly how play develops; the open-side player is on the other side. 'Flanker' is from a French word meaning 'side'.

Scrum half: standing strategically between the forwards and the backs, the scrum half is the player who puts the ball into the scrum and retrieves it as it comes out. The name dates from 1917 (*OED*).

Fly half: the fly half takes kicks at goal and to put the ball out of play. The name dates from 1918 (*OED*).

Rugby league also has a 'fullback', the last line of defence, and a 'stand-off' behind the scrum half.

Southpaw. A tradition has it that in the nineteenth-century United States, when permanent baseball parks were being established, it became customary to site the diamond so that in the afternoon batters would face east rather than have to look into the sun. This would put a left-handed pitcher with his pitching hand on his 'south' side, thus a 'south paw'. The term transferred to be used more in boxing for left-handed fighters, whose strongest punches would be from the left hand, and so would 'lead' (get the aiming punch in) with the right. The first documented use of 'southpaw' in the *OED* dates to 1848. The equivalent expression in Australia is a 'mollydooker', drawn from a long-standing association of the left with ideas of the 'unnatural or unreliable' – 'molly' here is slang for an 'effeminate man', while 'dook' is a variant of 'duke'.

Sportsman, sportswoman. The *OED* proposes that the sense of a sportsman as someone who engages in 'athletic sports' took prominence over someone who engages in 'hunting sports' as late as the mid-twentieth century. The word 'sporteer' was used, rarely, in the seventeenth century, and 'sporter' from the eighteenth century, developing from the sense of someone who enjoyed a good time, which has survived in the description of someone as 'a good sport'. 'Sporter' does not appear in Johnson's *Dictionary* but is in Webster's 1828 *American Dictionary*, and, though occasionally used in the nineteenth and twentieth centuries, it looks archaic. Though the word 'sportswoman' has been used since 1900 to mean a woman who participates in sports, it was in use from two hundred years earlier to indicate a prostitute; though this meaning has disappeared, the gender imbalance in sports terminology is persistent, and, as John Hargreaves points out in *Sport, Power and Culture* (2005), sport is still an area of cultural life that is dominated by men. It can be seen in such distinctions as 'football' and 'women's football', and the continued use of these in such events as the Lady Jockeys' Handicap (Newbury, October 2009).

Striker. 'Striker', 'centre-forward' (both football), 'centre' (basketball, American football, ice-hockey), 'forward' (rugby), 'full forward' (Australian rules football), 'driver' (water polo): there is a wide variety of names for the person whose prime job is to score the points. The ones that most clearly announce their roles are 'power attacker' (volleyball), 'goal shooter' (netball) and 'attacker' (handball, Gaelic football). Football 'centre-forwards' began to give way to 'strikers' in the early 1950s; occasionally the phrase 'old-fashioned centre-forward' is used, usually in reference to a tall strong forward.

Team. When 'team' was first used in Old English it meant the 'bringing forth of children', a 'line of descendants' and a 'set of draught animals yoked together', as in a 'team of oxen'. There was also the meaning very early (about AD 700) of a group of people acting together for the legal recovery of stolen property. From these the sense developed by about 1500 of a group of persons brought together for a specific purpose, but the usage for a group working together in a sporting sense is from the mid-nineteenth century, the word previously used for this being 'side'.

Thoroughbred. There is a tradition that three stallions brought to England between 1690 and 1730 provided the bloodline that produced all thoroughbred racehorses: the Byerley Turk, the Darley Arabian and the Godolphin Barb (short for Barbary – the horse was supposedly given by the Bey of Tunis to Louis XV, who sold him to an English trader, who sold him to Lord Godolphin). The Byerley Turk was captured from Turkish forces at the Battle of Buda in 1686. These horses were considered so fine that their genes were more profitable than their potential to win prize money. Flying Childers, foaled in 1712 and offspring of the Darley Arabian, was thought to be the fastest horse of his day, yet raced only twice. Thomas Darley found his sire in Aleppo and shipped him back to his father's stud farm in Yorkshire; the Darley Arabian is possibly the ancestor of almost all modern racehorses.

The first use of the term 'throbred' was in 1713; at this time 'thorough' carried the meaning of 'through', so that a 'thoroughbred horse' was one in which a known line was bred through from mare and stallion to foal. The three original thoroughbreds never raced at all.

Underdog. Supposedly the term 'underdog' comes from the business of sawing planks with a vertical saw, an operation performed by a senior partner who stood on the plank, the 'top-dog', and the junior standing in a pit below, the 'underdog'. Nobody has found any evidence for this, and it must be consigned to folk etymology. The 'underdog' was the one being beaten in a dog-fight. The *OED* records the word in use in 1887 as an obviously new term : '"under-dog" as the saying is.'

Welterweight. To 'welt' in Suffolk dialect meant to 'beat or thrash', but this did not lead directly to 'welterweight', which has been in use in boxing and wrestling since the end of the nineteenth century to describe a participant between light and middle weight. 'Welter' was used earlier to describe a 'heavy horseman' and a heavy prizefighter. After the term 'heavyweight' came into use in the 1870s, 'welterweight' moved down the scale.

Wicket-keeper. The wicket-keeper has occasionally been called the 'stumper', part of his job being to knock the bail off the stumps, but it is unclear whether this was a term of familiarity, semi-slang, or a *bona fide* expression in itself. Neither Hotten nor Partridge gives it in dictionaries of slang, but it appears in *Nuttall's Popular Dictionary* of 1934, so it may have been an accepted term around that time. Nineteenth-century *Laws of Cricket* and similar books refer only to the 'wicket-keeper'.

Prizes

America's Cup. The America's Cup is named after the yacht *America*, which won the first trophy, given for the race round the Isle of Wight in 1851 against fifteen yachts of the Royal Yacht Squadron. After the longest documented winning streak in sport, the New York Yacht Club relinquished the trophy in 1983 to the Royal Perth Yacht Club.

Ashes. In 1882 the Australian cricket side touring England notched up (the term is still used to mean 'to build up a score') a healthy record of wins before the only test match. In the first innings Australia were bowled out for 63, but England scored only 101 in reply. In the second innings Australia put on 122 runs, leaving England to score 85 to win. In an outcome all too familiar to followers of English cricket, what followed perfectly matches the headline 'England batting collapse'. The score went to 51 for 3, then 66 for 5, but with 77 runs on the board England were all out. The following day the *Sporting Times* published a mock obituary:

In affectionate remembrance of English cricket which died at the Oval on 29th August, 1882.

> Deeply lamented by a large circle of sorrowing
> friends and acquaintances.
> R.I.P.
> NB: the body will be cremated and the ashes taken to
> Australia.

The next English tour to Australia was called by the press 'the quest to regain the Ashes', and a group of Melbourne ladies presented to the England captain a terracotta urn supposedly containing the ashes of a bail. This is the trophy that has ever since been contested by England and Australia cricket teams; the actual urn stays at Lord's Cricket Ground, and the team that wins the series gets a replica to cherish.

Blue. These words of Robert Collis in his autobiography, published in 1939, are part of the world of privileged Varsity amateurism, recognisable in *Chariots of Fire*, but scarcely at all in the twenty-first century:

> In England the gaining of a 'blue' is generally
> regarded as a more desirable achievement than
> becoming an M.P., or being made a knight. The
> social position it confers lasts for many years, for to
> be an 'old blue' is to have an assured status for the
> rest of life.

In the first Boat Race between Cambridge and Oxford, in 1829, Oxford wore dark blue and white stripes, while Cambridge wore pink sashes over white shirts. For the second race, in 1836, the Cambridge boat had a light blue ribbon attached to its prow, and, following their victory, they adopted the colour permanently. 'Blues' are awarded to athletes who compete for either university against the other.

Blue ribbon. Why as slight a thing as a blue ribbon should be attached to the idea of victory or competition is not immediately obvious. It may be connected to the *cordon bleu*, which was the blue ribbon from which hung the Order of the Holy Spirit, an ancient French award of high honour, or from the Order of the Garter, an English honour of great exclusivity. The term was first used in a sporting context to describe the Derby, as the 'blue ribbon of the turf', in 1848.

Calcutta Cup. Attempts to play rugby football in India were so unsuccessful that in 1877 the secretary of the Calcutta Football Club passed on to the Rugby Football Union the last decision of the club members that the rupees constituting the club's funds would be withdrawn from the bank and melted down to make a cup to be competed for annually by the England and Scotland rugby teams. The cup was made in India and looks more like a tankard, with three handles modelled on cobras and a small elephant for the lid handle.

Davis Cup. In 1900 Dwight Filley Davis donated a cup that was to be awarded to the national team victorious in an international tennis tournament. The first match was between the United States and Great Britain in 1900, the next in 1902, and in 1905 the tournament included Belgium, Austria, France and a combined team from Australia and New Zealand. Currently 132 nations compete.

Pennant. Until 1968, a pennant was awarded to the club winning the league of the National League of Professional Baseball Clubs (the National League) since 1876, and to the winner of the American League since 1908. In 1968 the leagues divided into two divisions, and the winners of each obtained the pennant, playing each other in play-offs to decide an eventual winner. The 'Pennant' came to be a term meaning the league championship itself. Pennants have also been major trophies in Australian Rules Football since 1895, and the term survived the introduction of a cup in 1959 (the pennant was usually known as 'the Flag'). The word 'pennant' is derived from 'pendant', meaning 'hanging', and 'pennon', a 'small flag hanging from a lance or helmet', which in turn came from a number of variations of *pinnon*, an Anglo-Norman French word for 'feather or wing'.

Prize. In medieval sports, particularly wrestling, the prize was often a ram, though in the fifteenth-century *A Mery Geste of Robyn Hode* the prize at an archery contest is:

> an Arrowe, the Shafte of sylver white,
> The head, and fethers of rich red Gold.

Cash prizes appear where the rich are involved: in the fourteenth-century romance *Sir Bevis of Hampton*, there is a horse-race for 'forty pounds of redy golde', and at one of the first public race-meetings, at Enfield Chase in the seventeenth century, the prize was 'a golden ball'.

In the early eighteenth century the prize for a sporting event in provincial fairs was usually a hat for a man and a smock for a woman. In *A Match at Football* (1721), the victorious team is awarded 'six Holland caps with ribbons bound', with 'three pairs of gloves for the vanquish'd' (presumably one glove per team member), while in 1726 Voltaire saw a foot-race for women for which the prize was a chemise. A variation on the theme was Doggett's Coat and Badge, given since 1715 for an individual rowing race on the Thames.

Later professional challenge matches in sports such as pedestrianism, prizefighting, rowing, swimming and quoits were usually for money, but championship tournaments might award other prestigious prizes. In 1860 the Prestwick Club awarded a Challenge Belt for the champion golfer, the belt being of red morocco leather with silver plates, with the stipulation that it could be kept by whoever won it three times in succession. A belt was also given as a prize for a foot-race, as reported in the *Sporting Gazette* for 1 November 1862, and the first boxing championship belt, the Lonsdale Belt, was given in 1909.

Prizes for amateur contests tended to be prestigious rather than financially valuable: medals, cups and shields, on which the winner's name was engraved, conferring symbolic immortality rather than cash, or such things as a clock or a case of fish-knives, which had the useful side-effect of appealing to class segregation. However, the same effect was achieved much earlier in horse-racing by the Act of Parliament in 1740 that decreed that race-meetings could offer no prize smaller than £50, a limit that effectively closed down smaller race-meetings for the poorer owners and punters.

The wooden spoon was a traditional award at Cambridge University in the nineteenth century, given to the student with the lowest marks in the Maths Tripos who still managed to get a degree. The spoons themselves gradually grew in size, until the last one awarded was nearly 5 feet long, before the award was banned from 1909. The wooden spoon was in use in sports reporting, appearing in the *Glasgow Herald* in 1888, and by 1894 was being used in the Rugby Home Nations tournaments.

'Prize' was a variant of 'price', meaning a 'sum of money', and is related to 'praise', in the sense of 'value'. It entered English via Anglo-Norman French and is first recorded from about 1250 (*OED*).

Purse. From around 1600 a 'purse' was a sum of money collected for a purpose, for example to enable a trading venture; from this it came to mean the sum collected as prize money in a horse-race, and then a prize-fight. It is still used for the money earned by a boxer in a fight. The word comes from the medieval Latin *bursa*, meaning 'hide', which also developed into words such as 'bursary', 'reimburse' and the French *bourse*.

Ryder Cup. The Ryder Cup, played for in biennial matches between American and European teams, was donated by Samuel Ryder following the second match, between the United States and Great Britain, in 1926, the first having been in 1921. From 1947 Irish players joined the British, and from 1979 the team has been European. The Ryder Cup is rare among trophies in that it portrays an actual person, Abe Mitchell, Samuel Ryder's golfing coach.

Triple Crown. The Triple Crown is competed for in a number of sports: rugby union (defeating the other nations of the British Isles in the Six Nations Championship); horse-racing in the United States (the Preakness Stakes at Pimlico, Baltimore, the Belmont Stakes, and the Kentucky Derby); horse-racing in Britain (the Two Thousand Guineas at Newmarket, the Epsom Derby, and the St Leger at Doncaster); and motor-racing (the Indianapolis 500, the Le Mans 24-hour race, and the Monaco Grand Prix). These are the most famous Triple Crowns, but there are about twenty others, in cycling, golf, surfing, wrestling, and so on. The notion of a triple crown may come from James I's sovereignty over England, Scotland and Ireland, but more likely from the earlier papal tiara incorporating three crowns, whose numerical significance was clearly referred to in the quadruple-crowned ceremonial helmet commissioned by the Ottoman Sultan Suleiman in 1532. The 'grand slam' originated in card games in the seventeenth century; in the nineteenth century winning all the tricks in a game of whist was a 'slam'.

Rules (and breaking them)

Balk. A 'balk' is a foul in baseball, when the pitcher steps outside his lines, the equivalent of a 'no-ball' in cricket. It most likely comes from the use of the word to designate a line accidentally missed when ploughing a field, and thus a missed opportunity. One of the earliest *Laws of Tennis*, published in 1877, has a 'baulk line', which appears to mean the side lines of the court.

Bung. 'Bung' is probably a development from the Old English *pung*, meaning a 'purse', but it may also be a 'stopper', a bribe to stop someone talking. The *OED* records it in this sense from 1958. To 'bung' meant to 'lie' in the mid-nineteenth century. Hockey at one time seems to have been played with a 'bung', which in this case was probably similar to a 'puck'. An 1882 set of rules for hockey refers to the 'bung and stick'. The *Rules of Hockey* from 1887 state that 'the ball is an ordinary cricket ball painted white. This to anyone who has played with a bung will seem a great innovation.'

Cards, red and yellow. The story goes that the system of yellow and red cards for cautions and sendings-off in football was invented by the chairman of the FIFA International Referee Committee, after there was some dispute as to whether two players had been cautioned during a match in the 1966 World Cup finals. Apparently Kenneth Aston, while driving home, came up against four sets of traffic lights that turned from green to amber to red as he drove up to them. The immediate need was for a sign that would be instantly intelligible without need for translation, and 'yellow card' and 'red card', and their ancillary words, such as to 'red-card' someone, have been translated rather than adopted into other languages.

Cheat. 'Cheat' is a wonderful instance of lexical rebranding. In 1360 'purveyors' responsible for purchasing on behalf of the Crown realised that their reputation for corruption was such that their jobs needed to be renamed. They became 'achatours' (from the French *acheter*, meaning 'to buy'); unfortunately awareness of their dishonesty continued, and their name, which evolved into 'escheators', developed into the word 'cheat'.

One of the most bizarre accusations of 'cheating' occurred in 1674, when a tailor, James Bullocke, beat a Virginia gentleman, Matthew Slader, in a horse-race, which carried a wager of 2,000 pounds of tobacco. The local law decided that it was illegal for a 'labourer' to challenge a 'gentleman', and both fined him and sentenced him to the stocks for being 'an apparent cheate'.

Double-cross. An issue of the *Sporting Life* in 1848 announced that 'All bets are off. It has been rumoured that a double-cross was intended' (*OED*). A 'cross' was early-nineteenth-century slang for a swindle, particularly where two people pretended enmity in order to deceive a third; so in a horse-race a jockey would double-cross the person who paid him to lose a race.

Fair play. Around 1880 the promotion of sports tended to emphasise mental and social benefits as much as physical gains. Much of this depended on the amateur ethos, and the idea that playing games within this mindset both helped to render permanent these values within sport, and firmed up the relationship between sport and the values. Neil Tranter in *Sport, Economy and Society in Britain 1750–1914* (1998) defines the values as 'purity, manliness and the virtues of stoicism, pluck, self-reliance, and an unshakeable commitment to fair dealing'. 'Fair play' is a term first used in Shakespeare's *King John*, and its place in English sports culture was confirmed in the combination of muscular Christianity, rule-writing and team spirit produced by the sports movement in the public schools and universities in the mid-nineteenth century. Typical of how long this idea lasted as the centre of a 'golden age of sport mentality' is this text from *Sport in Britain* (1975) by H. A. Harris:

> Towards the end of the nineteenth century, organised sport was taken up by many European countries and by North America, and in the first quarter of this century it spread over most of the world. Fortunately this happened at a time when the tradition of sportsmanship was still strong in Britain. Because this was a conception new to several countries, they had no word for it in their language and so borrowed the term with the idea. To this day, *Le fairplay* is international linguistic currency, another fact of which we in this country may be modestly proud.

While this text provides a field day for post-colonial deconstructivists, it does say something about how long the perception lasted that 'fair play' was something fundamentally British. It was certainly an opinion that was around long before high imperialism. In Thom's *Pedestrianism* (1813) a 'Mr Jackson' is quoted as saying that he was 'always of opinion that nothing tended to more preserve among the English peasantry those sentiments of good faith and honour which have ever distinguished them from the natives of Italy and Spain, than the frequent practice of fair and open Boxing.'

FIFA (the Fédération Internationale de Football Association) uses the expression 'fair play', particularly in its Fairplay Awards, in several languages. Within the history of football, this seems to have been a conscious imposition: Richard Holt in *Sport and the British* (1989) states that 'football [in the twentieth century] enshrined older forms of toughness and rudeness, which stoutly resisted the "civilising process" of fair play and sportsmanship.' And yet there is the Cornish hurling ball of some antiquity, which is coated with silver on which are engraved words in Cornish that translate as 'Fair play is good play'.

Baron de Coubertin proposed that the 'important thing about the Olympic Games is not winning, but taking part', a sentiment taken up by the American Sportsmanship Brotherhood in 1926, in the words 'not that you won or lost, but how you played the game'. The adoption of the word 'sportsmanship' in the sense of 'fair play' appears to have been American, from the 1920s – its previous use in British English was solely 'skill or knowledge of a sport'. Now synonymous with 'fair play', 'sportsmanship' has also produced 'unsportsmanship'.

Incidences of untypical fair play or typical absence of fair play see the rolling out of specialist phrases. When in 1997 footballer Robbie Fowler was awarded a penalty that he felt was unmerited he was put in a position of having to take the kick, with the option of deliberately missing; Cashmore points out that doing so could have brought a charge of 'ungentlemanly conduct' or 'acting against the spirit of the game'. Other charges might have been 'improper conduct' and 'bringing the game into disrepute', which though definitely archaic-sounding outside football, have been used throughout the history of the game. In 1985 UEFA banned the Skopje Vardar trainer for two matches for 'ungentlemanly conduct', and fined the Turkish club Fenerbahce £23,000 for 'unsportsmanlike behaviour'. The 1976 edition of the *Association Football Laws Illustrated* includes this text:

> It is the belief of the Board [the International
> Football Association Board] that the Spirit in which
> the Game is played is of paramount importance and
> that changes in the Laws to improve the Game as a
> spectacle are of little value if 'fair play' is not
> universally observed.

Later in the book, in the 'Code of Practice' section, is the following:

> To avoid bringing the game into disrepute players are
> expected to observe the following code of practice...
> Sportsmanship: Do not indulge in practices of
> cheating under the guise of 'gamesmanship'. Honour:
> to win without honour is a hollow victory.

'The Spirit of the Game', 'guise', 'honour'; it is odd that the terms used to encourage fair play are still those that defined the amateur ethos in the nineteenth century, in which the sanction against a player guilty of 'violent conduct' was to have his name sent to 'the committee of the Association under whose rules the game was played, in whom shall be vested the sole right of accepting an apology' (*A Guide to Football*, W. S. Forley, 1890).

Foul. The early meaning of 'unfair' came from the Old English word *ful*, meaning 'unclean'. By the fifteenth century this had developed the specific meaning of unfair conduct in a game. In the late eighteenth century 'foul' developed a number of nautical uses, such

as the 'fouled anchor', which became a symbol used by the Royal Navy. This probably lay behind the use of the word to describe the various aggressive actions in rowing races, especially smashing your opponent's oar, or ramming his boat.

A race between a Cambridge University eight and one from the Leander Club in 1838 involved a deliberate smashing of an oar by the challenging boat, and when the umpire was called to judge whether the race was 'fair or foul' he called 'foul', presumably on the grounds that the following boat had been squeezed out of the race, not because they had smashed their opponents' oar. When the race was resumed, they rammed the leading boat. The rules for the Durham Regatta in 1837 stated that 'in the case of skiffs fouling, all jostling is allowable which can be accomplished with the sculls in the rowlocks, and the rower on his seat.' A race between Eton and Westminster schools in 1835 began with the agreement that there would be no fouling in the first half-mile.

Fouling at Oxford and Cambridge eventually evolved into 'bumping', in which staggered starts mean that boats have to catch the boat in front and 'bump' it.

By 1887 'fouling' had been adopted by other sports such as hockey, football and rugby.

Fouls. Some illegal practices in team contact sports:

Blind-side hit: in rugby, American football and ice-hockey, hitting a player, intentionally or not, from a place where he cannot see.

Boarding: in ice-hockey, checking an opponent so that he crashes into the boards at the edge of the rink.

Earholing: in American football, charging the side of an opponent's head to cause an ear injury.

Roughing the snapper: in American football, tackling a player who has just made a kick before he has time to assume a defensive position.

Shirt front: in Australian rules football, any player can 'bump' any player who is within 5 metres of the ball. But a bump to the player's chest, a 'shirt front', is illegal.

Spearing: in American football, tackling or making contact with a player by using the helmet. In rugby union, rugby league and Australian rules football, a spear tackle is when one or more players lift an opposing player so that he falls on his head. In ice-hockey it is stabbing an opponent with the blade of the stick.

Gamesmanship. Gamesmanship is defined by *Collins English Dictionary* as 'the art of winning games or defeating opponents by cunning practices without actually cheating'. 'Gamesmanship' encompasses standing away from the wicket and pretending to have something in your eye when a fast bowler has nearly completed his thunderous run and so has to pull away, grunting at high volume when serving in tennis, or coughing as your golf opponent is about to drive off the tee. The word was invented by Stephen Potter as the title of a book published in 1947, whose full form was 'The theory and practice of gamesmanship, or the art of winning games without actually cheating'.

Let. The *Book of Sports* (1618) by King James I stated that:

> Our pleasure likewise is, Our good people be not
> disturbed, letted [obstructed], or discouraged from
> any lawful recreation, such as dancing, either of men
> or women, Archery for men, leaping, vaulting, or any
> other such harmlesse Recreation…

This usage of 'to let' is the key to the use of 'let' in tennis and other racket games, in which a 'let' is an announcement of an obstruction that allows the shot to be retaken. The first usage in sport is from the nineteenth century.

Off-side. Of all the rules in football over the past 150 years the off-side rule has changed the most and been the subject of most debate. In *The Football Man* (1971) the referee Arthur Hopcraft stated that away from the pitch the arguments he was 'mostly called to settle were those about interpretations of the off-side rule'.

Thomas Hughes, the author of *Tom Brown's Schooldays* (1857), wrote in a dispute about the origins of the method of playing rugby that:

> running in [running with the ball] was made lawful
> within these limitations: the ball must be caught on
> the rebound; the catcher was not 'off his side'...

Off-side in football as played in the public schools had, since the rules were developed in the 1830s and written down in 1846, meant 'no player between the ball and the opposition goal'. In the first published laws of the Football Association (8 December 1863) the off-side rule made it illegal to pass the ball forward. In 1866 it was changed so that now a player was 'onside' and could receive a forward pass so long as there were three players between him and the opposing goal. This remained the rule until 1925, when a change to 'one man and the keeper between the player and the goal' came into force. The change came about because so few goals were being scored that spectator numbers were falling, and it resulted in an increase of 50 per cent in the number of goals scored the following season, and the emergence of the famous 'W formation', with three forwards pressing the opposition goal.

'Off-side' rules were adopted in hockey in 1886, changed in 1972 to specify two rather than three players between an attacking player and the goal, changed again in 1987 to apply only within 25 yards of the goal, and abolished in 1996.

Queensberry Rules. Also known as the Marquess of Queensberry's rules, they were drawn up by A. G. Chambers and J. S. Douglas in 1865 and approved by the Marquess

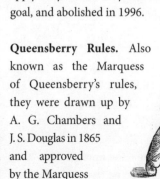

of Queensberry, a boxing enthusiast, in 1867. John Sholto Douglas, Marquess of Queensberry, was a Scottish peer and one of the founders of the Amateur Athletic Club in 1866; he refused to swear the religious oath of allegiance to Queen Victoria, being a noted atheist, and was thus barred from sitting in the House of Lords. As the father of Alfred 'Bosie' Douglas, he was also involved in the court case against Oscar Wilde (whose only known involvement in sports was, curiously, in boxing).

Ringer. In the late nineteenth century, as American sporting clubs began to be influenced by commercial interests, the need to win grew to be as strong as or stronger than the desire to play well. In certain situations, in this period before press photographs made players quickly recognisable, substitute players, or horses, sometimes took the place of the registered participant in major competitions. These were 'ringers', the term probably coming from the phrase 'to ring the changes'.

Rules. Rules in sport created a fair environment for betting, or for clarifying the ways of playing the game; this was particularly the case for horse-racing, where handicaps and other processes of evening the competition were applied in the seventeenth century. They could also function as a moral pressure on players. *The Compleat Gamester* (1674) states about billiards that:

> As this is a cleanly pastime, so there are laws or
> Orders against lolling slovenly Players, that by their
> forfeitures they may be reduced to Regularity and
> Decency.

The eighteenth century produced rule-making amongst the players, in cricket, boxing and horse-racing. The first laws of cricket date from 1727; Jack Broughton, the champion prizefighter, laid down the first rules of pugilism in 1743; and the Jockey Club was founded around 1750. The writing of rules clearly indicates the public-school hegemony of the nineteenth century. The first written rules for football were set down at Rugby School in 1845; the first laws of boat-racing by Oxford and Cambridge men with rowers from the leading London clubs in 1847; those of the Football Association by former public-school pupils who had founded the majority of the London clubs in 1863.

Gorn and Goldstein propose that the history of sport shows rules as among the things constantly being adjusted to create the optimum balance between defence and attack, to generate the largest number of spectators, directly or via the media. This is particularly clear from the twentieth century, with the creation or modification of rules to allow advertising or to create more dramatic results and partisanship.

'Rule' comes from an Old French form of the Latin *regula*, meaning 'bar, ruler, pattern'. The rules of cricket are still called 'laws', as are those of association football and rugby football, while lawn tennis and hockey have 'rules'.

Steroid. 'Steroid', a word bandied about whenever there is talk of athletes taking banned substances, has entered common usage to mean any performance-enhancing substance. 'Steroid' comes from 'sterol', which is a formative element in such substances as cholesterol or ergosterol (an alcohol present in ergot, yeasts and fungi). Steroids, first named as such in 1936, comprise a large number of organic and synthetic compounds, not all of which have pharmacological uses. The International Amateur Athletic Foundation banned the use of 'stimulating substances' in 1928.

Scoring

Ace. The game of lawn tennis, patented in 1874, took over some of the practices of 'rackets', including the scoring system of four by fifteen points to a game. Each point was known as an 'ace'. In early baseball, an 'ace' was a run. The term is also used in the United States

```
        SOMERSET—1st Innings.
J  C.  W. MacBryan,  c  Sinfield,  b
     Barnett  ..................... .....  12
Young, c Lyon, b Parker ..........  104
S.  G.  U.  Considine,  c  Lyon,  b
     Parker  ...  .... .................  63
R. A. Ingle, c Sinfield, b Parker ...  4
J. C. White, not out .............. .....  14
C. C. Case, not out ..................  31
          Extras  ....................  6
                                        ——
        Total  (for  4  wkts.)  .......  234
```

in golf where British English uses the term 'hole in one'. 'Ace' originally was the throw of one at dice, from the Old French, coming from the Latin word *as*, meaning a 'unit'.

Birdie. The word 'bird' was used from about 1840 in the United States as a term of praise for anyone or anything good, so its application to a good shot in a game of golf in 1899 (1903 in other accounts) at the Country Club in Atlantic City was fairly normal. But it was not until the early 1920s that the term was applied specifically to a score of one under par (one less than the expected score for a hole).

The idea was quickly extended to an 'eagle' (two under par), but only some time later, in 1937, to an 'albatross' (three under par); a 'condor' has been used for a hole in one, but 'hole in one' is such an iconic term that it is probably safe for a while.

Bogey. Initially, it is said, 'bogey' meant the same as 'par', the score expected for a golf hole. The appearance in 1892 of a song with the words 'I'm the Bogeyman, catch me if you can' led to the meaning of 'bogey' to golfers as 'something to be caught', i.e. the ideal score. The arrival of another song in the 1930s, 'Hush, hush, hush, here comes the Bogeyman, … he'll catch you if he can', changed the meaning of 'bogey' to 'something to be avoided', a score of one over (more than) par.

Another interpretation is that right from 1892 the 'bogeyman' was an imagined person always trying to make golfers make a mistake and play one shot above par. An alternative is that the 'bogeyman' would always make the perfect score, so 'bogey' did mean the same as 'par'. But the introduction of the dimpled golf ball in 1898 meant truer flight and better scores, thus 'par' (itself originally an Americanism) came to be 'one below bogey'. Or the idea of a 'ground score' (an ideal score for a particular course) was for a certain Major

Wellman in 1890 nothing but a 'bogeyman', a joke that was extended to create the bogeyman's score.

Down. In American football, the team holding the ball has four chances or 'downs' to run or pass the ball 10 yards forwards. If successful, it has another four 'downs' to make another 10 yards. If the ball is intercepted, or fumbled and captured, the team loses possession, and the other team tries to take the ball forwards. The first use of 'down' in this way was in 1882.

Duck. A 'duck' in cricket is short for a 'duck's egg', that is a score of zero, and was for long called a 'duck's egg'. One story is that it originated with a spectator making a quacking sound at a batsman who had failed to score. A 'golden duck' is being out first ball, a 'diamond duck' is when this happens on the first ball of a match, and if it happens that a batsman is out first ball twice in a match that is a 'golden pair' or 'king pair'. If a batsman later overcomes this misfortune, or even scores one run, he 'breaks his duck', thereby avoiding the most common score in cricket (mathematically it has to be, since zero is the only score that every batsman has to be on, at some stage in his innings). There is a thematic similarity to the generally debunked idea that 'love' in tennis is derived from the French for 'egg', *l'oeuf*, but 'duck' in cricket is not recorded

before 1868. Since the 1880s a 'goose egg' has been the term for a score of zero in American sports, especially baseball. In *Passing English of the Victorian Era* (1905) J. Redding Ware states that '"Blob" has taken the place of "duck" or "duck's egg"'.

Goal. To 'score' a goal sounds so natural that it is hard to think that any other phrase was used. But in the nineteenth century goals were 'won', 'shot', 'made', 'taken' and 'obtained', which sounds quite formal and polite. In early-twentieth-century rugby a successful kick between the posts after a try was called a 'goal', or a 'converted goal', not becoming a 'conversion' until the 1920s. The current laws of rugby union describe this as a 'conversion goal'. There are a few documentations of this expressed as a verb, 'to goal', as in 'Bennett … scored a try, which Tebbutt goaled' (1922 – *OED*); now 'goaled' would be replaced by 'converted'.

CITY FOOTBALL AND ATHLETIC OUTFITTER.
GOOD OUTFIT—GOOD KICK—and the GOAL IS WON.

Handicap. A handicap, in the sense of a deliberate disadvantage given to a stronger competitor in a contest, developed from a game called 'hand in cap' or 'hand in the cap', which was played by Samuel Pepys in September 1660 – 'Some of us fell to handicap, a sport that I never knew before, which was very good.' The game is mentioned in *Piers Plowman*, a fourteenth-century poem, and is found in a statute from 1477 as 'Hondyn & Hondoute'.

A good description of it is found in *The Slang Dictionary* (1865) by J. C. Hotten:

> Player A wishes to obtain some article belonging to
> B, say a horse; and offers to 'challenge' his watch

against it. B agrees; and C is chosen to 'make the
award' – that is, to name the sum of money that the
owner of the article of lesser value shall give with it,
in exchange for the more valuable one. The three
parties ... put down a certain stake each, and then
the handicapper makes his award. If A and B are
both satisfied with the award, the exchange is made
between the horse and the watch, and the
handicapper wins, and takes up the stakes. Or if
neither be satisfied with the award, the handicapper
takes the stakes; but if A be satisfied and B not, or
vice versa, the party who declares himself satisfied
gets the stakes. It is the object of the handicapper to
make such an award as will cause the challenger
and challenged to be of the same mind; and
considerable ingenuity is required and exhibited on
his part.

The three parties would hold their stakes in their hands in a cap or
hat, and the two deciders would show their acceptance of the decision
by leaving the money in the hat. The handicapper would try to
confuse the amount of the difference (the award) by expressing it as,
for example, 'two guineas, five crowns, and twenty five shillings'
requiring the others to decide immediately.

The idea of an act of equalising in a contest was transferred to
other sports about 1660. 'Handicapping' in foot-races seems to have
been common during the reign of Charles II (1660–85); faster
runners were required to wear heavy boots. Macaulay's *History*
states that the Duke of Monmouth used to win 'foot-races in his
boots against fleet runners in shoes'. No doubt an arbiter was
chosen to approve the handicap. The development to horse-racing
usage seems to have happened around the middle of the eighteenth

century, where people who wanted to race against each other would use the rules of 'hand in the cap' with a weight differential in place of cash. In cases of disagreement a third person would be involved as referee, again following the pattern of the game 'hand in the cap'. Within thirty years referees were being asked to judge on the different weights to be carried by horses in a race in order to equalise the contest. By the 1870s this principle was being applied to timing and distance in foot-races. Ratting matches in New York from about 1830 involved 'classic' matches, in which a dog would try to kill as many rats in an arena as possible in a set time, or a 'handicap' in which a dog was timed as to how long it took to kill its own weight in rats.

The word did not feature much in eighteenth-century dictionaries: Johnson in 1755 did not include it, though he describes a game called 'shufflecap' – 'a play at which money is shaken in a cap'.

Hat-trick. A 'hat-trick' or 'hat trick' possibly originates from the custom whereby a cricket club would give a new hat to a bowler who took three wickets in successive balls. Ice-hockey spectators throw hats on to the rink to celebrate the success of a player who scores a hat-trick. The term may come from the old custom of crowds throwing their hats in the air at good news. Another source may be the custom of awarding a hat as a prize in athletics festivals in eighteenth-century England. Bob Wilson in *Googlies, Nutmegs and Bogeys* (2006) is specific about the origin – a match in Sheffield in 1858 in which H. H. Stephenson playing for All-England took three wickets with three balls, and was presented with a hat bought with money from a collection (made by passing round the hat, maybe). Another suggestion is that any bowler managing the feat was entitled to pass round his own hat. The first documentation in the *OED* (1877) is of an achievement rather more than the usual hat-trick:

'Having on one occasion taken six wickets in seven balls, thus performing the hat-trick successfully.'

In baseball, to achieve a 'hat-trick' a batter has to hit in one game a single, double, triple and home run.

Home run. Around 1850 'home' came to mean in team games the place to get to in order to score or be free from attack. The 'home run' took on an added poignancy during the American Civil War, where baseball flourished in prisoner-of-war camps. The term 'homer' was first recorded in 1891.

Nil. *The Times* in 1920 and 1921 reported football matches with scores of 'four goals to none' and 'one goal to none'. A sixteenth-century contraction of the Latin *nihil*, meaning 'nothing', 'nil' began to be used for sports scores around 1914. Curiously *The Slang Dictionary* (1865) gives its meaning as 'half; half profits'.

Run. The terminology of cricket was changing when the laws were first printed. The *Laws for Cricket* published in 1755 use the word 'notch' instead of 'run', while the 'Rules of the game as played on the Artillery Ground' printed in the *New Universal Magazine* in 1752 used both 'runs' and 'notches', the latter when quoting an older authority. 'Runs' are documented from 1746, but 'notches' were still in use in 1800 in the MCC *Laws of Cricket*. 'Notch' can still be found in nineteenth-century cricketing accounts but it had come from a technology – keeping a tally by marking a notch in a stick – that had been rendered obsolete by education and the growing culture of record-keeping in cricket.

Camping, or campball, is recorded as having used the term 'notches' for points, but games similar to cricket use 'runs', though early baseball used 'aces' instead. Modern baseball has runs: a 'single run' or 'single', a hit that allows the batter enough time to reach the first base; a 'double', which allows him to reach second base, and so on. A 'home run' or 'homer' gives the batter time to get round all the bases, either by being hit beyond the boundary or, for a fast runner, to the edge of the field of play.

Tennis scoring. In 1558 a French visitor to England and Scotland wrote that 'you may commonly see artisans and joiners playing at tennis for a crown, which is not often seen elsewhere, particularly on a working day.' This is improbable since sixty years later a crown was a month's salary for a schoolteacher. The proposal is that a crown was 5 shillings (60 pence), which divided into 15 pence per point. This would have made the simplest set of six games worth six crowns, about six months' income for an artisan. The use of the word 'love' for 'no points', which came into use in the eighteenth century, has various explanations. One suggestion is that players played for money or love, and that no points meant no money, therefore 'love'; Hotten points out the paradoxes that can be produced by this expression, such as 'fighting a man for love, i.e. for the mere satisfaction of beating him, and not for a stake'. Alternatively 'love' is from the French *l'oeuf*, meaning an 'egg', the shape of zero – there is little academic support for this, but much popular belief. Palmer offers another possibility: the Icelandic *lyf*, meaning 'something small or worthless', similar to words in Old Danish, Old High German and Swedish. But he accepts that the idea of love as the antithesis of money is more likely.

'Love' was in use in card games in the eighteenth century, and people were puzzling over its origin then. Partridge notes its earliest uses as from south-east England, so possibly with a French influence.

Deuce (40 each) clearly is a term adopted from French, but its meaning is uncertain. One suggestion is *à deux de jeu*, or *à deux*, meaning 'at two to play', or 'two points to win'. Another is *deux* alone, meaning 'two' or a 'pair'. 'Deuce' was also a name for a demon, which became an oath, though there is little to connect it to the tennis score. A 'deuce' in baseball is a curveball.

In the *Laws of Tennis* published in 1877, a game lasted until one player had won 15 points, by a clear margin of two.

Try. In the 1830s the system of scoring in football was changed so that by carrying the ball over the end-line of the pitch you earned yourself a chance for a free kick at the goal, a 'try at goal'. Towards the end of the century this sense was retained in sports reporting. *The Guardian* for 20 January 1896 reported that 'Hainstock got a try at the corner flag, no goal resulting', and later 'scored another try for Leeds, no goal accruing'. The story that at Rugby School William Webb Ellis one afternoon ran with the ball to the end-line, placed it on the ground and then asked a master if it was a goal, getting the reply that it was not but it was a jolly good try, is, sadly, not supported by any documentation at all. In the period before 1890 a try did not count for points at all; later it was called a 'minor', as opposed to 'major', goal.

Players now call a 'try' a 'touchdown' (five points), which allows them a 'try' at converting the score into a goal, totalling seven points.

Skills, actions, techniques and styles

Alley-oop. A term for a basketball pass to a player near the hoop who jumps to catch and score, 'alley-oop' may have come from American soldiers returning from France after the First World War. However, the first documented use of this in basketball is from the 1950s (*OED*), though from the 1920s it was being used for acrobatic jumps. From the late 1980s it was being used to describe jumping 180-degree turns in skateboarding and snowboarding.

American seat. In the 1890s a large number of American jockeys, trainers and horses were forced to compete in the United Kingdom, following the suppression of racing in the United States as a result of widespread betting corruption. Their outstanding success in Britain was in large part due to the use of the 'American seat', first used in

Britain by the black jockey Willie Simms in 1895. Simms used short stirrups and appeared to be riding on his horse's neck. The technique was used in 1897 to great effect by another American jockey, Tod Sloan, along with a fast start, which frequently left Sloan isolated ahead of the field all the way to the finish. This, using the pattern of rhyming slang, is the origin of the expression 'on your tod'.

Backhand. Margot of Hainault was a celebrated French tennis player of the fifteenth century, who is credited with having invented or successfully used and developed the 'backhand' stroke. As backhand strokes for right-handed players involve using the left side of the court, this developed early on in English the sense of 'irregular', and its first documented use (1657, *OED*) is in this sense.

Back stroke. In 1595 Christopher Middleton published *A Short Introduction for to Learne to Swimme*, which was a translation of Everard Digbie's *De Arte Natandi* (1587). In this well-illustrated book, the instructions for the back stroke involved using the legs and feet only; the hands were placed on the belly. A later authority instructed that the arms should be used and lifted out of the water at the end of each stroke for the 'racing back stroke'. By 1941 the 'English back stroke' involved frog-kicks with the legs, with both arms simultaneously lifted clear of the water to reach above the head and down in a horizontal arc. *The Amateur Swimming Association Book on Swimming and Swimming Strokes* accepted that 'for speed purposes it has been superseded by the Back Crawl Stroke'. In the 1950s the term 'back stroke' or 'back crawl' came to be applied to the stroke that lifts the arms alternately clear of the water.

Bait. Bait is recorded as a dialect word in Dorset and northern counties of England for 'giving feed to a horse'. The word appears as 'bayte' in the fifteenth-century *Boke of St Albans* in a fishing context.

And 'Merry England' was characterised by bull-baiting and bear-baiting, and such blood sports. In the mid-nineteenth century in the United States 'to bait' was 'to take a portion of food or drink on a journey' (*Webster's Dictionary*, 1852). What all of these have in common is a root in the word 'bite', and from that to 'make an animal bite'. Baiting an animal involved setting one beast to bite another: the bait on the fish-hook was to make the fish bite, and Dorset farmers in baiting their horses gave them hay to bite. The sense of 'to harass' is a metaphorical development and can be found in Middle English.

Barani roll. A twist in the air in gymnastics is a 'barani roll'; it involves doing a front flip, but twisting the shoulders in mid-air to turn the body. If done well, the body is balanced, and the manoeuvre is named after the Austrian physicist Robert Barani, who won a Nobel Prize for his research into balance in the human body.

BMX. This term is rather a contradiction, BMX standing for 'Bicycle Moto Cross', because 'moto' here is the French contraction of motocycle, meaning 'motorcycle'.

Bowling (cricket). The term 'to bowl' in cricket derives from the game of bowling, a reminder that bowling the ball along the ground was the norm until the introduction of 'round-arm bowling' in the 1820s. The terms for distinct types of bowling in cricket go back to the period when bowling was all underarm; many have changed, indicating the way the culture of cricket has both acquired and abandoned terms in its long history. The *Cricketer's Pocket Companion* (1826) discusses the merits of a 'bailer', a ball that rises to the shoulder of the bat; a 'shooting ball', one that moves surprisingly quickly; and a 'twister', used in the nineteenth century rather than a 'spin ball'. A half-volley hit in cricket was called a 'barter' after Robert Barter, a teacher at Winchester College in the nineteenth century. The word, dating from about 1835, is no longer in use for this kind of stroke.

A confusion may arise with the word 'break'. This describes the way a ball's trajectory changes direction as a result of bouncing; an 'off-break' appears to be going to the 'off' side, but turns on the bounce to go towards the 'leg' side. A 'leg-break' does the opposite; the 'ball of the century', bowled by Shane Warne to Mike Gatting during the first test match between Australia and England in 1993, was an extreme leg-break, often called a 'flipper'. 'Off-spin' and 'leg-spin' are used in the same way. A 'left-arm spin', however, lands in the middle of the pitch and bounces towards the 'off' side. A 'leg-cutter' (first used in 1966), which sounds like a rogue cannonball, is a fast leg-break, but after bouncing on the seam may go in any direction, middle, leg or off. The famous 'googly' has an opposite, called the 'doosra', a ball that bounces apparently the wrong way, due to sleight of hand. 'Doosra' means 'second' or 'other' in Hindi and Panjabi, connecting it to the term 'wrong'un', sometimes used in Australia for a googly. A 'grubber', a ball that bounces low along the ground, dates from 1837, while a 'zooter', a ball that dips late in flight, originated with Shane Warne in the 1990s; there is a suspicion that a 'zooter' was the same as a 'flipper', and the term was invented just to confuse batsmen having to face an unidentified way of bowling.

When one side of the ball is polished more than the other, it offers less of a surface to the air and moves slightly more slowly, curving the ball's flight; this has been known as 'swing' since 1906 (*OED*). 'Seam' bowling, the term being used since the mid-twentieth century, uses the raised line of the seam on the ball to produce unpredictable bounce.

Any of these produces what is known as 'movement off the

SKILLS, ACTIONS, TECHNIQUES AND STYLES

pitch'. The most alarming movement is derived from the 'bouncer' (from 1913) or 'bumper' (from 1855). The opposite, a fast ball that bounces low, is a 'shooter'. There seems to be little but fashion in determining whether a cricket bowler is 'fast' or 'quick' or a 'pace bowler'. The *OED* records 'fast bowling' from 1886, 'quick bowling' from 1899, and 'pace bowling' from 1955.

Break. When the ball or puck, etc., 'breaks' for a player, it comes out of a melée of some kind advantageously for that person – this use of 'break' dates from the Old English period. In 1884 *Lillywhite's Cricket Companion* talked about a bowler 'breaking a ball two or three feet' (*OED*), that is, making it change direction, while for an athlete, 'breaking' means 'making a false start'. In billiards 'breaks' or passages of continuous scoring were recorded from 1865.

Breast stroke. The Amateur Swimming Association in 1921 reckoned the breast stroke 'is the most graceful form of progression through the water when the movements are performed with rhythmic precision'. In the sixteenth century there was a kind of breast stroke, but clearly the dog paddle was more familiar. In the mid-eighteenth century there was a stroke called the 'frog stroke', and in 1797 the *Encyclopaedia Britannica* recommended keeping frogs in a tub to watch and learn from them how to swim. The kick that is peculiar to the breast stroke was in the nineteenth century called the 'wedge', from the feet coming together at the end of the kick. The term 'breast stroke' first appeared in *The Times* in 1875, describing the technique used by Captain Matthew Webb in his swim across the Channel.

Butterfly stroke. The butterfly, described by H. A. Harris in *Sport in Britain* (1975) as an 'unnatural movement', 'hideously ugly' and without merits, was invented in the 1940s as a permissible alternative to the breast-stroke movement. Harris likens it to hopping backwards, as a 'difficult and strenuous exercise, but no one in his right senses would demand races on the track for it as part of the Olympics athletics programme'. The invention of the butterfly stroke, by swimmers in the United States or Britain, is hotly contested. In 1933 swimmers in the United States invented the arm movement as a way of decreasing drag, and the 'dolphin fishtail kick' soon afterwards. Some years earlier, swimmers in Britain and Ireland used similar arm and leg movements, which were, according to one story, disqualified by the Irish Board of Swimming Ethics, which described them as 'ungodly'.

Butterfly was considered a variant of the breast stroke until 1952, when it was accepted officially as a distinct stroke. It is sometimes known as 'the fly'.

Canter. Andrew Marvell wrote in 1673 of priests 'canterburing' from one place to another. 'Canter' is short for 'Canterbury', originally the pace recommended for Canterbury pilgrims. It was supposed that the pilgrimage to Canterbury was done at a gentle pace, though a 'canter' is now midway between a trot and a gallop.

Catch. 'Catch', in the form 'cacchen' or 'cahten', was adopted from the Anglo-Norman French *cacher*, meaning to 'capture', before 1200. The past tense form of 'catch' used to be 'catched', but as the standard form it was superseded by 'caught' only in the nineteenth century.

Chop. The action of bringing the surface of the bat or racket down on to the ball, the 'chop', is used in tennis, table tennis, cricket, baseball and other sports. The word is documented from 1888 (*OED*) for cricket, in which it was used for a hard downward stroke; it was used also in this way in baseball, notably in the 'Baltimore chop', a technique that involved hitting the ball down hard on to the hard ground in front of the home plate to ensure a high bounce, and time

for the batter to get to first base.
Conversely, a 'chop' in tennis
and table tennis slows the ball
down and puts a spin on it. The
word appeared in Middle
English and is probably a
development of 'chap', meaning
'crack', as in the cracks that
appear on the hands.

Christy. A quick turn in skiing,
a 'christy' or 'christiana', was invented in Norway in the nineteenth
century and named after the capital, then called Christiana
(now Oslo).

Crawl. When the crawl stroke appeared, few in Europe believed
that it would be good for anything except short sprints. Authorities
vary as to when it was introduced to Europe, from as late as the
1920 Olympic Games in Antwerp by American swimmers, to as
early as 1897 by an Australian swimmer. Early documentation of
the stroke after its 1897 introduction refer to the 'crawl' and the
'Australian crawl', though in 1930 Johnny Weissmuller's book was
called *Swimming the American Crawl*. Ralph Thomas reported
George Catlin describing the front crawl in 1841, in *Letters on the
North American Indians*, as a stroke used by the Mandans, and
'brought to London in 1873 by Mr Trudgen'. Thomas also called the
stroke the 'hand-over-hand or Indian stroke (also by some called
the Payton or Trudgeon)'. The 'Indian stroke' has been noted by
other writers as a term used by white settlers in North America.
The stroke was probably first used in Britain as early as 1844, in a
swimming demonstration by two North Americans, named Flying
Gull and Tobacco, who according to *The Times* of 22 April 1844

'lash[ed] the water violently with their arms, like the sails of a windmill, and beat downwards with their feet'. The first use of the word 'crawl' to describe the stroke in *The Times* was on 2 September 1913, and in *The Guardian* on 30 July 1912. Early versions of the stroke lifted the legs clear out of the water, a practice dropped after 1908. By the 1930s it was being referred to as 'the perfection of the dynamics of swimming' (Royal Life Saving Society handbook, 1937).

Dive. In his book *Swimming* (1904) Ralph Thomas tried to sort out the muddle of the meanings of the various words then in use to describe what is now usually called 'diving', i.e. entering the water head-first with the arms more or less stretched out in front. He lists a selection of terms and usages: 'diving' was used for jumping into the water feet-first as well as head and arms first in *Every Boy's Book* (1855); in the *Dictionary of Daily Wants* (1861) 'diving' means 'swimming under water', while 'plunging' means 'springing into the water'. By the mid-nineteenth century, he reports, there were the words 'header' for a dive, 'to spring' meant 'to dive' (head-first), and in 1879 a 'shooter' was a flat dive into water. For Thomas, 'header' and 'spring' were the correct words for entering the water, and 'dive' for 'swim under the surface'; to go down from a standing or swimming position in the water was a 'dolphin dive' or 'porpoise dive'. Considering the word 'dive', he says:

> it will be thus seen that the modern corrupt meaning has, without a note of warning or caution against the disaster that had occurred to the word, been adopted by the OED.

The *OED* currently does not give any idea that 'dive' can mean 'swim under the surface'. Thomas himself preferred 'spring' for any way of entering the water suddenly, and 'header' for a head-first dive into the water. At the end of his investigation into 'plunge' and 'dive' he writes:

> The word plunge has settled down to a quiet life;
> there are not likely to be any more changes for the
> Amateur Swimming Association has settled its
> meaning.

The 1904 St Louis Olympic Games had a category called 'Plunge for Distance', a static dive from the side of the pool, 'the body to be kept motionless – face downwards – and no progressive action to be imparted to it other than the impetus of the dive.' The distance achieved was measured after a minute, or less if the contestant's breath gave out. The record was 82 feet. 'Plunge' in this sense did not last long – *The Guardian* in 1895, reporting on a swimming contest, described an exhibition plunge by McHugh, 'the amateur champion plunger. The item was rather a novelty, but the interest created disappeared with the end of his long plunge.'

Earlier usages were little clearer: Middleton in 1595 used the phrase 'to dive underneath the water', meaning 'to dive in' (there were curious ways of doing this in 1595, including running and somersaulting forwards with the hands behind the neck, and cartwheeling in sideways). Benjamin Franklin in *Experiments and Observations* (1769) used 'plunge', while *Captain Stevens' System of Swimming* (1845) used 'dive' and 'plunge' indiscriminately.

By 1941 'diving' was as we know it, either a 'swallow dive' or an 'English header' (totally straight). Past-tense forms are 'dived' in Britain and Australia, but 'dove' in the United States and Canada. The 'pike' posture used in diving from a high board is a translation of German and Dutch expressions, *Hechtsprung* and *snoeksprong*, both derived from the shape of the head of the fish.

Dog paddle. Ralph Thomas in *Swimming* (1904) called dog paddle, or 'doggy paddle', the 'human stroke', probably because it is thought of as the first instinctive stroke used by a young child; *Captain Stevens' System of Swimming* (1845) called it 'dog-fashion'. In 1823 the Vicomte de Courtivron called the stroke 'swimming like a dog', the same term used by Christopher Middleton in 1595. Ralph Thomas describes it as 'the European stroke to about the year 1500', and suggests it was the stroke used by Beowulf, 'popularly but incorrectly known as the dog paddle'.

Dribble. Montague Shearman states that it was not until some years after the 1870s that:

> captains and [football] teams … discovered that the
> way to win a match was not to dribble cleverly and to
> 'back up' the dribblers, but to pass and to trust to
> combination alone.

Nottingham Forest Football Club in the 1860s pioneered the use of two defenders, three midfielders and five forwards, finding ways of confounding the off-side rule, which prohibited forward passing. 'Dribble' was first recorded in football in the same year as the founding of the Football Association, 1863, and was applied to the same kind of tactic in hockey, appearing in the first rules of hockey, published in 1887. 'Indian dribbling' in hockey, running the ball from right to left and back while moving forwards, was first shown to the world by the Indian hockey team at the 1956 Olympics. Somehow 'dribbling' was involved even in rugby, for it is found in a *Guardian* report of a match from 20 January 1896. The word ultimately comes from the word 'drip', imitating the sound of water dripping.

English. In billiards, 'to put the English' on a ball, or 'to English' it, meant 'to give it some spin'. The term appeared in the United States in 1869 in a text by Mark Twain. It was later used in bowls and tennis and, according to one story, originated with a display of putting spin on the billiard cue-ball by a British player in the United States, his name being English.

Fluke. This term, meaning a 'lucky hit' in billiards and later other sports, is recorded from the mid-nineteenth century; its origin is unclear but it may be connected to a dialect word for a 'guess'.

Follow-through. The 1879 *Encyclopedia of Sport* proposed that 'both force and direction are imparted by what is technically known as the "follow-through"' (*OED*). Logically, how you affect the force or direction produced by hitting something after you have hit it must be a bit of a mystery; perhaps of greater value is the continuation of the stroke and so maintaining the movement of the muscle, thus avoiding muscle strain or injury. The follow-through may be static, as in archery, nearly static, as in putting, or as active as the rest of the stroke, as in tennis; in cricket it sometimes seems to be as much about style and grace as anything else.

Fosbury flop. The Fosbury flop sounds like a film about an overrated sporting venture, but it is actually one of the most successful innovations in athletics. Richard Fosbury experimented in 1968 with a way of throwing himself at the high jump head-first and face upwards, winning the Olympic gold medal that year, and breaking the Olympic and world records. His eponymous recognition is due to his role as the perfector rather than the inventor of the technique.

Gallop. This word was effectively adopted twice, first from a lost Old French form *waloper*, which gave the Middle English 'wallop', which originally meant 'gallop'. This died out in the sixteenth century, when it was superseded by the French *galoper*, which became 'gallop'.

Garryowen. Between 1924 and 1926 the Garryowen Football Club (playing rugby union) used to great effect the tactic of back kicking a ball high and, calculating where it would land, rushing forwards to that spot while the opposition were looking up at it. The tactic was associated with the club and got the name as a result.

Googly. One of the most infamous terms in cricket, a 'googly' is a deceptively bowled ball sent by a leg-spin bowler (one who bowls in such a way that the balls hit the pitch in line with the batsman's legs, but bounce away to the off side), so that it bounces in the opposite direction from that expected. The mechanics of this involve the ball coming out of the back of the hand, therefore being difficult for the batsman to see. The style was developed by the bowler B. J. T. Bosanquet and is thus known in Australia as a 'bosey' or 'bosie'. The supposed origin of the word 'googly' is that the first uses of the ball, in the early twentieth century, were so surprising that they caused people to 'goggle', or 'google', a contemporary variant. 'Google' is the verb developed from this, and 'googler' is the bowler who manages to use it.

Grounder. This is a ball hit along the ground in baseball, and during the nineteenth century in cricket; it has largely disappeared from cricket usage.

Hacking. The ploy of trying to bring an opponent down by kicking at his shins was one of the major points in the divergence of rugby and football. At the historic meeting that marked the separation between these two sports, 'hacking' was banned by the association code followers, while the rugby code supporters felt that its removal would 'do away with all the pluck and courage of the game'.

The word derived from a Germanic source and is first noted about 1200, meaning a heavy cutting blow. Incidentally, it may be one of the sources for the words 'haggle' and 'haggis', a pudding containing hacked meat.

Header. Before its association with football, a 'header' was a boxer's blow to the head, and a swimmer's head-first dive. Early rules of football do not mention players being allowed to head the ball; the first mention of the practice is in 1906 (*OED*).

Hook. The curving line of a hook made it the natural word for a boxer's swing round towards his opponent, and for a golfer's mis-hit that takes the ball to the side, and for the cricketer's hit over his shoulder to the leg side. All of these are recorded from the 1890s (*OED*).

Infighting. Daniel Mendoza, the prizefighter, was an exponent of the practice of standing close to his opponent, recorded in 1816 as 'infighting'. The term developed its meaning to express 'fighting within a group' about thirty years later, but was still in use in the 1920s to describe close fighting.

Jump. Appearing about 1500, 'jump' seems to have sprung into existence from nowhere. It is possibly onomatopoeic, a kind of sound-picture of the action (and presumably the landing). Eric Partridge gives a Medieval Latin word *jumpare*, and the *OED* gives similar imitative words in Germanic languages, but these are not otherwise related.

The nineteenth century preferred the words 'leap' or 'vault' for athletic movement. *Walker's Manly Exercises* (1839) gives instructions as to how to perform 'vaulting over a fence', the 'high leap', the 'long leap', and the 'deep leap', which was jumping down off a wall.

Lob. The 'lob', a ball in tennis sent to the back of the court over the opponent, was supposedly invented on the spur of the moment during the finals of the 1878 Wimbledon championships. Patrick Hadow found it was the only way he could deal with Spencer Gore's net volley game. At first called a 'toss', though 'high lob' had been in use in cricket since the 1850s, 'lob' has been used in writing about tennis since 1890 (*OED*). The general sense of the early forms of the word in English and other Germanic languages is of 'looseness' and 'clumsiness'; a 'lob' was a 'fool' or 'clown', thus a 'lob' is a simple throw or hit and, though intentionally placed in tennis, implies some guileless optimism.

Mankad. Not a word that has made it into the *OED*, 'mankad' comes from the name of Mulvantrai Mankad, an Indian cricketer, who, while coming up to bowl during a test match in 1947, noticed that the non-facing batsman was out of his crease, and ran him out instead of bowling. This was permissible within the rules of cricket but provoked heated debate, on the grounds of sportsmanship. But the same bowler in a previous match with the same batsman had first warned his opponent that this might happen and had then carried out the same action, which is now called a 'mankad'.

Nelson. The wrestling arm-hold, involving surrounding the opponent's arm or arms from behind, supposedly comes from the tactics applied by Nelson at the battles of the Nile and Trafalgar, though the main thrust of the attack at Trafalgar was to do with cutting the opposing fleet in two rather than surrounding it; so this might stand as false or folk etymology. Similar uncertainty surrounds the 'nelson' in cricket scoring, the superstitious 111, which sends nervous players and umpires into a variety of supposedly placatory actions, including taking both feet off the ground. Explanations include the false story that Nelson had only

Three-Quarter Nelson

one arm, one leg and one eye, and the slightly more plausible observation that the three stripes on the collar of a naval uniform represent Nelson's three major victories, the Nile, Copenhagen and Trafalgar, thus 'won, won, won'.

Overarm bowling. The development in cricket from underarm to 'round-arm' (with the arm swung out to the height of the shoulder, legalised in 1835) and then to overarm bowling took about sixty years. The incident that forced the MCC's hand with regard to allowing overarm bowling may have been a set-up, but it was successful. In 1862 Edgar Willsher was given a 'no-ball' on six consecutive balls and stormed off the field, taking his colleagues with him. The umpire who called the 'no-balls' was replaced and the game continued, and nobody was disqualified from bowling overarm after that. It later transpired that bowler and umpire were good friends. 'Overarm' is recorded from 1864; but bowlers still used the round-arm action into the 1890s.

Overtake. When Isaac Ford and William Leek raced each other in 1845, 'the former led the latter for about three hundred yards, when his opponent gave him the "go-by" and won easily' (*Bell's Life in*

London and Sporting Chronicle). 'Overtake' had been in use from about 1225, originally with the meaning of 'to hit', but by 1800 it was developing the meaning of 'to pass'.

Pass. Schoolboy football games used to comprise one boy with the ball and all his team-mates shouting 'Pass!' When the 'dribbling' game gave way to the 'passing' game around the 1880s, 'passing' was more commonly known as 'passing on'. Hockey and football players 'sidled' – passed to the side – or 'middled' – passed to the centre. From the late 1960s a 'wall pass', passing to a colleague who passes back, came to be called a 'one-two' in the United Kingdom, though it remained a 'wall-pass' in the United States; in basketball the action is called 'give-and-go'.

Passing shot. A 'passing shot' in tennis, where the successful player sends the ball wide of his or her opponent's reach, is first documented from 1928 (*OED*).

Punch. 'To punch' as in boxing is a development from the earliest meaning in English, which was 'to make a hole'; we still have the expression 'to punch a hole in something'. The first documented use of the word as 'hit' is dated 1530.

Punt. A punt is used for a 'more or less optimistic kick at goal'; also, for the *Concise Oxford Dictionary* it means a 'drop-kick (rugby) hit before the ball hits the ground'. 'Punt' comes from 'bunt', a forceful push or stop; in baseball 'bunt' is used for the action of stopping the ball without swinging the bat, dating from 1872.

The idea of an optimistic venture is carried also in the use of 'punt' to mean a 'bet'; originally a bet against the bank in card games, it developed into any kind of bet, but especially on a horse. This probably developed from the French *ponter*, from *ponte*, meaning 'in card games any player other than the bank'. In the United States 'horseplayer' is the usual expression for someone who bets on horses. 'Punter' in Britain also came to mean in the nineteenth century a prostitute's client, and from this anyone purchasing a service with an uncertain outcome.

Putt. 'Putt' was a Scottish variant of 'put' and is known from the late-seventeenth century in the golfing context. ('Putt' was also a seventeenth-century card game.) 'Putting out' to end a hole (get the ball in the hole) has been in use since the 1870s.

Ruck and maul. 'To come in with the ruck' in 1865 meant to arrive at the winning post behind the winning horses. A 'ruck', once meaning 'the undistinguished crowd', is now commonly found in rugby union, in which since about 1905 a 'ruck' forms when a player holding the ball falls to the ground, and players from both sides pile on top, making sure that their opponents cannot move forward, and trying to 'ruck' the ball out from the 'ruck' with their feet, in order to move it back to free players behind them. If the same thing happens but the player with the ball stays on his feet, the resulting mobile melée is a 'maul'. In Australian rules football, a 'ruck' is a group of three players without fixed positions who can follow the play anywhere on the field. A 'ruck' was originally a 'pile' and is connected to 'rick' as in 'hayrick'. The more alarming-sounding 'maul' comes via Anglo-Norman French from the Latin *malleus*, meaning a 'hammer'.

Scull. 'Sculling' is rowing with a pair of oars, though in the nineteenth century it came to mean 'to propel through water by any means'; the 'propeller stroke' involved a swimmer lying on his back with arms stretched out above the head in a line with the body, and using the hands to 'scull' – to propel himself feet first, presumably quite slowly. Mid-twentieth-century swimming manuals advise 'sculling' with the hands as part of treading water.

The first championship of sculling as a professional sport took place in 1831; though it did not provide a living for a large number of scullers, there were major sporting figures, such as Robert Coombes and Harry Clasper, and a great rivalry between watermen of the Thames and the Tyne. Sculling did not just involve rowing: the rules for the Durham Regatta in 1837 provided that 'in the case of skiffs fouling, all jostling is allowable which can be accomplished with the sculls in the rowlocks, and the rower on his seat.' This text shows that the 'scull' was the oar, originally one used by sweeping it from side to side over the back of the boat, and later one with a shorter shaft. The word is of unknown origin.

Shoot. The earliest documented use of 'shoot' to describe what is done optimistically in football, polo, ice-hockey, etc., is from 1882 (*OED*). This is an obvious transference from using a gun (itself first documented from the sixteenth century for a large gun, and 1644 for a musket), which had in turn used the term from archery. In 1665 Colonel Hutchinson shot 'with bows and guns, and much used them for his exercise'. The first use for using a bow in a sporting context dates from around 1200, and the word comes from the Old English *sceotan*. By 1889 the term 'shooting service' was in use in tennis to give the idea of a very fast service. Golf uses the term differently: players 'shoot' a score of, for example, three under par. This usage dates from the 1920s.

Side stroke. *Captain Stevens' System of Swimming* (1845) described a stroke called 'side-swimming or thrusting'; this involved an open kick, with one arm doing a dog-paddle and the other a crawl. Steedman's *Manual of Swimming* (1867) described it as having five movements – three for the legs and two for the arms (*OED*). By 1900 this became the 'English side-stroke' or 'English racing stroke', as opposed to the 'North of England side stroke', in which all the limbs were moved independently. The stroke was considered decorous as it did not involve splashing. By the 1960s it had become the 'old-fashioned side-stroke' (*OED*).

Slam dunk. In basketball, a 'slam dunk' is jumping to a height that allows the player to push the ball down through the hoop with one or both hands above the hoop. The shot was banned between 1967 and 1976 in North American college basketball because of its dominant use by the 7-foot 2-inch Lew Alcindor, who also developed the reverse slam dunk, with his hands above and behind his head. 'Dunk' comes from Pennsylvanian German *dunken*, meaning to 'dip'.

Slice. When the golfer 'slices' the ball, it goes away from the intended line, in the direction away from the golfer's face. This can happen to anyone playing a ball-based sport and tends to be bad news, unless, as in tennis or snooker or squash, it is done deliberately, to give the ball spin. 'Slicing' the ball dates from 1890 (*OED*).

Sliding. Strutt in 1801 was careful to distinguish between 'skating', with skates, and 'sliding', on ice but without skates.

Slogging. The *Rules of Hockey* (1887) state 'No slogging'. Routledge's *Pronouncing Dictionary of the English Language* (1879) does not have an entry for 'slog', as then it was still considered a slang word. Hotten's *The Slang Dictionary* (1865) defines 'slog' as 'beat, baste or wallop', possibly from the German *schlagen*, meaning 'to hit'. Hotten quotes a *Punch* cartoon of 4 May 1859 in which a small boy excuses his use of the word in front of his grandmother by pretending that it comes from the Greek *slogo*, which naturally does not exist. 'Slogging' has been cricketing slang since the 1860s.

Smash. The 'smash' in tennis was first used by William and Ernest Renshaw in 1881 and is documented from the following year. This was a development of the use of the word in the sense of a 'heavy blow'. The word was probably originally imitative and seems to be limited in its use to racket sports.

Snapshot. In the 1960s and 1970s the word 'snapshot' had a vogue in sports reporting for a quickly taken shot in football, polo, hockey, etc. 'Snap' is the action of the centre passing the ball back to the quarterback in American football; short for 'snap-back', it is documented from 1922.

Spar. Gloves were used in 'sparring' in the world of boxing in 1781, by which time the word had been used in the sense of practice boxing for about twenty-five years. It had a long association with cock-fighting, for the action of the cocks making darting actions with their spurs. While the *OED* deems the etymology to be obscure, Eric Partridge connects it to the Middle French word *s'esparer*, meaning 'to kick', which is effectively what a cock does with its spurs (an unconnected word).

Sprint. Sprint derives originally from Old Norse *sprenten*, which appears in Icelandic as *spretta* and Swedish as *spritta*. Though the *OED* records it from 1566, it was evidently not a common word, appearing in neither Johnson, nor Webster, nor *Chambers Etymological Dictionary* (1867). For Partridge, it derived from the

Middle English *sprenten*, meaning 'to run', itself from either the Old Norse word or the Old English *ge-sprintan*, meaning 'to burst forth'. For the *Chambers Dictionary of Etymology* (1988) the word is linked to the Old English *spyrd*, meaning 'a racecourse'. The original sense was most likely 'to leap forward' and it was recorded in 1842 as a type of race at the running track where Lord's Cricket Ground now is.

'Dash' was the word used for a short foot-race for a period in twentieth-century Britain. It appeared in the nineteenth century in the United States and was still in use in 1984 for races up to 200 yards. In 1889 the athletics and football volume of the *Badminton Library of Sports and Pastimes* pointed out that the previous generation had decided that 300 yards was the limit of sprinting distance.

The Greek word *stadion*, from which we have 'stadium', meant 'a short foot-race or sprint'.

Strokes (cricket). The names of cricket strokes are fairly simple. The 'sweep' (from 1888) is done with the bat sideways, being swung across the line of the ball from 'off' to 'leg' (a 'reverse sweep' goes the other way); the body is low for the sweep, sometimes with the knee of the 'back' leg touching the ground. The 'pull' is similar, but with the body kept upright. A 'cut' is done with the bat swung in a pendulum-like movement, with the weight on the foot nearer to the wicket; the 'drive' is similar, but with the weight on the forward, or 'front', foot.

The defensive strokes are known as 'forward defensive' and 'backward defensive' (with the body moving forward or backward); in 1800 the forward defensive stroke was known as 'stopping the ball forwards' (*Rules and Instructions for Playing the Game of Cricket*, T. Boxall).

Strokes (early swimming and lifesaving). Among the strokes and swimming actions that appear in Middleton's *Short Introduction* (1595), the author advises the swimmer to learn how to 'swim with

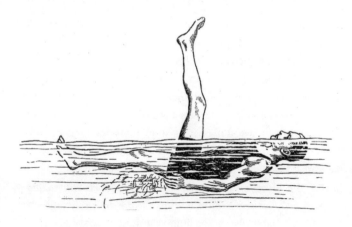

one hand and one foot upon his back', to 'pare his toes in the water' (with a knife, while floating), and to 'swim with one leg right up'. The last of these was not unlike a stroke called 'imitation of a submarine', found in the Royal Life Saving Society handbook for 1937, presumably a way of being seen from a distance. The same book contains instructions for how to perform the 'water wheel', also known as the 'bicycle', the 'washing tub', the 'mill', the 'Manx wheel', the 'cart wheel' and the 'Catherine wheel'; this involved rotating the body around the axis of the shoulders. There were also 'imitation of a porpoise', 'pendulum floating', 'paddlewheel' and 'oyster'.

Tackle. 'Takel' was a Middle English word of Germanic origin, meaning 'apparatus, equipment, gear', which developed into the word 'tackle', meaning 'to equip a ship'; this in turn developed into the meaning 'to deal with a problem mentally or physically'. It was thus ideal as the word for dealing with a member of an opposing team in rugby, and then football, first being used in this way in the 1880s.

Throw. The *OED* defines 'throw' specifically as 'to cast by a sudden jerk or straightening of the arm', rather than by using the momentum of the arm straight throughout the entire movement. The word originally meant 'to use a twisting movement', as in 'to throw a pot', and in sporting terms until the nineteenth century 'cast' was often the preferred word. 'Casting the barre' was the Tudor version of the modern 'throwing the hammer', and Strutt in 1833 talks about 'casting the javelin'. The exception to this was in wrestling and boxing, where 'throwing' an opponent often involved a twisting action – Carew described it as to 'overthrow an opponent' in 1600. 'Tossing the caber' is recorded from about the same time as 'throwing the caber' – the 1860s and 1870s. The 'throw-in' replaced the kick-in in association football in 1892, but at this time a 'throw-in' for a 'line-out' in rugby union was still called a 'throw-out'.

Trot. 'Trot' was adopted from the French *trotter* in the fourteenth century. Harness racing, more popular in the United States than Britain, though introduced to North America by the colonial British, involves horses 'trotting' or 'pacing'. The chariot is called a 'sulky', apparently because the driver has to be alone – in eighteenth-century England such an apparatus was called a 'desobligeant'. There is evidence of chariot-racing from 3,300 years ago.

Trudgeon. *The Amateur Swimming Association Book on Swimming and Swimming Strokes* (1941) states that the trudgeon stroke in its early days used to be referred to as 'double overarm' as often as by its proper name. The trudgeon involved a shortened alternating crawl stroke with the arms, and an alternating scissor-kick action with the legs. It involved some rolling of the lower body, while keeping the head forward and out of the water. Sometimes called the 'racing stroke' or, curiously, the 'East Indian stroke', it was named after John Trudgen, who used it when winning the English 100-yards race in 1875. Trudgen claimed that he had learned to 'trudge' from indigenous people in South America. The *OED* gives the first documented use as 1893, but there is some confusion as to whether the word is 'trudgen' or 'trudgeon'. A 'trudgeon' was originally a 'toddling child or a person who trudges' (*OED*), and the earliest-known spelling for the stroke is 'trudgeon'. It may be that the spelling of the name of the stroke was affected by the spelling of 'gudgeon', 'bludgeon', 'dudgeon', etc.

Vardon grip. It seems to be the way in sport that eponymous recognition goes not to the inventor of a technique, but to the person who uses it with the most publicity. Harry Vardon was the first professional golfer to play in knickerbockers, the winner of sixty-two tournaments, including six Open Championships, and

was ranked thirteenth best golfer in golfing history. He used an overlapping grip on the golf club, with the last finger of the lower hand tucking over the space between the first and second fingers of the upper hand. Previously it was called the 'overlapping grip', but it is now known as the 'Vardon grip'.

Volley. Playing, kicking or hitting a ball before it hits the ground has been called a volley since 1596, when the term is first recorded as being used in tennis. It is derived via Middle French from the Latin *volare*, meaning 'to fly'. The volley in lawn tennis was first used at Wimbledon in 1877 by the eventual champion, Spencer Gore.

Yorker. A ball in cricket bowled to land under the bat, a 'yorker' comes from an eighteenth-century slang expression 'to York' or 'pull Yorkshire' on someone, meaning to deceive them. Hotten's *Slang Dictionary* (1865) quotes 'Yorshar, to put Yorkshire to a man, is to trick or deceive him', from *Lancashire Dialect* (1757).

Slang and metaphor

A game of two halves. Though this wonderful truism is recorded from the 1950s, its heyday was in the late 1960s and 1970s. In *The Guardian* of 26 November 1971 Eric Todd wrote:

> Years ago some anonymous sportswriter gave birth
> to the phrase 'It was a game of two halves'. This
> implied that one of them was good, the other poor,
> and not that both lasted for 45 minutes. Like many
> another cliché it has withstood the challenge of age.

An anonymous sportswriter may have given birth to the phrase, but in the imagination it is always spoken in a rather nondescript voice by a footballer in a post-match interview, for some reason preceded by 'Well, John…' While few would now dare to use the phrase in sports reporting, away from sport it seems less of a cliché.

Annie's room. Dating from the First World War, when 'in Annie's room' was a stock response to the question regarding the whereabouts of someone missing from his post, this phrase is used in darts to mean 'double one'. In darts games, where doubles have to be thrown, a player can end up finding himself or herself having to throw a double one to finish: 'Annie's room' is the place not to be. The phrase reputedly originated with Australian troops.

Bagel. A set in a tennis match won 6-0 is a 'bagel', from the shape like a zero. The phrase is supposed to have originated with the American doubles players Eddie Dibbs and Harold Solomon, after Dibbs described a set won 6-0 as a 'bagel job'.

Ball. Colloquial terms for the ball in baseball include 'pea' (nineteenth century) and 'apple' (from the 1920s). From 'apple' comes the occasional phrase 'apple orchard' for a ballpark.

Barmy Army. The raucous supporters of the England cricket team appeared about 1995, though the name was also given to English football and rugby supporters, and to the members of the Tory party who tried to rattle Prime Minister John Major in 1995.

Bleachers. The cheaper part of an American sports ground, especially a baseball ground, is called this because the sun would bleach the painted wooden slats of the seats; 'bleachers' dates from 1889. In Spanish bullrings, the cheapest seats are in the sun (*sol*), the expensive seats in the shade (*sombra*), and the medium-priced seats are located where they will be partly in the sun and partly in the shade as the sun moves round (*sol y sombra*).

Boxing slang. In *Boxiana* (1812–29) Pierce Egan gives an enthusiastic display of boxing slang from the end of the eighteenth century:

> The milling coves, it is urged, are treading so fast
> upon the heels of one another, that the amateurs
> complain that before they can get scarcely three
> whiffs out of their steamer (pipe), or cool their
> chaffer (mouth) with a drop of the heavy wet (stout
> or porter), their ogles (eyes) are made to wink at the
> sight of a benefit ticket, and to prevent being thought
> scaly (mean), three bobs (shillings) are punished
> beyond redemption.

'Milling' was the general term for fighting, though boxers were not called 'millers' so much as 'bruisers' ('the Milling Corps' as in *Bell's Life in London*, 1833, was the 'Fancy', and a 'mill' was a fight); 'to mill' had previously meant 'to kill', but by 1700 had come to mean just 'to beat'. Other terms that appear in Egan are: 'bottleman', who held the boxer's bottle of drink; 'chancery suit', a headlock; 'daffy' or 'daffy's elixir', which was gin; 'daffy club', a social-sporting club meeting at the Castle Tavern, near Chancery Lane in London; 'facer', a blow to the face; 'ivories', teeth. 'Bottom' (endurance) supposedly developed a rhyming slang form, 'bottom' replaced by 'arse', leading to 'bottle and glass', leading to the modern 'bottle'. 'Bottom' disappeared about 1870. Hotten added a few more in 1865, for example 'topper', 'lobb' and 'nut' for 'head', 'noser' for 'a bloody nose', 'pepper' for 'thrash',

THE RING.

FIGHTS TO COME.

Jan 24.—Smith and Reardon—£25 a side, London.
    31.—Millard and Sawney—£20 a side, Bristol.
Feb 7.—Hicks and Nolan—£60 a side, London.
    13.—Farr and Sladen—£25 a side, Derby.
    21.—Bob Travers and Jem Mace—£100 a side, London.
March 13.—Sullivan and Tyler—£25 a side, London.
April 16.—Sayers and the Benicia Boy—£200 a side and the Belt, London.

'draw off' for leaning back before throwing a punch, 'bore' for 'press your opponent down on the ropes', 'fib' for 'hit', 'peel' for 'get ready for a fight'. 'Bursting your crust' meant 'bleeding heavily', while 'daddles' were hands. 'Dropping' or 'tumbling' was a way of using Broughton's rules to your advantage – these stated that if a boxer fell on one knee his opponent had to retire to his corner, giving him time to recover; 'tumbling' boxers used to go down deliberately for a breather. 'Articles of agreement' might be arranged between boxers that, for example, the first one to 'tumble' would forfeit the fight.

Burying the ball. A footballer who scores or a golfer who putts successfully may be said to 'bury the ball'. In 1913 *The Guardian* reported that a 'good drive buried the ball' in a golf context, while 'Rowley buried the ball in the crowd' during a football match in 1935, and in 1979 a striker 'buried the ball in the net'. The phrase was familiar by the time it was used in a Manchester United fanzine in 1994, along with 'heading the ball home' – curiously the ball is never 'kicked home'. In 1958 it was reported that at the Ashbourne football game, 'after a goal had been scored because players had dug a hole and buried the ball, there was talk of introducing rules into the game' (*The Guardian*, 20 February 1958). The Down'ards had buried the ball for four hours and walked six miles to put the Up'ards off the scent.

Claret. 'Claret' is known from the early seventeenth century as an alternative term for 'blood', but it is difficult to know whether the usage was a euphemism, or a florid metaphor, or downright revelling in the sight of blood, or any combination of these. Partridge puts its use in boxing from about 1770. In the nineteenth century 'Bordeaux' was used in the same way in boxing circles, as was, improbably, 'Badminton', from a red-wine-based drink popular between 1860 and 1890.

Corinthian. The 'Corinthian years', the 'Corinthian spirit', even 'Corinthianism', are still with us: in 2003 *The Guardian* challenged readers as to whether football should be viewed as 'Corinthian values or pantomime with boots'. 'Corinthians' was the name of a team of footballers formed in 1882 by N. L. Jackson, assistant Honorary Secretary of the Football Association, partly with the intention of keeping together the best university players after they had left college. Early Corinthian teams maintained a rigorous amateur ethic, not entering competitions, but regularly supplying England team members, and frequently successfully challenging the winners of the Football League. The selection of the word 'Corinthian' allegedly came from an early-nineteenth-century meaning of 'man of fashion', with implications of wealth and leisure, and a certain amount of dissipation.

Cricket slang. A slip of paper pasted into a nineteenth-century dictionary of slang contained these expressions:

Aunt Sally: caught or stumped by the wicket-keeper.

Bagged the fruit: failed to score in either innings.

Balloons, or Skyscrapers: lofty hit [this was in cricketing use seventeen years before the first use of the word to refer to a building; a term currently in use is 'air hostess', a 'fly ball' or 'airball' in baseball].

Feed with dollies: bowling easy balls.

Googlie: donkey drop.

Making the ball talk: break or turn the ball.

Pair of carpetbags: hands of a good fieldsman.

Play the cow shot: full bowling from the off side.

Poucher: easy catch.

Sitting on the splice, or Goose game: playing carefully.

Snorter: ball that is difficult to play.

Timberyard: wicket [still in use at the present time].

Timberyard watcher: wicket-keeper.

Other slang expressions of the time include 'to butter a catch', meaning 'to drop an easy catch'.

As Russell and Stevens said in *The Budding Cricketer* (1926), one has to learn 'the terms which become the mysteries of the game'.

Dead and buried. 'Dead and buried', meaning 'losing with no hope of retrieval', was first noted in this sense in 1934 (*OED*). In a sporting context *The Guardian* used it from 1980: 'Coventry should have been dead and buried after forty minutes.'

Dead ball. 'When the ball crosses either line it is dead and out of play', wrote Montague Shearman of football in 1889. The *OED* gives an instance from the seventeenth century of the expression being used in bowling; the sense of 'inactive' or 'not in use' is very clear. The familiar 'dead-ball situation' in football, meaning 'play following on from a free kick', dates from the late 1960s, but dead-ball situations feature in other sports, including baseball, cricket, basketball and American football.

Dukes. 'Dukes' is a Cockney rhyming slang expression, the 'Duke of Yorks', meaning the 'forks', i.e. the fingers, and from that extended to the hands, and thus the fists. Another possibility offered by Partridge is that it comes from a mistaken belief that the Queensberry Rules were made under the auspices of a duke rather than a marquis.

Footer, Footie, Fitba. Fairly well recognised still, but used now only as upper-class archaisms, 'footer' and 'rugger' were public-school slang expressions for football and rugby. Both expressions date from the mid-nineteenth-century heyday of the public schools but were extended at Oxford University in the early twentieth century to other expressions – 'eccers' for 'exercise' for example. Around 1890 'rugger' and 'soccer' were first documented, 'soccer' developing from 'association football', with alternative spellings 'socca' and 'socker'. 'Footer' had been used previously in the late eighteenth century for a kick as used in football. As an alternative to 'football', 'footer' spread to all classes; a First World War soldier's diary from 1915 refers to 'footer' in recording scores in the Poperinge League. While 'footer' died out in the 1940s, frequent appearances in football club fanzines show 'footy' becoming common in the 1990s. 'Fitba', a common Scottish dialect word, has not yet been included in the *OED*.

Game on. 'Game on' originated with darts matches in the 1980s, to let people know that a match had been arranged. 'Game' in the sense of 'tough and prepared to take a risk' developed in the early eighteenth century.

Hit the wall. Primarily an expression used by long-distance runners when they run out of reserves of glycogen (stored sugar), the metaphor aptly describes the feeling of the impossibility of progressing. Cycling has its own term, 'bonking', said to describe the banging in the stomach as the body starts to burn body fat, having used up every other resource.

Hospital pass. A rugby or American football player who is thrown a pass such that he will be immediately on the receiving end of a crunching tackle that may put him in hospital is said to be getting a 'hospital pass'. The expression has been in use since the late 1970s.

Left field (out of). 'Left-field thinking' is something people are regularly encouraged to do, while few people know what it means (or whether saying 'left-field thinking' is an example of left-field thinking). In baseball, the left field is the part of the field to the left of the batter – it assumes a right-handed batter. New York Yankees

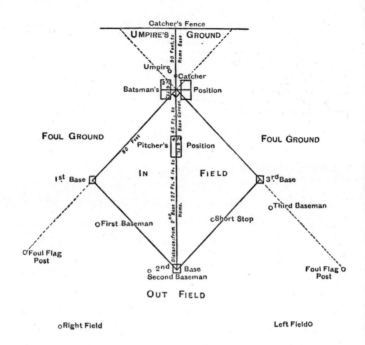

fans in the 1920s preferred the right-field seats, because Babe Ruth was left-handed and preferred to field on the right field. Deliberately buying left-field seats seemed odd, unorthodox, even perverse.

An alternative story is that the Neuropsychiatric Institute was located beyond the northern boundary of Chicago's former baseball park, West Side Park, and that anything that came 'out of left field' had dubious credentials as regards mental stability.

Money slang used in betting. The following have been among the most frequently used expressions:

Buck: $100 (mid-nineteenth century).

Burlington: £30, rhyming slang from 'Burlington Bertie', a
    nineteenth-century music-hall song.

Dime: $1,000 (1950s).

Grand: £1,000 (1920s, originally American).

Monkey: £500 (1827, *OED*).

Nickel: $500 (1970s).

Pony: £25 (1827, *OED*).

Score: £20 (late nineteenth century).

Ton: £100 (since the 1940s).

Nutmeg. The origin of this expression, meaning 'to make an opponent look foolish by a simple deception or skilful action', is supposed to derive from the actions of nineteenth-century spice traders who used to cheat customers by exchanging wooden substitutes for the expensive nutmegs. Alternatively, it may be Cockney rhyming slang for 'legs', as in football 'to nutmeg' an opponent is to kick the ball between his outstretched legs: Partridge's 1937 *Dictionary of Slang and Unconventional English* gives 'nutmegs' as part of the male anatomy – 'to nutmeg' someone in this case might be a metaphor for 'to neutralise or symbolically emasculate'. Hotten's 1865 *Slang Dictionary* gives the following definition for 'nutted': 'taken in by a man who professed to be "nuts" upon you'.

Over the moon. A common response in post-match interviews, 'over the moon' first came into common use in the 1970s. Eric Partridge in *A Dictionary of Slang and Unconventional English* (1937) records a single unpublished example from the mid-nineteenth century, but the phrase is recorded from 1857, as typical of the repertoire of a group of Victorian and Edwardian aesthetes who called themselves 'The Souls' and who used highly specialised and elevated phraseology.

Perform. 'We didn't really perform today', say a weary series of losing teams, or, if disgruntled at the result, 'the ref didn't perform'. 'Perform' in the sense of 'do well' is very recent. It is always in the negative – successful players are not described as having 'performed'. On 29 March 1991 *The Guardian* reported the England football manager, Graham Taylor, as saying 'What happened Wednesday was that we didn't perform', adding to a handful of notable remarks associated with him; but 'We didn't perform' had been the assessment of the England rugby union captain, Steve Smith, in 1982 (*The Times*, 17 February).

Pillar to post. In *jeu de paume*, the earliest form of tennis, the court was bounded by pillars and the net held up by posts. Because of the unpredictability of where the ball would land, due to the multifarious nature of the features of the court, the players could find themselves forced to rush 'from post to pillar', which, probably because the rhythm is easier, became 'from pillar to post'.

Public-school slang. Given that nineteenth-century public schools developed the rules and codes of many sports, it is not surprising that they developed their own terms. What is surprising is that the greatest variety describe the scrum in mass football. They are:

Bully: Eton, Rossall, Uppingham, Westminster.

Grovel: Sherborne.

Gutter: Tonbridge.

Hot: Bradfield, Winchester.

Pudding: Radley.

Rouge: Charterhouse.

Scrimmage: Repton, Shrewsbury.

Scrummage: Rugby.

Shindy: Downside.

Squash: Charterhouse, Cheltenham, Harrow, Marlborough, Stoneyhurst.

Apart from these, Lancing had its version of simple cricket called 'pintle', and Charterhouse and Marlborough had their versions called 'gownboy cricket' and 'snob' respectively. Eton cricketers were called 'dry bobs', while rowers were called 'wet bobs'.

Showboat. 'Showboating', showing off after victory is more or less assured, to humiliate your opponent, has been in use in Britain since the 1970s. It is derived from the paddle-steamers of the Mississippi, on which glamorous entertainments were presented.

Show pony. A player who tries to impress the crowd with too many fancy tricks is a 'show pony', a term introduced from Australia in the 1960s as meaning someone overly concerned with looks. The phrase began to be applied to certain footballers in the early 2000s, meeting with considerable favour amongst sports journalists.

Sick as a parrot. There was a phrase 'as melancholy as a parrot', which was used in the seventeenth and eighteenth centuries, but the phrase as used especially by defeated football players and managers in post-match interviews probably owes a lot to the Monty Python 'Dead Parrot' sketch, first broadcast in 1969. By the mid-1980s losers were more likely to feel 'gutted'.

Sledge. Though 'sledging' in cricket sounds as though it would be hitting the ball with more emphasis on force than control, it is actually a low-level barrage of insults usually directed by the fielders at the batsmen. The practice has been around since the 1970s, but the origin of the term is unknown, though there is a story that it was related to the Australian expression 'as subtle as a sledgehammer'.

Tennis slang. Expressions in use in 2010 include:
  Bagel: losing a set 6-0.

Banger: a power-hitter.

Dinker: a player who prefers slice shots to power shots.

Dirtballer: a player who prefers to play on clay.

Moonball: a high looping ball with top spin.

Pusher: a player who does not use specialist strokes but keeps the ball in play, waiting for the other player to make a mistake.

Sandbagging: pretending to be a worse player than you are, for the sake of winning.

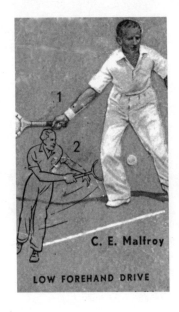

C. E. Malfroy

LOW FOREHAND DRIVE

Shank: a mis-hit or a ball hitting the frame of the racket.

S&V: an internet term for a 'serve and power-volley specialist'.

Throw your hat in the ring. In the early-nineteenth-century heyday of prizefighting, the heavily backed fighters would arrive at the site of the contest gaudily dressed, and the first thing they would do would be to throw their hats in the ring, to declare both their arrival and their readiness to fight. The choice of the hat may have had something to do with the tradition of awarding a hat as a prize in a sporting contest.

Turf. The turf has since the mid-eighteenth century been the name for both the racing fraternity and the course of a horse-race, though Partridge gives it as public-school slang for the short grass of a cricket pitch, as opposed to the 'long grass' of the rest of the field (now 'infield' and 'outfield'). The word was the same in Old English.

We was robbed. In 1937 *The Guardian* reported a player stating 'We were robbed of the game', and by 1962 the phrase had become the straight 'We were robbed' (the *Guardian* article was perhaps slightly tongue-in-cheek, as the paragraph began 'Whither Wolverhampton Wanderers?'). On 16 September 1952 their reporter wrote that as the players, including George Robb, were walking off at half-time 'some inveterate punster yelled out "We was robbed".

Willow. The phrase 'the sound of leather on willow' is instantly resonant to those who enjoy cricket, and meaningless, or cringingly nostalgic, to those who do not. 'Willow' here refers to the wood used for the blade of a cricket bat (in the nineteenth century the handles were made of whalebone, that is the stiffer part of a whale's 'sieve', also used for stiffening corsets). 'Lumber' (wood) is used for a baseball bat, particularly when wielded by a strong hitter; according to the *OED*, 'willow' has also been used for a baseball bat, though these are traditionally made of ash. The use of the word for the raw material as an image for the finished product has a long history in English. Old English poetry makes frequent use of this, often in 'kennings', metaphors that require for their explanation some inside knowledge or lateral thinking (though this would be in a society more familiar with the relationship between raw material and product). Thus in the *Anglo-Saxon Chronicle* entry for year 973, the phrase *hamera lafum*, meaning 'leavings of hammers' is used for 'swords', and in the seventh-century poem *The Dream of the Rood* the Cross tells its story from the point where it is cut down as a tree. 'Willow' has been in use as a metaphor for a cricket bat since the mid-nineteenth century.

Spectators

Cheerleader. 'Cheerleaders' were known in the early twentieth century. The earliest documentation in the *OED* (1903) cites Franklin D. Roosevelt as a 'cheer leader'; but the preamble to a 1721 poem about a football match states that 'it is customary for the Maids to dance for Cakes, and have several other sports before the Foot-ball is begun'. 'Cheerleading' now embraces static acrobatics and group acrobatics, with high numbers of injuries.

Fan. 'Fan' immediately looks as though it would be an obvious abbreviation of 'fanatic'. In Johnson's *Dictionary* (1755), the word appears as 'fanatick', following contemporary spellings such as 'musick' or 'garlick', which persisted till the end of the century, but in 1828 Webster gave the spelling as 'fanatic'. A fanatic was originally someone in a religious frenzy, the word deriving from the Latin *fanum*, meaning 'a temple'.

But such an obvious derivation should ring warning bells. The *OED* gives one early documentation of the word 'phan', though it arrived in English in the United States, as 'baseball fan', in 1889. Another possibility is that 'the fancy', originally the posh set who followed bare-fist fighting, became shortened to 'the fance' in both Britain and the United States, and then to 'the fans'. The word crossed the Atlantic in the early years of the twentieth century, with the first football fans noted around 1914, the fans previously being known as 'club followers'.

Hooligan. Football lost its public-school aura quickly between 1875 and 1890, and the presence of large numbers of spectators changed the nature of both the game and of watching it. The reaction of amateur players of the sport was that professionalism was demanding a spectator presence, which was partisan, which in turn led to a greater emphasis on winning. This in turn influenced attitudes on the terraces, and increased aggression among supporters was noted from 1876. However, this was not limited to football. The crowd rioted at a cricket match in Sydney in 1879, and again in 1903 during a test match. Alcohol and other social pressures were brought in as explanations, and in the 1980s 'hooliganism' was seen as part of young male working-class culture; football 'hooliganism' was common until the crowd segregation and all-seating stadiums of the 1990s.

The association of hooliganism with football is limiting, as riots and uprisings had always occurred at cock-fights, prize-fights and horse-races, with the militia or police being regularly called out. Boxing events still employ 'whips', whose job it is to run the minor business; their name comes from the 'heavies' using whips who were employed at prize-fights to stop spectators from crowding down the edges of the ring.

The word 'hooligan' appeared in the summer of 1898, and the common story is that it was derived from the name of a particular family, the Hooleys, or their gang – Hooley's gang, or from a different family called the Houlihans. There is no documentary proof for either story. The word has the distinction of being exported to a number of languages as part of football culture: *der Hooligan* in German, *houligan* in French, *huligaani* in Finnish, *huligán* in Hungarian.

Mexican wave. While the Mexican wave began as a spectator phenomenon during the World Cup in Mexico in 1986, it was by no means the first orchestrated spectator cheer; this may have been the 'locomotive', an increasing rhythmical cheer, which originated at a Princeton football game in 1871.

Spectators. While the ancient world provided vast stadiums with room for thousands of spectators, 'spectatorism' was seen by nineteenth-century amateurs as the antithesis of sport, a movement that would lead to the predominance of partisanship, which in turn would making winning the immediate goal of sport. The first documentation of the word in Britain in the *OED* notably is from the magazine of Winchester College, one of the foremost Victorian schools: 'there are distinct limits to the use of "spectatorism"' (1889). Richard Holt proposes that it was the drive to play and the lack of space that forced people into the position of being spectators in late-nineteenth-century cities, while Ellis Cashmore indicates the role of the spectator in creating the 'ritual' of sport, underlined by the fact that the 'performers' were usually the empowered class in society, while the spectators were the unempowered.

Spectator numbers in the era before public transport were vast (ten thousand for a cricket match at the Honourable Artillery Ground in London in 1743), while pedestrian races in the early nineteenth century could easily attract four thousand spectators. Cricket matches in the 1820s and 1830s might attract a crowd of twenty thousand, while major horse-races in North America were attended by several thousands. *The Guardian*, reporting the FA Cup Final in 1883, stated that it was played 'in the presence of an enormous number of people'.

Spectator figures have been affected by many factors; the change to the off-side rule in football in 1925 brought larger crowds, while the halving of attendance at matches between 1951 and 1984 may be due to television, hooliganism, and widespread changes to disposable income and leisure activities. For some reason, cricket attendances fell by a third between 1949 and 1954. In the United States in the 1950s there was so much television coverage of boxing that, in Cashmore's words, it became in effect a 'studio sport', achieving one third of the possible television audience. But at the same time, between 1952 and 1959, 83 per cent of the small boxing clubs closed down. While television is regularly blamed for the loss of live spectators, it may increase active participation, Richard Holt claiming that watching on television and taking part 'are not so much mutually exclusive as part of a balanced human cycle of passive and active involvement' (*Sport and the British*, 1989). The practice by Channel 4 of introducing to television audiences Australian rules football, sumo, basketball and other sports from 1982 not only increased awareness and created a following for these sports, but brought their vocabulary into British homes. Ultimately, it may be the television audience that controls the sport – in the United States ABC television redesigned the National Football League in order to give it more television advertising potential, and from 1958 more time-outs were allowed specifically to provide television advertising time.

The term 'spectator' dates from the end of the sixteenth century, while 'spectator sport' dates from 1943 (*OED*). The use of 'viewers' rather than 'spectators' for those watching sport on television comes from the choice of that word as a counterpart to radio 'listeners'; 'viewer' dates from 1935. Another term was 'gazers', used of people watching skating on the Serpentine (*Everyday Book*, 22 January 1830), and found in *Bell's Life in London and Sporting Chronicle* in reports of horse-races at Ascot in 1838 and a cricket match in 1841; by the end of the nineteenth century it had all but disappeared. The 'crowd' at a sporting event can be found in nineteenth-century sports reporting, though it is not common; the word dates back to the late fourteenth century, when it meant a 'crush of people'. It may come from the term 'crowder', used in the late nineteenth century to denote a full house at a theatre.

Sponsor. Sports facilities have for centuries been provided by taverns, inns, pubs, hostelries and so on; such places were the obvious sites for bowling alleys, cockpits, quoits matches and billiards tables. Clear evidence of sponsorship of sporting events is seen in the publicans who built pedestrian tracks next to their pubs in the nineteenth century, such as the Snipe Inn Course owned by Betty Berry in 1842, or the White Lion at Hackney Wick, scene of Deerfoot's first British race in 1861. In North America there is documentation of this from the early eighteenth century. From the late nineteenth century commercial companies realised that the audience for sport meant that sponsorship could provide massive advertising opportunities, from companies sponsoring football teams like Thames Ironworks Football Club, through the appearance of 'official' suppliers to the 1932 Olympics, such as Ovaltine and Omega, to the 'guerrilla marketing' at the 2010 World Cup. W. G. Grace endorsed products at the end of the nineteenth century, including mustard as well as cricket-related products. Spalding in the United States quickly realised the commercial potential of sport, sponsoring the 1904 Olympics by designing the stadium, organising the games and supplying the equipment; they also encouraged endorsement of products by players. The curious case of the Gillette sponsorship of cricket from 1963 shows the limitations of sponsorship; by 1981 it was reported that few people still associated the Gillette Cup with razors, and some believed it to have been named after a Dr W. G. Gillette (reported in Polley, *Moving the Goalposts*, 1998).

The curious process by which television viewers will see a perfectly squared-up design on a cricket field, while the players will be playing on a distorted and unreadable spread of colour dates from 1994, but it is a surprise how quickly over the past decades visual sponsorship moved from the area around the playing field on to the field and the players themselves. In 1975 cricketers were still wearing clothes without logos, and the *Sydney Morning Herald* painted a curious picture of a bowler coming into bowl with a logo for a cigarette manufacturer on his shirt – 'Could this ever happen at Lord's? Would we wear it at the SCG?' (21 January 1975). By 1992 the umpires at international test matches were being sponsored by private companies, and wearing logos. The blatant flouting of amateurism was an affront to many who held on to the non-commercial traditions of cricket.

A 'sponsor' was originally a godfather or godmother, the word deriving from the Latin *spondere*, meaning to 'pledge'.

Support. 'Support' is a curious term for the emotional relationship between an individual and a sports club or team. A boy may ask an adult 'Whom do you support?' in the hope of finding grounds for confirming a friendship, or support may entail no more than vague interest in a national team. The fact that support usually involves teams or individuals in sports based on one-to-one competition – cricket, tennis, rugby – rather than open competition may give some idea of what is happening; you back a horse, but you don't 'support' one, and, while you may want a particular athlete to win a contest, you are unlikely to 'support' that athlete across the competitions of a year or more. 'Supporting' perhaps involves the idea of 'willing on' or 'giving adherence', something that can be done mentally without ever having to be in the same stadium as the team or person supported. Indeed, adherence to a particular club may be so strong that the supporter cannot bear to watch a game in progress; Simon Barnes in *The Meaning of Sport* (2007) tells the story of a supporter for whom the worst thing that could happen was his side scoring, as this would antagonise and galvanise the opposition. Football fans talk about the team 'choosing them' rather than the reverse, while others openly decide to support a club on the basis of the way it plays; some supporters at football matches will applaud everything their team does and revile the opposition continuously, no matter how either side plays. The sense of 'belonging' is a key notion – the supporter and the club both belong to the same place and are linked by this; a club's premises may move within the area, but not away from the area, a potential upheaval explored in the film *Major League* (1989). Gorn and Goldstein in *A Brief History of American Sports* (2004) describe the relationship between supporter and club as being highlighted by failure:

> The close relationship between the city and the team
> … has never been in question… The hostility a fan
> directs towards a losing team is largely self-directed;
> such feelings gnaw at, even poison, many fans'
> feelings about themselves and the place they live.

This seems far from the formalism of *The Guardian*'s report (1 January 1900) of a match between Leicester Fosse and Woolwich Arsenal: 'Both clubs were well represented.'

'Support' seems to embrace a wealth of concepts – tribalism (Tony Adams, a former Arsenal player, in 2009 talked about being in the crowd watching a match where some of the people around him were interested in their side winning to the exclusion of everything else), fear, hope, despair, belonging, home, identity, continuity, hero-worship, family, and sometimes appreciation of how a game is played. The word 'support' is documented in this sense from 1390 (*OED*) and ultimately comes from a Latin word meaning 'carry'. In the United States the word 'root' appeared in the 1880s, famously occurring in the 1908 song 'Take me out to the ball game':

> Let me root, root, root for the home team.

Originally meaning 'cheer', 'root' quickly transferred to the sense of 'support', though for *The Observer* in November 1924, reporting on a baseball match played in London, 'rooters perform the same function at a baseball match as barrackers at a cricket ground.' 'Barracking' at that time meant 'jeering'.

Success and failure

Catch a crab. The phrase found in rowing applied originally to plunging the oar so deeply into the water that pulling power was lost, and the onward movement of the boat would jam the oar against the rower's chest. It was supposed that this was as if a crab's pincers had caught the oar underwater. Francis Grose's *The Vulgar Tongue* (1785) applied the phrase to 'missing one's stroke in rowing'; though this is an entirely different action, the effect is similar, and 'catching a crab' became applicable to either mishap. The crab has been since antiquity associated with sourness, ill-fortune and hidden adversity, as seen in the application of its Latin name to the disease cancer.

Champion. A 'champion' was originally a 'man in a field', from the Latin *campus*, which had a meaning of a 'field for military exercises', as well as a simple 'field'. The Late Latin word *campio* meant a 'combatant in the arena', and thus 'gladiator'. The word was adopted into English twice, first as the Old English *cempa* (Beowulf is described as a *cempa*), and in the thirteenth century as 'champiun' from the French, by which time the 'champion' was a knight who fought either to uphold someone's right or in a tournament. The legal role of the 'King's or Queen's Champion', who at a coronation offers to fight any challenger to the new monarch's right to the crown, offers a model for the champion–challenger relationship in, for example, boxing title fights, while the champion at a chivalric tournament is the model for contests such as the Olympic Games.

The first uses in a sporting context appeared in the eighteenth century, applied to cricket and boxing.

Dead heat. The use of the word 'dead' to mean 'absolute' dates from the seventeenth century, and a 'dead heat' for an 'equal finish' from the end of the eighteenth century, when a 'heat' meant a 'warm-up race' or 'one course of a race'.

Defeat. 'Defeat' appeared in English at the end of the sixteenth century, from a French root. Among the list of imaginative synonyms for defeat are 'choking' – particularly in tennis, for 'snatching defeat from the jaws of victory'; 'shellacking', often used in baseball, and dating from the 1930s; and Billie Jean King's reaction to her defeat by the teenage Andrea Jaeger in 1983 – 'she just cleaned my clock'.

Draw. There was a good, but sadly unfounded, story, that if there was no clear winner in a fight the referee would pull up the stakes at the corners of the ring, drawing them out of the ground – the contest would thus be a 'draw'. In fact, an inconclusive contest would result in the betting participants withdrawing their stakes, hence the match being 'drawn'; this usage dates from the early seventeenth century. To 'draw', and a match ending up as a 'draw', date from the nineteenth century, with newspaper reports from the late Victorian period often stating that a match 'became a draw'.

Hole out. When a golfer 'holes out', he or she putts successfully to end play on that hole, but if a cricketer 'holes out' he is caught. The golf usage dates from 1867 (*OED*), but the cricket usage is more recent, from the 1960s. Given that many phrases and terms cross from one sport to another, it is curious that 'hole out' should mean success in golf and failure in cricket.

Losingest. American sports reporting has produced 'losingest' and 'winningest', for the team with the longest consecutive run of lost or won games. 'Losingest' came first, first used in the *New York Times* in 1941 ('the losingest pitcher in the league'), and 'winningest' two years later, but in inverted commas, indicating that it was still a new word. Neither is currently recognised by the *OED*.

Pipped at the post. There is a story that 'pipped at the post' derives from the idea that black balls used in voting for gentlemen's club membership (giving the word 'blackball') were originally called 'pips' after olive stones used in Greek and Roman voting procedures. However, olive stones had been referred to as 'stones' rather than 'pips' since the sixteenth century. While there are late-nineteenth-century usages of 'pipped' to mean 'annoyed, irritated', and much earlier usages to describe a 'pipped' nut as one having no kernel (thus 'spoiled' and 'worthless'), the earliest *OED* documentation for 'pipped', meaning 'beaten', is from 1838; the sense of being 'rejected' is recorded only from 1908; and 'pipped on [not at] the post' from 1924. From around the beginning of the twentieth century there was the use of 'to pip' in the sense of 'to hit with a shot from a gun', and this would tie in with the use of the word 'pip' to mean 'a small ball or shot' (*English Phrases*, Penguin, 2006). 'Pipped' would thus mean 'brought down with a small shot', in keeping with its usage to convey a sense that the situation is less than disastrous.

Record. The ancient Olympic Games kept a strict record of results, though presumably not of times. At the first modern Olympics times were recorded, in fifths of a second; no records were broken. Given the variety of challenges available to pedestrian racers in the eighteenth century, it is not surprising that there were a vast number of 'records', including pedestrians beating their own records.

The term is naturally a result of keeping records, as in 'the greatest performance on record', the assessment by *Bell's Life in London* of Henry Rayner's 5-mile run in twenty-two minutes in April 1822, and Chadwick's 1885 book, *The Art of Pitching and Fielding, together with the best pitching and fielding records*. In Montague Shearman's *Athletics and Football* (1889) we see the use of the term 'record-breaking', though it appears in inverted commas, indicating its novelty (records had previously been 'cut'). It seemed to stay an unfamiliar term for some time: in 1909 the new world record for the 120 yards (11.25 seconds) was broken, with the announcement in *The Observer*: 'World's record broken.' 'Record' entered English from Anglo-Norman French in the fourteenth century.

What constitutes a record was thrown into confusion by the decision by the Union Cycliste Internationale in 2000 to reinstate Eddie Merckx's record for the hour (49.431 km), set in 1972 and broken many times on technologically improved cycles. The implications of an unlimited 'level playing field' might suggest athletics records should stand until they are broken on cinder tracks with uncomfortable shoes and a Corinthian disdain for training.

Result. Delahunty, in *Talking Balls*, points out that there is a world of difference between 'the result' of a match and 'getting a result', meaning winning or at least avoiding defeat. For Jonathon Green in the Cassell *Dictionary of Slang*, this dates from the 1950s and was originally criminal slang for a successful burglary. The first entry for 'getting a result' in the *OED* in a sporting context is in 1976, and the phrase was fairly common by the time of the first football fanzines in the 1980s.

Cashmore in *Making Sense of Sports* proposes that one similarity between now-banned blood sports and sporting contests is the importance of the result. Betting acted as an incentive for the need for a result, and presumably this provided the sense that the gambler, having won, could walk away from the scene of the contest, while for the losing gambler there would be a feeling of unfinished business. The 'result' then would only be winning. It is an interesting interpretation, especially as the word 'getting' is involved – the winner does not 'see', is not 'awarded' a result. The result is 'got'; it is taken, grasped, seized.

Runner-up. This is a generous term, within the amateur ethos, for a defeated finalist; the term originated in greyhounds being set to chase hares (hare-coursing) in the mid-nineteenth century, though there is no usage of 'run up', meaning 'come second'.

Save. A 'save' in football, hockey and other team games dates from the early 1890s, shots previously having been 'stopped'.

Score. The idea that 'to score' came from the act of cutting a groove in a piece of wood, even the upright of a football goal, is often proposed, though by the time of goalposts this would have been very unlikely. 'Score' did originally mean a 'cut' or 'notch', from the Old English *scoru*.

Win. 'Win' originally meant 'work', 'contend' or 'strive'; in *Beowulf* Unferth asks Beowulf if he is that Beowulf who contended with Breca in a swimming match – *Eart thu se Beowulf, se the with Brecan wunne*? About three hundred years later it was being used in the sense of 'conquer', 'defeat' or 'be victorious'. The progression of meaning is a fair reflection of the myth of sportsmanship that changed over the hundred years or so from the emergence of amateurism, from the much misquoted 'It matters not who won or lost, but how you played the game.' It is not just in recent years that sport has been about winning. Mussolini sent a telegram to the Italian football team as they were about to take on Hungary in the World Cup Final in 1938; it read 'Win or die'. Mihir Bose, reporting on the 2008 Beijing Olympics, said that the Olympics were not to do with participating, but with winning. We may feel that something is lost in this attitude – fairness, enjoyment of sport for sport's sake, a discomfort that greed might underlie the need to win. A more challenging thought is that reported by Simon Barnes in *The Meaning of Sport* (2006): there was an American gambler who summed up not just gambling, but all sport, for all time. He said: 'The most exciting thing in life is winning. And the second most exciting thing is losing.'

Training and injuries

Exercise. Thomas Elyot's *The Governour* (1531) proposes wrestling, running, swimming, swordplay and riding as 'exercises whereby should grow both recreation and profit'. Richard Burton, in his *Anatomy of Melancholy* (1621), sees exercise as a way of profitably channelling activity that would otherwise be for its own sake; he quotes a number of authorities who recommend gentle exercise, including Galen, who 'prefers exercise before all physic, rectification of diet, or any regimen in what kind soever; 'tis nature's physician.' Galen's recommendation is to exercise 'till the body be ready to sweat', and 'roused up' in Burton's words. In his assessment of the authorities he quotes, 'The most forbid, and by no means will have it go farther than a beginning sweat, as being perilous if it exceed.'

The activities recommended were:

> to play at ball, be it with the hand or racket, in
> tennis-courts or otherwise, hawking, hunting,

> fishing, ringing [quoits], bowling, shooting [archery]
> … keelpins, trunks, pitching bars, hurling, wrestling,
> leaping, running, fencing, mustring, swimming,
> wasters, foils, football, baloon, quintan, and many
> such, which are the common recreations of the
> countryfolks. Riding of great horses, running at
> rings, tilts and tournaments, horse-races, wild-goose
> chases, which are the disports of greater men…

But Burton's most recommended 'exercises' are:

> a merry journey now and then with some good
> companions, to visit friends, see cities, castles, towns,
> … To walk among orchards, gardens, … and such
> like pleasant places…

This sounds more like a day out than an hour in the gym.

A more rigorous view is given by writers such as John Winthrop, governor of the Massachusetts Bay Colony from 1630 to 1649, for whom 'a moderate exercise' might 'recreate my mind with some outward recreation'. For the New England puritans, 'exercise' did not include shuffleboard, quoits and lawn-bowling, which they legislated against.

Samuel Johnson wrote in 1755 that 'exercise is labour used only while it produces pleasure', and gave the following definitions:

1. Labour of the body; labour considered as
   conducive to the cure and prevention of diseases.
2. Something done for amusement.
3. Habitual action by which the body is formed to
   gracefulness, air and agility.

From definition 3 we can see the development of 'exercises', specific activities to build up the body.

Fit. 'Fit' in the usage of 'get fit' and 'to be fit' developed from a later-nineteenth-century use of 'fit' to mean 'in good condition', itself from the sense of 'being fit for something'. As being 'fit' became an end in itself, it enveloped the word 'fitness', which came to mean 'the state of being healthy and robust' in the early twentieth century. *Recreation and Physical Fitness* (1937) included a chapter on a 'Keep fit' scheme.

Gymnastic march. The 'gymnastic march', as directed in the *Model Course of Physical Training* (1902), involved walking with the hands on hips, lifting up the forward knee, pushing the calf forward and the foot out, not unlike a horse pacing. This was part of Swedish drill, a regimen of bending, twisting and stretching, based on Swedish therapeutic gymnastics, originally set out by Pehr Henrik Ling, and recognised by the Swedish government in 1813. The exercises were pedagogical, military, medical and aesthetic, and gained wide support in the United Kingdom in the late nineteenth century, being used in schools and the army and navy. Though Swedish drill was eventually phased out between 1910 and 1930, a display was given at the 1948 Olympic Games in London.

Hamstring. The 'hamstring' is recorded from the mid-sixteenth century, deriving from two Old English words. The 'Achilles tendon' was also formerly called a 'string' but by the mid-eighteenth century had acquired its modern name, from the Latin *tendo* and the name of the Greek hero from the *Iliad*.

Injury. From the Latin word *injurius*, meaning 'unjust or wrongful', the word 'injury' was first used in Wycliffe's translation of the Bible in the fourteenth century to mean 'a wrong done to someone'. The idea of an injury as a 'physical hurt' comes later, in the sixteenth century. About one third of all injuries received by children are sports-related, though not necessarily through those sports usually reckoned as dangerous. In high schools and colleges in the United States cheerleading accounts for more spinal and head injuries than all other sports together.

PE and PT. The differences between PE and PT would at first appear to be of intention, style and time. As a school subject, the terms 'PE' (Physical Education) and 'PT' (Physical Training) were in use from the end of the nineteenth century, while *Physical Jerks* (1921) by Captain T. A. Lowe uses both 'physical training' and 'physical education'. 'Physical training' appears to indicate a specific purpose – *Competitive Sports in Schools and Colleges* (New York, 1951) states that 'Since the beginning of civilization physical training has been used to condition men for warfare'; however, this text also uses the term 'physical education'. 'PT' was the term used in London schools in the 1960s, while *The Curriculum of the Secondary School* (1952) has 'Physical Education' as a heading, but also uses 'training' in this context. John Hargreaves in *Sport, Power and Culture* (2005) uses 'PE' in a context discussing gender pressure in schools.

Physical jerks. This curious term was the title of a small book by Captain T. A. Lowe, published in 1921, which contained instructions for exercise programmes using skipping, trunk-bending, lunging and similar activities; few of them were in any way jerky, most of them involving either stretching, bending or turning. The *OED* records the phrase from 1917 in a military context.

Press-up. In the *Model Course of Physical Training* for the Board of Education in 1902, press-ups were called 'pressing from the ground'.

The first documented use of 'press-up' is in 1928 (OED). Its absence from *Recreation and Physical Fitness for Girls and Women* (1937) implies that this exercise was then deemed suitable for boys only.

Stamina. Stamina is generally now thought of as the power to sustain exertion or recover from injury or illness. Its development to this meaning involves both weaving, mythology and early scientific medical thought. *Stamina* is the plural form of the Latin word *stamen*, now the word for part of the reproductive apparatus of a flower, but in the seventeenth century 'stamina' meant both the warp of a woven cloth (the threads lying vertically on an upright loom) and the threads of life woven by the Fates. From these together came the idea of the vital essence of an organism, that from which it developed, and which sustained it through life, and which indeed determined the length of life. During the eighteenth century experimental science observed the rudiments of teeth in mammalian embryos and termed these 'stamina'. This developed also a figurative use, in the sense of the 'seeds' of something; thus Johnson talked about the 'stamina' of an essay, the ideas from which it grew.

The current meaning, 'staying power', developed in the eighteenth century and is curiously similar to the most unlikely idea above, that of what determines how long a body could keep going – except that now stamina can be topped up, in any number of acceptable or unacceptable ways.

Strain. 'In cold weather muscles strain or snap without any warning,' wrote Montague Shearman in an article on training in 1889. 'Strain' comes via Middle English 'streyne' and Old French *estreindre* from the Latin *stringere*, meaning to 'bind tightly'. 'Snap' here appears to mean to 'seize up quickly'.

Train. From 1609 the word 'train' was used for animals, in the sense of getting them to perform specific acts, and the word was used for preparing the military and for studying for the professions. In the early nineteenth century it was used for athletes: in *Boxiana* (1812–29) Egan describes Tom Cribb as a 'trained man', who used 'regimen and discipline'.

In *Pedestrianism* (1813) Walter Thom describes a training regime for a pedestrian athlete:

> The art of training for athletic exercises, consists in purifying the body and strengthening its powers, by certain processes, which thus qualify the person for the accomplishment of laborious exercises.

The 'trainer' has a 'patient', to whom he gives initially 'three dozes of Glauber Salts' (a mild laxative).

> He [the athlete] must rise at five in the morning, run half a mile at the top of his speed uphill, and then walk six miles at a moderate pace, coming in about seven to breakfast, which should consist of beef-steaks or mutton-chops under-done, with stale bread and old beer … The pedestrian must … run four miles, in flannel, at the top of his speed. Immediately on returning, a hot liquor is prescribed, in order to promote the perspiration, of which he must drink one English pint. It is termed 'the Sweating Liquor', and is composed of the following ingredients, viz: one ounce of caraway seed, half an ounce of coriander seed, one ounce of root liquorice, and half of sugar-candy, mixed with two bottles of cyder, and boiled down to one half. He is then put to bed in his

> flannels, and being covered with six or eight pairs of
> blankets, and a feather-bed, must remain in this state
> from twenty-five to thirty-five minutes, when he is
> taken out and rubbed perfectly dry. Being then well
> wrapt in his greatcoat, he walks out gently for two
> miles, and returns to breakfast.

This use of regimen and conditioning, as well as exercise, was Captain Barclay's practice; he seemed to do well on it.

The Victorian amateur attitude to training was that it was bad form. When Blackburn Olympic had the temerity to beat the Old Etonians in the 1883 FA Cup Final, the *Eton College Chronicle* wrote:

> So great was their desire to wrest the Cup from the
> holders that they introduced into football a practice
> which has excited the greatest disapprobation in the
> South. For three weeks before the final match they
> went into a strict course of training...

However, even as confirmed an amateur as Montague Shearman, co-founder of the Amateur Athletics Association, had a good word for professional trainers (*Athletics and Football*, 1889):

> Well can we recollect the vigorous rubbings of Bob
> Rogers and the cast-iron hand of old Harry Andrews
> at Lillie Bridge ... your amateur rubber is too
> perfunctory in his ministrations, and cannot vie with
> the professional exponent of the art.

'Train' comes from the Latin *trahere*, meaning 'drag or pull'; it appeared in Middle English with the sense of 'persuade' and 'induce', as well as 'manipulate towards a desired state'.

Select bibliography

Simon Barnes. *The Meaning of Sport*. Short Books, 2006.

Ellis Cashmore. *Making Sense of Sports*. Routledge, 2001.

J. J. Coakley. *Sport in Society*. Mosby, 1978.

Andrew Delahunty. *Talking Balls*. Weidenfeld & Nicolson, 2006.

Norbert Elias. *An Essay on Sport and Violence*. 1986.

Elliot Gorn. *The Manly Art: Bareknuckle Prizefighting in America*. Cornell University Press, 1986.

E. Gorn and W. Goldstein. *A Brief History of American Sports*. University of Illinois Press, 2004.

John Hargreaves. *Sport, Power and Culture*. Polity Press, 2005.

H. A. Harris. *Sport in Britain*. Paul, 1975.

R. Holt. *Sport and the British*. Clarendon Press, 1989.

Nick Hornby. *Fever Pitch*. Penguin, 1992.

C. L. R. James. *Beyond a Boundary*. Yellow Jersey, 1963.

Norman Mailer. *The Fight*. Penguin, 1975.

Joyce Carol Oates. *On Boxing*. Harper Collins, 1987.

Oxford Encyclopedia of World Sport (1998)

Martin Polley. *Moving the Goalposts*. Routledge, 1999.

Al Silverman. *The Twentieth Century Treasury of Sports*. Viking, 1992.

The Sports Book. Dorling Kindersley, 2007.

Ralph Thomas. *Swimming*. Marston & company, 1904.

Neil Tranter. *Sport, Economy and Society in Britain 1750–1914*. Cambridge University Press, 1998.

David Wallechinsky. *The Complete Book of the Olympics*. Aurum Press, 1984.

Bob Wilson. *Ultimate Collection of Peculiar Sporting Lingo*. Icon Books, 2004.

Bob Wilson. *Googlies, Nutmegs and Bogeys*. Icon Books, 2006.

Index

Ace 258,
Acrobat 231
Aerobics 75
Alley-oop 267
Also-ran 231
Amateur and professional approaches 38, 40–7, 134–5, 144, 170, 188, 236,
American and British usages 9, 91
American seat 267
America's Cup 241
Anchor man 231
Angling 77
Animal blood-sports 21–2, 50–1, 68, 183, 286
Annie's room 292
Aquatics 78, 157
Archery 78–9, 151, 192
Arena 228
Arlott, John 63, 68, 71
Arnold, Thomas 11, 52
Arrow 192
Artisans clause 36, 42
Ascham, Roger 79, 187
Ashes 241
Athlete 232
Athletics 38, 79–80, 135, 232
Astroturf 209
Back stroke 268
Backhand 268
Badminton 80–1
Bagel 292
Baggy green 169
Bails 98, 192
Bait 268–9
Balbis 107
Ball 143, 153, 192–3, 222, 292
Balloon 81
Ballpark 228
Ban, the 58

Bandy 81–2, 123, 198,
Bantamweight 232
Barani roll 269
Barbell 194
Barclay, Captain 132–3, 135, 170, 324
Barleybreak 82
Barmy Army 40, 292
Baseball 19, 33, 55, 68, 83–5, 176, 182, 189, 191, 193, 195, 236, 243, 261, 264, 265, 292, 303
Basketball 85–6, 194, 239, 285
Bat 100, 194
Batsman 98, 232
Battery 236
Battle royal 178
Battledore 86–7, 153
Balk 247
Beowulf 2, 138, 276, 317
Bergman-Österburg, Martina 131, 173
Betting 27–30, 99, 103, 160–7
Betting terms 162–4
Bias 89
Billiards 87–8, 186, 198, 256, 277
Birdie 259
Blazer 168
Bleachers 292
Block hole 209
Blue 242
Blue ribbon 243
BMX 269
Boat Race 63, 242
Bobsleigh 195
Bodyline series 23, 47
Bogey 259
Bonspiel 104
Bookmaker 161
Boot 168
Bottleman 220
Bounce 194
Bout 178
Bottle 293
Bow 196

Bowl 269–71, 278, 290
Bowler 98
Bowling, bowls 50, 88–90, 216
Boxing 16, 18, 22, 29, 39, 40, 62, 68, 90–4, 151, 172, 200, 215, 226, 240, 246, 255, 286, 292–4, 305
Break 88, 222, 271
Breast stroke 271
British bulldog 83, 178
Broadcasting 5, 63–4
Broughton, Jack 91, 161, 172, 236, 257
Bullseye 209–10
Bully 222–3
Bung 247
Bunker 210
Burton, Robert 27, 82, 318–19
Bury the ball 294
Butterfly stroke 271–2
Butts 207
Bye 223
Caber 196
Caddie 218
Cage-fighting 74
Calcio 111
Calcutta Cup 243
Callisthenics 94
Camp, Walter 75, 76
Campball 94, 111, 264
Cannon 223
Canoe 196
Canter 272
Canvas 210
Cap 169
Card, red or yellow 248
Carew, Richard 58, 288
Catamaran 197
Catch 272
Catch a crab 312
Catgut 197
Centre-forward 239
Century 99, 100
Chadwick, Henry 53, 84, 315
Challenge 179
Champion 313